Donated by the estate of Nick Dragisic
Midland, Texas, October 2005

WAITING FOR WINTER TO END

WAITING
FOR
WINTER TO END

─────────⬥─────────

*An Extraordinary Journey
Through Soviet Central Asia*

Georgie Anne Geyer

Brassey's
Washington · London

Library of Congress Cataloging-in-Publication Data
Geyer, Georgie Anne
Waiting for winter to end: an extraordinary journey through
Soviet Central Asia/Georgie Anne Geyer.
p.   cm.
Includes bibliographical references and index.
ISBN 0-02-881110-0
1. Asia, Central—Description and travel. 2. Geyer, Georgie Anne—
Journeys—Asia, Central. I. Title.
DK854.G4 1994
915.804'41—dc20   94-9519

Designed by Oksana Kushnir
Map by Derrick Chamlee/D.C. Design

10 9 8 7 6 5 4 3 2 1
Printed in the United States of America

For Enders Wimbush—
without his rare collegial support
and profound knowledge of Central Asia,
this book would never have been written

Contents

Preface

One day in 1967, when I first visited the Soviet Union and Central Asia, I happened to be sitting near to the legendary English explorer Freya Stark in the restaurant of a Bukhara hotel. A buxom, sturdy woman who had fearlessly entered the world of the Heartland of Empires tribesmen and its great and fearsome deserts and mountains, she invited me to lunch with her. I gladly changed tables and found myself in the company of a woman who, like all great explorers of the Silk Road and its little-known environs, was an eccentric world of knowledge and perception in herself.

I remember two things about that long-ago meal: first, that she was wearing a very, very big and floppy hat with flowers on it, which seemed quite incongruous in Bukhara; and second, that her enthusiastic talk about the whole forgotten region left me with a yearning to know more about it that would not be satisfied for many years.

The chance to visit Central Asia in some depth came unexpectedly in the fall of 1991. The Radio Free Europe Fund, a private group formed to support Radio Free Europe and Radio Liberty, the Munich-based radio networks that did such superb work in broadcasting genuine news behind the Iron Curtain, decided to give small grants to a number of journalists to write about the newly independent Soviet republics. There were no strings attached; the group just wanted good journalists to fill in the yawning gaps in our knowledge and coverage.

I looked at a map of the Soviet Union with relish (at the opportunity) but also with trepidation (at the potential dangers involved). It took not even a minute to point my finger as far away from Moscow as I could go—to Kazakhstan in the far east of the former U.S.S.R. Then I filled in the route—why not Kyrgyzstan, followed by Tatarstan, Uzbekistan, Azerbaijan, and of course Russia itself? On January 2, 1992, I was on my way.

It was a singular opportunity. While we journalists spend our time at best rummaging about in other people's minds, usually those minds are already known to the world—other rummagers have already been there. But in this case it was different: outside of tourist attractions such as Samarkand and Bukhara, Central Asia had been locked tight during seven decades of Bolshevik dictatorship. This time, I could play a political Freya Stark and be one of the first to roam and rummage across one of the most fascinating, legendary, and least-known areas of the world. Now, not only were borders suddenly opened but, more important, minds were.

My first thanks, then, go to the Radio Free Europe Fund, whose perceptive generosity allowed me to take such an unusual trip at such a propitious time (Leonard Marks, chairman of the Radio Free Europe/Radio Liberty Fund, deserves special acknowledgment). Very special thanks go to Enders Wimbush, then the director of Radio Liberty, and to his wife, Jane Ann. Without their support—and particularly without Enders putting the local Central Asian journalists of Radio Liberty at my disposal as guides and mentors—I could never have seen so much and gotten so much information in such a short time. My thanks also to Enders and to Paul Goble, two brilliant Central Asian scholars, for reading this manuscript for historic errors; this is particularly important in a geographic area so complex, where myriad scripts need transliteration into English and where one can be forgiven for drawing lots on any one day as to whether you are going to call the Dungans the Tungans.

The beautiful photographs were kindly supplied by photographers Judith Olney and Hermine Dreyfuss, and through the offices of Shafiq Kombargi, director of public affairs for Aramco in Houston, who made pictures that had appeared in *Aramco World* available to the author. I am grateful to them all.

Special thanks go to my wonderful literary agent, Richard Curtis, and to the splendid staff at Brassey's for their professionalism and enthusiasm. While many there worked on this book, I especially want to thank Don McKeon, who was the primary editor, Sybil Pincus, who did a superb job of copy editing—linguistically and historically—an unusually complicated manuscript, and Franklin Margiotta, president and publisher, for taking a chance on a different kind of book.

Finally, I want to thank all those Central Asian intellectuals, politicians, tribesmen and women, dreamers and realists, who opened their lives to me so generously at their extraordinary and unexpected moment of awakening.

Georgie Anne Geyer
Washington, D.C.
April 1994

FORMER SOVIET CENTRAL ASIA

Moscow

Kaz

RUSSIA

Black Sea

GEORGIA

Baku

Istanbul

TURKEY

ARMENIA

AZERBAIJA

Caspia

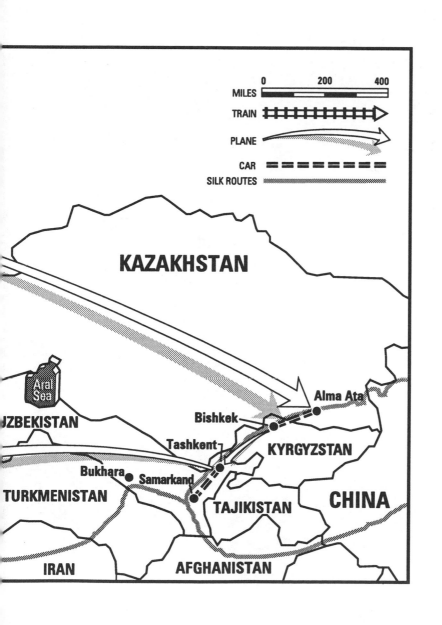

WAITING FOR WINTER TO END

Chapter 1

Waiting for Winter
The Ruins of Utopianism

And empires gleam,
like wrecks of a dissolving dream.

Percy Bysshe Shelley,
Hellas

In the late sixties and early seventies, the advice given by smug and arrogant Russian officers to the armies of "their" Third World surrogates was often curious indeed. In those now nearly forgotten days, the two superpowers were vying for dominance through an unprecedented historic competition for the hearts and minds (and oil and minerals, and strategic geopolitical positioning) of the poor nations of Latin America, the Middle East, and Asia. In such hot, remote, and unlikely places as Aden, Huambo, and Cienfuegos, Russian "advisers" would expound with great seriousness upon military tactics and strategy to use in the fight for Communism and against American imperialism.

Finally, like people all over the world, the Soviets would fall back on the only experience they really knew: their own. They would soberly advise the Third World officers, "Then, if everything else fails, *wait for winter!*"

This genre of true story was first regaled to me by Egyptian officers in Cairo in 1969. We were chatting congenially at an Egyptian army base one day in the searing Nile heat. We were so far away from the frozen gray steppes of central Russia and any idea of winter, we might as well have been on another planet. "Imagine," one officer cried that day, tears of laughter welling up in his eyes as he spoke, "to tell us to 'wait for winter'—in Egypt!"

I would be told such stories repeatedly; such tales were often advanced as ironic evidence of the foolhardiness of the powerful imperialists of the great force from the East (not that the American empire was not capable of it as well).

But the Russian officers' sage advice was no joke at all to the Russians themselves. For centuries, they had lived bundled up in their historic reality, but they existed also with an abiding fear of the outsider and in dire trepidation as to their own continued existence.

In that inner core of the convoluted but fascinating Russian mind, they could see as if it were yesterday the Mongol hordes, with their sturdy ponies shadowing the horizons of the East as they swept down upon them out of Central Asia in those dark years between 1207 and 1227. Those brilliant, cruel, and utterly relentless horsemen had destroyed many flourishing cultures and kingdoms of the then known world. From budding Persia to ancient China to young Muscovy and to Western-leaning Christian Kievan Rus, great cities were left in ruins, cultures were cut off at their earliest moment of bloom, and mountains of skulls loomed against the evening skies.

The memory of the pugnacious Swedes sailing down the Volga between 1741 and 1743 and seizing the great commercial city of Novgorod was as fresh in their minds as was World War II. Nor could the Russians ever forget Napoleon I invading all of Russia in 1812; much less could they bury the memory of Adolf Hitler's voracious legions, starving out Leningrad during those three terrible years of the early forties and finally marching as far as Stalingrad on the plains of southern Russia before Dame Winter stepped in and again defeated still another of Mother Russia's enemies.

Winter defined Russia. Over and over it shut the Russians off from the rest of the world, protecting the homeland from pillage, from further humiliation, and even from obliteration. It was their friend and almost always their enemies' principal enemy. The throne of the Romanovs, Aleksandr Kerensky's provisional government, and Mikhail Gorbachev's Soviet Union all collapsed and disintegrated while the snows were deep and impenetrable. And when President Boris Yeltsin phoned President-elect Bill Clinton in the fall of 1992, the words he spoke to the young American were a mirror of the melancholy Russian soul and of Russian history. "It's winter here," he said, "and you know, winter is always hard for us."

But it was hardly surprising that the Russians should also have seen winter as their friend, for in each onslaught of modern times the Russians were finally saved by just that. Out on the steppes of Russia, winter inevitably tamed man's aggressive ferocity, because winter could outlast any human impulse, however savage. Winter was the great equalizer, and it confirmed in the Russians their natural proclivity to a brooding patience in the face of all odds. That patience, of course, was unknown to the activist, optimistic, and relentlessly positive West; those blessed but less soulful lands could afford to be hopeful about human nature.

And so, winter came to symbolize the Russians' entire dependent, traditional, long-suffering view of life. Winter strengthened and reinforced in them their tendency, born of the long snows and the frigid steppes, to feel that passivity in the face of an overwhelmingly powerful enemy could serve them far better than that ceaseless and childlike ebullient confidence of the West. It was natural: they were employing the sheer absorptive qualities of nature, the one thing they had in abundance.

This was my first trip to Russia in winter. I had traveled to that closed and enigmatic land in the fall of 1967 for the grand and somewhat frightening fiftieth anniversary of the Glorious Russian Revolution. That was the Soviets' supreme age of arrogant assurance, as day after day that fall, enormous military parades spread like fingers of power across the city and finally into Red Square. The entire country had become one marching confirmation of the sobering potency of that other superpower.

When I returned to the Soviet Union in 1971, I was continuing the in-depth study of the new generation of Russians that I had begun in 1967. I did what other journalists had not done: I spoke at length to young men and women and to their interpreters about themselves, their country, their hopes. But when I published my findings—that there was an entirely different new generation arising, one that cared little for ideology and a great deal for living a decent, personally rewarding, and essentially normal life—the Western Sovietologists disdained and derided me.

They could not believe that there could be any changes in that monolith of a forced and obedient society that could move it toward even the beginnings of an open and liberal society.

But they were wrong. I had found, analyzed, and catalogued what after 1985 would be seen as the transformational "Gorbachev generation." But I was too early with my well-documented predictions—fourteen years, to be exact—and no establishment voices anywhere ever really forgive prophecies that come to pass when they themselves did not make them.

When I returned in 1988 and then again in 1990, I could see further how profoundly the whole society was changing. The economy was dangerously slowing; there were no trucks on the streets of Moscow that spring of 1988; the country was beginning to disintegrate in a slow-motion breakdown as region after region quietly held back its products—and the decline began. The Eastern empire was so far behind the West by then that there was no longer any serious thought of any competition save a military one. Yet even that competition loomed as unrealistic because powerful military machines in the modern world need sound economies and reasonably satisfied, productive people behind them to make them work.

In this winter of 1992, I was traveling to Russia for the fifth time. But what a different Russia I was visiting, compared to the unbending and imperious superpower I had struggled with in those previous years! With the economy in a free fall, the standard of living was lower than it had been in 1945, and then, at the end of World War II, the Russian people had hope.

Now, empty-eyed people walked about the fiercely cold and snow-covered streets of Moscow as if they no longer knew who or what they were—or, worse, why? In demonstrations, the elliptical posters held up by the exhausted "citizens-of-what?" best encompassed the sense of hopeless irony that has always appeared and reappeared across Russian history: 74 YEARS ON THE ROAD TO NOWHERE . . . HUNDREDS OF MILLIONS HAVE BEEN TWISTED IN THIS LUNATIC EXPERIMENT . . . WE WANT TO BE A NORMAL SOCIETY.

I soon realized that what I was seeing before me was a different winter. Today this winter was a winter of the mind, a winter of cultures that are not easily amenable to modernization. This winter marked a new and ambiguous kind of defeat that the Russians had never dreamed of in their earlier military defeats, which now looked remarkably simple. This time around, Moscow had the distinctive feeling about it of a great city ambivalently and ambiguously defeated. An economic defeat is not a Douglas MacArthur standing valiantly on the battleship *Missouri* taking the total surrender of the emperor of Japan; no, an economic defeat is complicated, imprecise, and amorphous. It defeats most of all through its irresolution.

This was not Napoleon but Novotel; not Sweden but Swissair; not Adolf but Arpège.

For the first time in history—without having been defeated in war and with its armed forces intact—a superpower had collapsed, imploded, disintegrated. As the Oxford philosopher Isaiah Berlin put it, "Never before has there been a case of an empire that caved in without a war, revolution or invasion." Even the collapse of the Roman Empire occurred only because of the barbarian attacks from the north; the Soviet state simply . . . withered . . . away.

At the same time, the Russians had to move successfully through three impossible transformations all at once: from totalitarianism to democracy, from a command economy to a free-market one, and from the total powers of a multinational empire to the relative powers of a nation-state.

Even worse, the Russians now had to adopt the very economic and political philosophies of their former enemies, and those philosophies were the hated antithesis of the historic "redemptive" ideologies of Communism and collectivism. Without knowing even what those new and foreign truths were, they needed to absorb the truths of modern organizations—to know that horizontal organizational links are more important than the vertical links they knew, to learn that palpable things of worth must be built from the bottom up and not from the top down.

And unlike the "lucky" Germans and Japanese after World War II, they had no outside authority to take over for a period of time, to relieve them of responsibility while they learned the new and victorious system. They had to do it alone, against every possible odd, and they did not really know what it was they had to do!

The Russians had known what to do in those other winters, and in those seasons their qualities of stoic patience suited the temperatures well. But it was no idle question to ask: What do you do in the face of this other winter, where the implacable economic face of the West now stands immeasurably more dangerous and more bloodcurdling before the gates of Moscow than those old faces of the worst khans from the East?

The great Communist dream, with the Marxist ideology that

was to make brothers of "new men" who would readily share their lives and their production, had all burst apart so quickly, not from year to year but from week to week!

One day, the citizens of the Soviet Union were still part of an empire, of a universe of peoples, nationalities, and coherent groups. Their armies and navies strode the soils and the waves of the world. A continent of diverse peoples had grown up reciting the Soviet Great Power catechisms: a world that traversed eleven time zones . . . nearly 300 million people . . . production figures so boring they could have put Catherine the Great to sleep even while waiting for one of her favorite lovers . . .

And then, not only was it all gone, but nobody knew how to put in its place what the world told them they *must* put in its place.

Few people spoke on the flight that Sunday in early January of 1992, as the afternoon Lufthansa jet from Munich made its way above the plains of central Europe.

On those plains, Western military planners had always feared that the Russians would attack in massive tank wars, but now the Western tanks massed there were dinosaurs of an age already past. Perhaps no one was speaking out of some inner fear; we had all heard too many times that this was the winter when Russia would probably collapse into a final anarchy. The Soviet racketeers, the "Russian mafia," were, we knew, poised to take over vast areas of Russia's failed economic life, and had already done so in the crucially important area of foreign trade.

But my imagination focused on a modern Russian equivalent not of the Mafia but of "highwaymen," and I knew full well that my greatest fear must be those hoodlums who roamed the streets at will, feeding off the unagile and unsuspecting foreigner, whose money alone still had value.

It was "dangerous" even to take a taxi from the city to Sheretmetyevo Airport, "dangerous" to take a cab anywhere, "dangerous" to carry money anywhere except around your waist . . .

Most international flights have a certain sense of high spirits about them somewhere along the way, but not this plane. On our Lufthansa flight, an unmistakable sense of gloom and unease hung over us all, and no one was more uneasy than I. It seemed to me at one point that we were moving as a new army: a silent, well-meaning, but inexorable and relentless new kind of invader, far more dangerous than the Mongols because we were marching toward them only to rob them of their very souls and, by the way, to refuse them the assurance that once again something as simple as winter would save them.

Without guns or tanks, with airline coupon clubs and credit cards and *the best of wishes for all,* we came on the wings of our airplanes and our airwaves.

But I had no intention this time of staying in Moscow. Indeed, I would remain there for only a week before moving out, however possible, to Central Asia: to Kazakhstan, Kyrgyzstan, Uzbekistan, and Azerbaijan. En route, I would pause in Tatarstan, which, while not precisely in historic Central Asia, was also Muslim and related.

Why was I doing this? I still was not certain, except that those proclaimed republics of Central Asia constituted the last most remote and exotic parts of the earth. In truth, I felt a breathless romantic pull to that vast area of 55 million people and immense plains, of rivers that crashed down from the Arctic in the spring like the very tongues of raging river gods and of sacred mountain ranges that stretched from the caviar-rich Caspian Sea to the vast Gobi Desert and from the wastes of Siberia in the north to Iran and Afghanistan in the south.

Not only had few modern-day adventurers been able to reach these peoples—who were mostly Turkic, with admixtures of everything from Mongol to Tungan to Persian—but almost all of Central Asia had been closed for decades under the omnipotent "Soviet power."

It was the last unknown part of the world. And the collapse had come so swiftly that few from the West had grasped the fact that finally—for the first time since the 1917 Revolution—all of Central Asia was open to us.

So if, on some levels, I felt myself walking in the footsteps of Marco Polo, or Alexander the Great, or Ibn Battuta, so be it! (I am not ashamed to admit that I have always been a romantic explorer in my heart and soul.) If, in nocturnal revels, I was having dreams of the Silk Road or of crossing the sacred Tien Shan mountains, I will not take issue with such accusations! For almost no Westerners were "out there" in Central Asia this new winter; and when I looked at the map, it seemed to me to be only some huge and empty blackness, some chasmlike emptiness, nothing more.

But on another level, I had to admit that I also nursed a distinct phobia. I feared—no, I *knew*—that I would be killed, that I would probably disappear from this very earth, most probably on the very first part of the trip. It would most probably happen on the Train to Kazan, which would ostensibly take me the very next Sunday from Moscow to the capital of Tatarstan. Indeed, I had so focused all my fears on that poor train, from which I would fall off the map and perhaps also off that suddenly opened world, that I gave rather little thought to the highwaymen lurking elsewhere.

To put it mildly, I did not feel comfortable about the whole trip. I kept asking myself: What will I find? What will I do? *Why* am I doing this? And, even more importantly, How will I ever get back once I get there? And so, the Train to Kazan the next Sunday emerged from my inner fears as the symbol and representation of all those other fears that attended that entire unprecedented winter.

Only a few times in my life as a foreign correspondent had I been really afraid, and each time I had somehow dealt with my fears by focusing those fears on some object, appropriate or inappropriate. When I first went overseas as a correspondent in 1964, to Latin America, I decided that I would almost immediately be bitten by the Chagas bug, a nasty black fellow that inhabited the Amazon basin, and I would die of the withering Chagas disease.

("She never had a chance," I could hear my editors at the *Chicago Daily News* saying. "Poor girl!"

"A life snuffed out so early—and by a damnable Chagas bug! Lying in wait for her, no doubt!"

And, "Do you think the *Tribune* could have told the Chagas bug she was coming?")

As it happened, as far as I can tell, I never met the dreaded Chagas bug, and the fear passed swiftly into history.

Still I feared the Train to Kazan. They couldn't fool me: that was where the highwaymen were, and they were waiting for me as surely as winter had so patiently prepared itself for Napoleon and Hitler.

As our jet descended into Moscow and our wheels slowly lowered to land in this new Russia at 4:30 P.M., Sunday afternoon, I thought that I had never seen such a rich collage of steel-grays and jet-blacks as was displayed before me on the earth below. As we slowly inched downward, toward Sheretmetyevo Airport, we glimpsed villages covered with snow and surrounded by the birch trees of Russian literature and legend. There seemed to be only one light burning in each village.

It reminded me of what European life must have been like fifty years ago, or what it was like a hundred years ago when at four o'clock in the afternoon it was already pitch-dark. The landscape was as dim and foreboding as an old witches' tale.

Always when I entered Sheretmetyevo, I gritted my teeth before facing the Bolshevik Revolution's leaden wall of bureaucrats and police, arm in steel arm protecting the riddle inside the enigma from the nosy likes of us. Now the borders were open; you could get visas right there in the airport. But there was still something even more impossible to believe.

There were signs in English everywhere, advertising those very worlds that had defeated them and that this time around would not be stopped by winter. MasterCard! Baskin-Robbins (with a delicious picture of a feast of ice creams)! Novotel, with a brazen hotel right outside Sheretmetyevo Airport!

Was this possible? I posed that question to two correspondents from Radio Free Europe and Radio Liberty who were also on the flight, and then I realized that they themselves were the very human, walking, intrusive embodiment of those signs; those American-sponsored, Munich-based radio stations were the main vehicles used for years and years to break down the wall against information reaching the U.S.S.R.

I did get outside the terminal, and I did get a taxi to take me to my hotel, the Radisson's Radomir Slavyanskaya Hotel across from the Kiev Railway Station. And, no, the highwaymen did not get me—not yet. I knew why, of course—because the plan was that they would be waiting on the Train to Kazan.

The week in Moscow was a week of ceaseless, difficult preparation, while I tried in some desperation to figure out how to deal with the first story I had ever covered that was not a war, a revolution, a rebellion, an uprising, or a civil war, but instead a devolution, a collapse, a slow-motion breakdown.

Revolutions are easy. Everything is speeded up and the adrenaline is flowing: it will be a new world, a pure world, a perfect and perfecting world!

How different, this! So long, so gradual, so painful, so without any promise of relief—like a divorce that goes on for twenty years until you don't even quite remember who the man was or why you married him.

Before, in 1967 and 1971, I had always worked with the Soviet Novosti Press Agency, which assured that you at least got some interviews in a society where people were always too terrified to speak to you. Now I had to arrange everything myself, and all in a society where no one really knew from moment to moment who was in power, much less where they could be found.

When I walked into the spacious, pleasant lobby of the Slavyan-skaya, the music was invariably dirgish, and foreign businessmen sat around reading *Moscow* magazine, which gave would-be investors every bit of information on what they seemed or wanted to think was the "great potential" of this new era in the new Russia. One sample advertisement:

> Want to climb volcanos in Kamchatka or cycle in the Crimea? If you have a yen for horseback riding in Central Asia or salmon fishing on the Kola Peninsula, call Soviet Travels, one of the new hard-currency coop adventure travel service. (248-0360; FAX, 288-9587)

For a moment, I was actually miffed. I had not come all this way to Dr.-Zhivago-it alone across Central Asia only to be met in Bish-kek or Bukhara with a friendly wave by Rotarians from Oklahoma City on horseback!

But this mood—unworthy, I admit—soon passed.

Mikhail Gorbachev was across town at his new Gorbachev Foundation, and President Yeltsin was down the river a fifteen-minute walk away at what is called the Belii Dom (White House), where his people were working night and day to construct a constitution, to build a modern bureaucracy, and to assure a kind of new democracy never before known in the world. It was all totally unreal, and this was only the beginning.

By the first afternoon, Monday, I was doing what a good foreign correspondent does everywhere: I got phone numbers from various sources, and from my room for five hours I phoned, and phoned, and phoned. It got to be two o'clock, and while I was somewhat reassured at not having encountered any highwaymen yet, I was also coming down with a Russian form of cabin fever. I knew the sun would begin seriously dropping at three, and that by four o'clock the city would be eerily dark.

So I rushed down to the lobby, caught one of the taxis (by this time, all of the cabdrivers cruising the big hotels catering to foreigners charged five dollars for any and all drives around town), and told him deftly in Russian, "Take me to Red Square." I badly needed some air and I knew the area from my earlier trips, when I had always happily stayed at the elegant old National Hotel. Lenin had lived there in the early, halcyon, world-shaking days of the Revolution. I wanted to look around, but above all I wanted to get out before locking myself overnight in the Slavyanskaya.

Nothing could have prepared me for what I was about to see, on this, my very first day in the new Russia.

Red Square was freezing cold that waning January afternoon, as the temperature dipped to 30 to 40 degrees below zero. The sun seemed as unsure of itself as this new Mother Russia; perhaps, hectored by all the cold and by all the problems down here on earth, she was thinking about throwing in her towel for the night as well. People huddled deep inside their coats and they walked briskly, for on winter days like these there was no time to waste. As I approached the big, dull, hopelessly antiquated GUM department store directly across from Lenin's Tomb on Red Square, to my amazement I noticed that there was now a Christian Dior window that spread across the entire corner of GUM.

"How astonishing," I thought. Then, with a touch of our Western smugness, "Well, they *are* moving forward!"

Then my eyes swept to the otherworldly scene taking place in front of the Christian Dior window. At first, it seemed to me to be a money-raising scheme of some sort. A boy who looked to be about ten years old stood there all bundled up against the frigid weather. He had a face as round as a pumpkin, a fat and opaque face, and he seemed from a distance to be singing something, some chant from the Russian Orthodox Church, I assumed.

"Raaahhhrrrr," he would chant.

I walked closer.

"Rrruuurrhhh," he would howl for another five seconds.

Then, as I came nearer, the eeriness of this strange little drama assailed my senses. The boy was demented. "Crazy, crazy," Russians standing there kept saying to me, pointing to their heads. But there was something more than strange about the scene, something that arrested our attention and indeed mesmerized us. Over and over the boy kept letting out phantasmagorical five- or six-second howls, like a wolf lost in the tundra. Then he would pause for five seconds and begin to howl again. All the time, his eyes were closed, while the woman with him calmly collected donations in a small box.

Then, as I stood there, rapt, a handsome and well-dressed man, his impeccably trimmed gray hair tucked neatly under a smart fur hat, walked up and stopped, listening intently to the mantric howls, his eyes gleaming in the cold like some sophisticated animal of the valley hearing some primeval forest cries.

After only some instants, he fell to his knees on the packed snow before the fat-faced boy and bowed his head for some seconds. When he gracefully arose, he gave the expressionless woman some money and disappeared, in all his incongruous elegance, into the cold gray afternoon.

With both fright and excitement, I knew exactly what I had seen. The boy was what was called throughout Russian history a "holy fool." Across all those centuries of Russian Orthodoxy, with its stoic mysticism and its hauntingly beautiful music, the world of historic Russia was so insane that insane people were believed to speak in God's tongues.

As I left Red Square that day, still shaken and stunned by what I had seen, I noticed for the first time that my beautiful, mellow, old National Hotel, with its great salons and its stupendous views of the Kremlin, had protective scaffolding all around it. It was being renovated, and there was a big sign on it; the restoration was by ROGNER, AUSTRIA.

"Of course you saw a holy fool," a sensitive American diplomat assured me the next day at the American embassy, when I wondered aloud whether the Russian winter was getting to me. "It's the old holiness of insanity in an insane world . . . God speaking to a deranged world through the deranged, who know him." Then he shook his head slightly and added, "If you just look around here, you'll see a lot of things out of *Boris Godunov*."

At that very moment, as we were sitting and chatting in the well-used coffee shop of the embassy, Serge Schmemann, the superb correspondent of *The New York Times,* stopped by for a moment.

"Central Asia?" he said, and a dreamy kind of look crept into his eyes. "You're going to Central Asia?"

I nodded.

"Nobody's out there," Schmemann said then. "We don't have

any idea what's going on out there. Are you coming back through Moscow? If you do, please call us."

His words made me both happy and sad: happy that few foreigners were there to muck things up, and sad because, if they had holy fools in relatively advanced Moscow, what in God's name (literally) would they have out there?

I started to say that I was not coming back; I wanted to say that I thought that he, with his rich experience in and understanding of Russia, would understand that. But I only said quietly, lacing my tone of voice with a self-pitying edge of understated sacrifice, "No, I'm not coming back through Moscow."

Still, all I could focus on was the fact that I never dreamed that I would see a holy fool in our age, whatever that is. But strange things happen when one world collapses and no one knows what world will come next.

The week was not to grow any less strange. It was so cold and so gray that one could almost skate on the mood. There was so little food that people lived their days waiting in lines, and lines, and more lines. Nobody was starving—yet—but malnutrition was setting in, particularly among the vulnerable older population, who had fought the great wars and were now losing this one.

Underneath, I soon began to notice a strange and disturbing "etiquette" of hunger. Even though people were increasingly without food, everywhere I went they seemed repeatedly to refuse to accept either offers of food from me or invitations to dinner. It was only one first indication of the profound humiliation that people were feeling everywhere.

For those with hard currency, however, there was plenty of food. If you had money, particularly dollars or deutsche marks, you could buy almost anything. There were pineapples in the markets for five dollars, a month's salary for the average Russian, and gold- and ocher-colored spices from Samarkand. In every one of the six hotels I stayed in, there were dinners of chicken, noodles, and carrots (from roughly seventy-five cents to two dollars), caviar (five dollars for a good-sized tin, slipped to me for dollars by the waiter), and champagne (at a dollar a bottle). Of course, the Slavyanskaya had excellent buffets three times a day in a small, pleasant, Scandinavian-style restaurant, where all the food was imported from Europe or Scandinavia.

I, like most foreigners, found myself feeling distinctly guilty about not being hungry but did not know what to do about the problem, aside from inviting personal contacts to lunch and trying to slip them money or food. And that, as I've mentioned, was not all that easy.

The American embassy encountered and noted odd psychological reactions on just about everyone's part. One officer told me, as we walked down the corridors of the embassy, "See the junk food in the front of our food store? That wasn't there before. People are just stuffing themselves with junk food. It's compulsive, it's a response to the hunger outside."

Another day, I sat in the Slavyanskaya coffee shop, talking to the American manager. At one point he said, a strange smile on his lips, "When do you think they will get so hungry they will attack the hotels?"

Even more notable, there were now a number of new food shops where foreigners could go in and pay only with credit cards. Usually, for reasons that are obscure to me, they were situated right next door to Russian food stores, and so the Russians in their grim lines could watch the prosperous, credit-card-sporting, worldly denizens of those other worlds (their new and oddly unwilling conquerors) moving smartly in and out, in and out, quickly, because we're "awfully busy today, you know!"

Every time I saw these scenes, I wondered what all of this was doing to the Russians psychologically, and how long it would be before they would begin to explode from the sheer humiliation.

Even worse in terms of insulting the Russians were the new hotels, usually built by Europeans, which literally sparkled with a vulgar sheen of lights, gloss, and poor but expensive taste. The Penta was one of these, with its huge dining room that featured stalactites hanging from the ceiling and a girl in green singing "Merry Christmas" in January. All of these hotels were catering to foreign businessmen, and some, like the elegantly redone old Metropole, had a harpist playing at breakfast. They all cost between $400 and $500 a day, which struck me as unbelievably vulgar in a country on the verge of starvation and already in the depths of despair. They were a little like the old foreign sectors of Peking in the 1880s and 1890s, and those sectors were, of course, finally besieged and destroyed by the Chinese Boxers, enraged by the arrogance of the West.

Yet when I asked a young reporter, Ivan Kadulin, at *Komsomol-*

skaya Pravda, how much Russians resented these foreign shops and hotels, he only said wistfully, "There are a lot of things that disturb me a lot more!" Then he added that when he walked by the Kremlin, he used to see the Soviet flag and know who he was, that he was a citizen of the Soviet Union. "Now," he said poignantly, "we don't know who we are."

As for myself, I began to fit into, to adapt, to begin to try to understand, this strange new/old society in this, its most poignant winter of all. As I had readied (nervously) for this consummately unfashionable voyage through the ruins of utopianism, I had carefully packed. Since it was high winter everywhere, I took my good wool Gucci suit, in a dark and pleasing (but not too noticeably different) brown and black check, a change of skirts, two washable silk blouses, a sweater, and an appropriately dour dark green and black flannel nightgown. I began to give my tailored traveling companions names, so I would not be so alone out there. My beautiful, practical, rain-resistant German lodencloth cape-coat, forest green and bought in the Frankfurt airport (where any fool knows you can live out your life with any product your heart desires), I dubbed my "World-Famous Lodencloth Cape-Coat." My red bandanna, which was to make me look not-too-American, I called, not surprisingly, perhaps, "Babushka." And then there were my Okura slippers!

These nice simple leather scuffs had been one of the gifts at the glorious Okura Hotel in Tokyo several years before. Now, the Okura must be one of the most perfect hotels in the world, so you can imagine what the "Hearty Okura Slippers" were like: they saved me across Central Asia.

I also packed two complete medical kits, for I knew that the hospital services, always bad in the former Soviet Union, had by now completely broken down. I even carried my own clean syringes should I get into an accident or need an injection. (Often I put some of the syringes in the pockets of the World-Famous Lodencloth Cape-Coat just in case I got into an accident and needed a blood transfusion.) I packed reading matter: a rich lode of Russian history, several piles of magazines, entertainment reading, and of course some classic Soviet histories and commentaries, in particular my beloved Nikolay Berdyayev's *The Origin of Russian Communism.* I would discard them or leave them with people as I moved on. As it happened, the stacks of magazines that I brought to read and throw away were especially valuable; everyone so vied for them along the way that they almost, but not quite, took the place of money.

Since banks were largely nonexistent, most foreigners were out of necessity transmogrified into walking banks. I ended up carrying $3,000 in small bills in a money belt around my waist, which I removed only to bathe. By the time I was under way, I had so many things literally attached to me that I felt like a moving bulletin board or computer notebook.

So it was that I started on this strange journey, soon feeling that I was a kind of ship moving into uncharted seas. If I did not hit an iceberg or a torpedo (or even a high wave or a tree), everything would probably work. If I did hit anything, I, the ship, was in big trouble.

On Thursday, as the Train to Kazan approached more closely, I went to the international desk of Intourist to buy a ticket for the following week from Moscow to Alma-Ata in Kazakhstan. (In truth, this seemed like a rather silly expenditure to me because that would come *after* Kazan, and we all knew I was not returning from Kazan . . .)

What amazed me most of all was the depths to which Intourist had sunk. Intourist, after all, was the international tourism bureau of the superpower Soviet Union; it had sent Aeroflot planes all over the world and had handled tens of millions of passengers a year. Now, to get to the international or foreign desks, one went up through filthy, dirt-encrusted old hallways that smelled, as does everything in the former Soviet Union, of stale urine.

"It used to cost me $1,500 to fly to London," a British businessman standing next to me reminisced in the half hour or so it took to get our tickets. "Now it costs $5,600 because of the ruble problem."

"People are driving to Europe for the first time in decades," added his Russian partner, also a nice-looking young man.

"The money situation is almost comical," the Brit went on. "Businessmen are coming in here with $20,000 . . . $30,000 . . . $50,000 in their briefcases, because there is no place to put it. The banks that exist are hopeless. Often, they won't give you back your money . . ."

"Where are you going?" I finally asked them, as I watched the Intourist woman work on a computer. (In Moscow, at least, they do take Western credit cards, use computers, and are thus slowly entering the modern world.)

"Magadan," the Brit said.

Before my eyes flashed all the horror stories about Magadan in the far Far East of Russia, where the worst prison camp of all had stood for many years. Tens of thousands of prisoners would be dropped off on the ice floes. They would have to walk across the freezing ice for miles, some without shoes, many soon dropping to die, perhaps mercifully, in the snow.

"There is now a joint-venture hamburger stand in Magadan," the Brit said brightly.

I shook my head and said good-bye. It was getting hard to absorb it all.

If anyone thought Russia would change Bob Strauss, charming Texan and head of the Democratic party for many years, he was surely mistaken. No one could quite understand why Republican George Bush had sent Strauss, by then seventy, to be ambassador to Moscow. True, Strauss had monumental political skills. True, he could charm the hammer and sickle off a Warsaw Pact tank. But by his own admission, he knew nothing about Russia. Nobody's perfect.

So when I saw him that Thursday in January in the American embassy, I was pleased to see him filled with spirit, if a sometimes confused spirit.

"Georgie Anne," he said immediately upon my walking into his office, "this is one tough sonofabitch. It's the toughest job I've ever had . . .

"The economists tell me—the figure given to me—is that the value of the whole ruble market today is ten billion dollars. A foreigner could come in and buy that whole market—buy Russia. Then I talked to high government officials, and they told me they're out of wheat.

"Then a European businessman came in—and this will give you an idea of the way things are going here—and he told me, 'I've been working here for years, but suddenly strange things are going on. I owe different Russians about twenty million dollars, but they don't want me to pay them. Then suddenly they'll call and say they need one million dollars in medical supplies, or one million dollars of such-and-so: please pay us!' "

Bob Strauss leaned back in his chair in his small office and shook his head some more. "Now, I thought immediately that they wanted to put the money in an offshore bank—but no, that's *our* type of story! This isn't Central America or Miami. What's happening here is they're using this man as their barter bank. Why? Because that way, they don't have to pay any taxes on the money. And this is what's being done all over." He paused again.

"Georgie Anne, this is just one sonofabitch . . ."

Still, Bob Strauss had some hope, which gave me hope, and not incidentally took my mind off the Train to Kazan. He believed in the Boris Yeltsin team. He believed that the West should coordinate aid—not foolish aid, but practical aid—to help this stricken country emerge out of Communism and its attendant desperations.

"You can deliver food here," he said forcefully at one point in our talk. "You do it through the agencies or the European Community system. Almost every city has a crude commodity exchange and auction under sealed bids. You put the food in the stream and let the market function and use the proceeds for social benefits. I'm coming to the conclusion that's the way to go."

Still, at that freeze-frame moment in time, the reforms that had begun on January 2, only ten days before my arrival, were not working. Even Jeffrey Sachs, the Harvard economist who was the designer of the so-called "shock therapy," told me in some despair that they were not working. And a well-informed economist at a Western embassy in Moscow, trying to figure it all out, finally threw up his hands and asked:

"Is the food out there and they're hoarding it, or isn't it there? Nobody has the answer. The only thing is, something has to be done here. Nothing like this has ever been attempted before. It's like coming to a door, and it's blocked on the other side, and you don't know whether there's another room there or a dangerous staircase."

But what was unmistakable was the fact that the reforms begun on January 2, 1992—which were to jolt this turgid, decaying state into a semblance of modernity through the shock of freeing prices all at once—already were not working. Sachs kept shaking his head and wondering why there still wasn't food on the shelves. But more and more thoughtful people were counter-wondering whether a gradual policy of preparing Russians for this unknown new system would not have been wiser.

Moreover, it was these reforms that formed the crucial background to the mammoth changes that were occurring in Central Asia. Russia's economy had for decades been Central Asia's; Russia's stability was the stability of Kazakhstan, Kyrgyzstan, and Uzbekistan, so what was happening in Moscow was the fount of the rivers of change that I would be seeing "out there."

There had to be deeper reasons for why this was happening; there had to be profound historic tides that, despite the "originality" of Communism in its messianic ideological passion in history, could link the collapse of the powerful Soviet Union to other events in history.

I found some major reasons one bitter-cold morning when I walked briskly over to the Institute of the U.S.A. and Canada. Institutes like these had in Soviet times played a crucial role: they were the channels through which knowledge of and analyses of the West were carefully passed on to the appropriate *nomenklatura* of the Communist regime. To others, such information was forbidden, but these men and women, though by and large Communists, did generally express the truth about the threatening world outside.

This institute was housed in mellow old yellow buildings in a backstreet just off wide and busy Gorky Street. There, in the freezing cold, I found Boris Mihailov, a leading liberal political scientist, who gave me a good analysis of what more and more were coming to think was *the* mistake of the American-inspired "shock therapy."

"I was actually very concerned about just lifting prices as the first step," he said, as we sat talking, bundled up in his cold office. "I thought it was more important to privatize first, to establish readjustment training, and to use state procurements to fill the market in the first phase. Now I see that I was right. What happened was the prices are free, but the shops are still empty . . .

"What we are seeing on the larger scale is simply the classic process of the dissolving of empire," Professor Mihailov, a quiet, well-spoken, intelligent man, went on. "The old 'center' is dead, and that's good. We are now in the business of building classic nation-states. But there are problems."

I thought at that moment of Shelley, except nothing about the former Soviet Union seemed to "gleam," not even like junk! But I thought, too, about how, yes, the dissolution of the Soviet empire *did* compare to the collapse of other empires—the Abbasid in Baghdad in the ninth century, the Ottoman Turkish in the early twentieth century, the British Empire in our times, perhaps the American Empire in years to come.

That very night, my own problems seemed to loom larger. Late that same afternoon I received a call from "the representative of the Tatar Republic in Moscow." He had my ticket for the Train to Kazan, and could he please deliver it that very afternoon? This was it. My one last hope had been that the representative of the Tatar Republic, which had declared its sovereignty from Russia but was still within the new Russian state, would not exist; or he would not find me and would thus have to return the ticket. Another hope had been that there were so many breakdowns in the trains—there were no flights—that there would not even *be* any Train to Kazan.

Indeed, there were so many real possibilities for failure that I had to wonder, peevishly, to tell the truth, why it all had to work out so efficiently.

"Yes, all right, come over," was all I said, but I had seldom felt more depressed.

Sure enough, the Tatar chap, a baleful lad who insisted proudly upon showing me his full identification from the new Republic of Tatarstan, was standing there in the lobby, swaying slightly to the omnipresent dirgish music. He had a sturdy cap smacked down on his dark head, and he had my ticket securely in hand, as though he were holding the key to the gold supply of the old Soviet Union.

"Our people will meet you at the train on Monday morning," he told me; and then he left; and soon I would leave.

There was one last hope. My visa to Moscow was for only one week, obtained for me through the Radisson chain, which runs the Slavyanskaya, and no one really knew what to do once you got there. I was traveling, after all, to places like Kazakhstan and Kyrgyzstan and Uzbekistan. They had the historic nerve to think— and even to *declare*—that they were now countries, nations, republics of their own!

Did that mean you needed to have visas for each of these new "countries"? If so, where would you get them? They had no embassies or offices abroad, and most of them did not even have representation in Moscow. In short, if I could not get visas to these "entities" or get my pitiful week's visa extended to places that did not officially exist, then I did not really have to take the Train to Kazan.

Living in hope once again, on Thursday I brightly took my passport down to the desk of the Slavyanskaya. At first, the clerk, a holdover from the old Russia, said, *"Nyet vozmozhno"* ("It can't be done"). The first answer to any request was properly Old Soviet-negative.

I loved her. I wanted to embrace her. With more like her around, I might actually be able to announce my failure and turn around and go home. But then she, too, let me down.

It seemed there was some ruffian on the desk who pictured himself a modern Russian man, a kind of post–new socialist man, a Ross Perot of the steppes, who could "get things done."

I hated him, but I did give him my passport.

I snarled at him when he approached me in the lobby Friday morning with a big confident modern Russian "can-do" smile, obviously trained into his dark muzhik's heart by the well-meaning Radisson, and said in a manner that seemed to indicate that I should actually *thank* him, "We have got your visa extended—to February tenth, just as you wished!"

I tried to console myself by repeating to myself, "What is written in the sands is written," and/or "The moving hand has writ and, having writ, moves on. . . ." But, basically, I knew that now I was really going.

Saturday I wrote several columns. I tried to make them good, but not too good, because my dear editor, Elizabeth Anderson, would then later become so awfully saddened at the loss of such a talent.

And then—and then—there came a break.

A phone call came Friday to my room in the Slavyanskaya from a journalist visiting Moscow for *The Washington Times,* the paper in Washington, D.C., that buys my column. Her name was Judith Olney, and would I like to have a drink?

I was delighted with Judy. She was a tall, statuesque, utterly stunning blonde with a gorgeous smile and bearing that simply stopped men in their tracks. (Under normal circumstances, I might have been a trifle jealous, but my sex appeal or lack of it was, under these circumstances, at the very bottom of my list of concerns.) She was also a lot of fun. I also quickly caught on to the fact that she was also feeling more than a little uneasy about Russia, as was only smart; it was her first overseas assignment, and she was really the restaurant critic for the paper, so this political and economic world was, not unnaturally, all the more strange to her.

"I was dying to come," she said, "and I've been looking into some of these cults, run by Americans. I was thinking of going to St. Petersburg—I knew a man there who had fought in World War Two and . . . Where do you think I should go next?"

I looked at her very seriously. I looked at her searchingly. I wanted her to gain a proper appreciation for the gravity of what I was about to propose. Judy seemed quickly to grasp the tension of the moment and looked back at me with a kind of pleasant and open anticipation.

"You know, Judy," I finally said, "I never like to travel with people. I'm very much an individualist, and I can only really *see* things when I'm by myself. I've always had this thought that, in order to really feel everything and not miss things, one had to be by oneself."

She nodded politely while I paused for proper emphasis.

"But I'm going to Kazan in Tatarstan tomorrow night. It's supposed to be very interesting. They are the first people to have declared their independence within the Russian federation, but they are still within the Russian state, and, well, you seem so nice that I will break my rules for once. If you wanted to get a ticket tomorrow and go with me, well, that would be, well, okay!"

Judy looked very pleased indeed. "That would be terrific," she said. "And what is Kazan like? And what will we see there? And . . . where will we stay . . . and how much money should we take . . . ?"

Then, as I feared, she asked me how we were going to get there? This is how I, at least, remember it.

"There is a train," I answered. (I wasn't going to avoid or evade this truth.)

"And what is it like?" she asked. "I've heard there are a lot of criminals on the trains."

"No," I answered quickly. "Highwaymen."

She looked puzzled and crinkled up her eyes.

"Have you ever been on the Orient Express?" I asked.

"Oh, yes, actually I have . . ."

I nodded sagely.

"Ever taken the European Express from Washington, D.C., to Chicago?"

"As a matter of fact I have!" Now she was smiling.

"Ever taken the Empire State out West?"

She shook her head no.

I didn't say anything more. I only smiled like a person really sacrificing for her colleague, and in truth I didn't lie once.

"I'll bet you'll love it," was all I finally said. "You'll love the Train to Kazan."

Chapter 2

Tatarstan
Getting Even After 440 Years

If you scratch a Russian,
you find a Tatar.

Napoleon

I awoke early Monday morning, long before the dawn began to shower its light over this strange, dour world of the Russian steppes, and the Train to Kazan was working its doughty way across the plains in that methodical and unexcited manner of the true Russian railroad.

Unsparingly examining my feelings, I found them alternating between relief and disappointment. Relief that I had at least not yet been raped, robbed, or murdered. Disappointment that I would in the future be seen to have so inordinately feared something that was in truth so utterly ordinary.

The weakest of gray sunrises struggled to assert some guiding warmth outside, and the sun seemed to me to be also a little disappointed in that it, too, had to face still another day in such a contradictory continent and in such a confusing winter.

How could anyone have expected such a night on the feared Train to Kazan? How could one have anticipated that there would indeed be no highwaymen—not even one at all, not even some poor country-bumpkin muzhik or blundering party *paren* who looked sidewise at us—but only unsmiling, eternally unhappy Russians, Tatars, and perhaps a few history-weary Bashkirs?

I sighed, wondering to myself as I was thrown this way and that, as the train heaved and struggled to dominate the steppes: What should I worry about now?

The monumental train stations of Moscow are great, sobering behemoths, each one named after the noble destination of its vehicles: Kievsky, Belorussky, Kazansky, etc. Inevitably they evoked memories of those yearning and euphoric days of the Revolution, now long gone; of arrivals from Germany in closed trains whose movements would shake the world, now well past; and of open trains that would carry the suffering masses of exiles to unforgiving foreign parts, merely a memory.

At my insistence, Judy and I had gotten to the station far too early, and she tried to be a good sport about it, but she really didn't understand. For me, getting there early was a little like being sure you were at your own execution with plenty of time to think over what-might-have-been, perhaps even heroically give the sign to shoot.

Since we were going to Tatarstan for only three days, I had theatrically left almost all of my luggage at the Slavyanskaya, pretending that I would pick it up the following Thursday. That was all right; they had my syndicate's address, and they could easily ship the whole thing to them when I did not turn up. (I hoped that my editor, Elizabeth, would get the caviar I had purchased on Arbat Street.)

Judy, ever the vigilant restaurant critic and food editor, used her time to roam around the station buying bits of food: nothing special, a hard-boiled egg here, some meat pies there, some tea. The cavernous gray station, which in better days would have made a wonderful backdrop for Anna Karenina's heartbreaking farewell to Count Vronsky, now seemed to have plunged to a final Dostoevskian degradation.

The mood of smothering melancholia was not helped by the snow that was everywhere packed hard on the walkways, nor by the oppressive blackness of the deep winter night, through which only a few dim bulbs glowered. Outside, beautiful but determined snowflakes tumbled down upon us like damp manna from heaven, until we climbed into our first-class carriage and into our compact but comfortable compartment for four.

After all my fears, how could I possibly stoop to admit the embarrassing truth, which was that the Train to Kazan was utterly normal and woefully uneventful? How can I humiliate myself so, expose myself to the ridicule of friend and stranger alike? Well, the truth must emerge in this new era of *glasnost* for Russia, and the truth was that two friendly, chubby Russian-Tatar women climbed aboard who talked with us about the dismal situation in Kazan, with no food and all the enterprises closing and everybody wondering what under heaven was ever going to become of them.

Meanwhile, I quietly drank Scotch from the bottle I had carefully packed; I intended to make my last hours as frivolous and as happy as they could be.

"It's quite nice," Judy said, settling into one corner.

"Maybe this is just the start," I answered, cautious.

Judy giggled at me, and I giggled back. Then we sat back and talked about her two husbands (not at the same time), her son, her last divorce, our great loves and losses, our newspaper work and how nobody really appreciated us—until we both drifted into fitful sleep on the upper bunks that the other ladies insisted we take because they had "weakness in the knees."

As I lay there in the morning, thinking one more time that maybe the highwaymen might still attack (were they perhaps morning people?), the train's radio automatically switched on. Instead of the old Communist propaganda about the joys of the Communist party and the inevitable defeat of American imperialism, which was hated throughout the entire world, the announcements were:

"The German Christian Democrat party chief from Württemberg is visiting St. Petersburg this week . . .

"Experts from San Francisco on banking systems are meeting with President Boris Yeltsin in Moscow . . .

"The Ukrainian president has begun economic reforms designed to . . ."

The train lady brought us all hot tea: good, strong, black tea, which was one thing the Russians still had. The frosted windows slowly began to thaw, and, through the collage of melting ice and grime, I could see—with a certain breathless anticipation—the legendary "space" of central Russia, that vast unchanging panorama that had always emotionally swallowed up the spirit of the great Russian writers. We did not speak as we crossed the wide, frozen Volga, whose gray expanse made one think of its sister American rivers, like the Mississippi and the Ohio.

But how different its history! Actually, there are three Volgas—the upper, the middle, and the lower. The Volga has the honor of being the European continent's longest waterway, and, in Russia itself, it is the legendary subject of song, story, and national myth.

It is generally referred to lovingly as "Mother Volga."

Little wooden houses out of the nineteenth century sped by outside us; beside them all along the way were blurred and beautiful stands of white birch trees and an occasional modern city, always sporting those tall, gray, stolid Soviet buildings that Old Russians Turgenev and Tolstoy would most definitely not have liked.

"We are in Tatária!" one of the chubby women with the bad knees announced to us suddenly, in a hoarse whisper.

Outside, nothing had changed. I could see only more of the same rolling and hilly landscape, a universe stricken by the snows of Russia's eternal winters—a world forsaken even by *The New York Times*—a continent dug in until spring.

I thought at first it was a little like crossing from Iowa into Missouri, but in truth it was not. Tatarstan, which is the modern name for ancient Tatária, had long been one of the most closed parts of the Soviet Union. Indeed, the land of the Tatars, descendants of the Mongols, was until now almost entirely closed to the world because of its giant defense industries and huge oil industry. It had been opened only in 1988 after Mikhail Gorbachev began his reforms.

Yes, now we were in historic Tatarstan, where some of the Mongol hordes that had come sweeping across the plains of Central Asia in the thirteenth century under Genghis Khan settled down.

What kind of a fellow was Genghis Khan? Once asked by one of his aides what was life's sweetest pleasure—and after one horseman had volunteered that it was surely falconry—Genghis Khan replied coldly, "You're mistaken. Man's greatest good fortune is to chase and defeat his enemy, seize his total possessions, leave his married women weeping and wailing, ride his gelding, and use the bodies of his women as a nightshirt . . ."

Whether the khanates of Central Asia; whether the empires of China, the Arab world, or the Persians; whether the Kievan Rus or fledgling Muscovy, each empire was then at its moment of birth or in full bloom. Great civilized cities were beginning to emerge, with intricate cultures and art. Christian Kiev was developing strong contacts with Western Christian Europe. Muscovy might eventually have followed Kiev's example; it was Mongol suppression that inflicted upon Muscovy, for all time to come, its paranoid fear of outsiders from both East and West. On top of all that, being oppressed and conquered by what they considered to be a primitive and inferior people added fearsome and ultimately unfathomable dimensions of guilt and shame to the later Russians' psyche that exist to this day.

Had they been left alone, these cultures could have developed into mature and progressive societies. Instead, in the face of the frightful losses inflicted by the Mongols, all turned inward. As the legendary American intelligence officer and ranking adventurer Archie Roosevelt wrote, "In the Slavs' millennium-long confrontation with their Eastern neighbors lies the key to an understanding not only of Russian history, but Russian character."

Yet, nothing was ever simple in Central Asia. Historian Paul Goble, one of the world specialists on the area and a brilliant analyst, points out that roughly 30 percent of the hordes were some sort of Nestorian Christian, and that another third was Jewish! This only sounds strange—and it certainly does sound strange—if one does not realize that all religions were proselytizing and cross-proselytizing even in those remote areas and especially in those ancient days. Judaism had reached out there, at one point to convert a whole people, the Khazars of today's Azerbaijan, thus opening the historic opportunity for a Jewish state and possible empire in the Middle Ages.

Genghis Khan's successors subjugated Russia for a century and a half, and the European Renaissance and the Enlightenment never reached the gray steppes, the deep forests, or the impenetrable minds that the Mongol conquest had so cruelly formed and left behind. As Central Asian historian Robert C. Kaplan puts it, using interchangeably the word Tatar for Mongol: "The Tatars were, by and large, responsible for orientalizing Russia. And ever since the days of Ivan the Terrible, in the sixteenth century, the Russians, burdened with an inferiority complex and a need for revenge, have been on the offensive against the Turkic peoples."

Once the Mongol threat began to recede in the fifteenth and sixteenth centuries, khanates, city-states ruled by local khans, took the place of the imperial Mongol power. In the tenth century, the advanced kingdom of Bulgar, which was the ancestor polity of Kazan and whose ruins lie today just south of Kazan on the Volga, adopted Islam. From the thirteenth to the fourteenth centuries, princes of Muscovy were even vassals of the Tatar khans, while later Tatar feudal lords served the rulers of Muscovy.

But the Russians eventually got even. Finally resurgent, the Russians under Ivan the Terrible, whose own character certainly equaled in evil that of Genghis Khan, took Kazan, where the Tatars had by then settled. The year was 1552, and Ivan not only crushed the city, he constructed an astonishing White Kremlin atop the ruins of the old Tatar fortress; the White Kremlin still broods hauntingly over the confluence of the Volga and Kama rivers. Tatars were then moved en masse to the villages, so that the cities were totally Russified, and every attempt was made to wipe out Tatar culture, just as the Mongols had tried to wipe out Russian culture.

After 1917, the Soviets continued the, shall we say, tradition of getting even with the Tatars; they kept the area not only closed to the outside world but under the mailed fist. Stalin attempted to destroy historic memory by forcing first the Latin and then the Cyrillic alphabet on his Turkic subjects, a move designed both to Slavicize them and to destroy any attempts at unity among the Turkic peoples of Central Asia. It was all very deliberate and open; Stalin divided the Muslim communities of the middle Volga into different peoples, so that there was little possibility of their minds and souls turning again to the ancient dream of a (finally!) united "Turkestan."

Pondering all of that, as we watched the snow-covered forests pass by outside, I felt a rush of excitement. I knew that now those inexorable flows of history were being reversed once again. Now it was Tatar time to get even. The Tatars were the first people within Russia to declare independence from it; theirs was the first rift, the first rip in that tight and unforgiving national fabric so carefully woven by the Bolsheviks, the first threat to the territorial integrity of Russia itself.

I was riding toward one of the great stories in the world—and nobody had yet written it.

"We greet you officially on behalf of the Watan Society of Tatarstan, which is responsible for relations with one million Tatars abroad. You must know that only twenty-five percent of Tatars live on our territory. They are spread in forty different countries—Austria, Finland, Turkey, Romania, China, the United States. Here in Tatarstan live 1,750,000 Tatars, and there are more than five million who live in the former Soviet Union. The Tatar language is Turkic. The famous University of Kazan opened in 1804 and Tolstoy, Pushkin, and Gorky studied there. But as early as the ninth century, the Bulgar state was founded—that was the predecessor to

Kazan—and it adopted Islam. We celebrated the 1,100th anniversary of adopting Islam in 1989."

With that astonishing greeting, Damir Gismetdinov, a well-dressed, businesslike Tatar who had come to meet us at the arrival of the Train to Kazan, barely missed a breath as he immediately gave us this capsule history of Kazan. He stood there, in the snow, and began his unstoppable speech about his new country of Tatarstan. Damir, we soon learned, was from the newly formed Watan, or "Homeland" Society, and it was typical of the burning aspirations I was to find everywhere on this trip that these young Tatar professionals had immediately organized to reach out to their fellow countrymen who had gone abroad. That outreach for physical and spiritual support was a backup for getting out from under the cruel and officious thumb of Moscow (referred to as "the center"). My God, how they wanted out!

But our little scene was to become even more incongruous, minute by minute. Within half an hour, beautiful and sexy Judy (whom they did not, of course, expect and had no idea at all what to make of) and I had been duly checked into the Tatarstan Hotel in downtown Kazan and were sitting in an ornate Oriental-style private dining room in this hotel in "hungry" Russia. With us was the Radio Liberty correspondent, a handsome and charming roughneck named Rimzil Valeev, our interpreter, a slim and pretty young lady named Dania, and a striving *biznismyen* named Rimil. An extraordinary spread of soups, caviar, hard-boiled eggs, noodles, beet salad, vodka, and sliced beef was spread out on the formal table before us.

That, and optimism too!

"Soon our republic will become very famous worldwide and in Europe," Damir, the tireless propagandist, went on. "Now I'll explain why. We are going to have the same problems we had with 'the center' throughout history. The less the Russian leaders understand them, the more acute the problems will become. Because we have a leading position in the economy of Russia . . ."

The three others nodded enthusiastically. Having come out of the darkness of the cave, they were seeing Tatarstan as the new center not only of their world, but of *the* world.

"We produce more products than the three Baltic republics," Damir went on. "Oil, chemicals, chemical products, medical instruments, synthetic rubber, raw materials, rubber tires, computing, optical, high-quality motors for the defense of the army. Sixty percent of the trucks in Russia are from Tatarstan. We produce more than the three Baltic republics together, and we have the great fertile lands of the Volga." He paused, basically for breath. "Tatarstan could paralyze the whole country's economy," he finally summed up proudly, as we all downed another vodka.

Then Rimzil added, with his hopeful and mischievous smile, "After declaring independence, we started negotiating with Czechoslovakia, Yugoslavia, Hungary, the United States, Germany, Finland, and Turkey. Moscow calls our economic and political acts illegal, and they have imposed a sort of economic blockade and won't allow some raw materials to pass to us. It seems, however," he added archly, "that we understand market relations better than they do in Moscow. We don't want their old empire system; no, we are much closer in our thinking to a world integration system."

Then, as we tore into the incredible lunch, which made me feel guilty again, Damir took still another swig of vodka and gazed adoringly (again) at Judy.

"Where did you come from?" he finally asked.

Since in truth it was hard to explain, I answered for her, saying only, "Well, we met Saturday night in the hotel. And she writes for one of my papers and all her life she has been dying to come to Kazan—on the train!"

This pleased everyone. Everyone smiled happily at such good sense.

Before we left for a tour around the city, the Tatar gentlemen smiled devilishly at one point and began to tell the interesting story of Soviet space genius Roald Sagdeev, who had stunned and delighted and made immensely proud all of Tatardom by marrying Susan Eisenhower, the beautiful, charming, and intelligent granddaughter of President Dwight D. Eisenhower.

Roald was a Tatar to his bones, they assured me, and he and Susan had come back to visit "free" Kazan only the year before. "They were asked on television whether Roald wanted to be president of an independent Tatarstan." Rimzil told the story, as they all smiled broadly. "And he said no, but Susan said yes!"

I almost asked them whether Roald and Susan had come to Kazan on the train, but at the last minute I controlled myself.

Whenever I think about the unexpected in life, I shall think of Kazan. The city was simply beautiful. Oh, it was worn down, decaying, peeling, weeping, sleeping, dreaming, hallucinating, hoping, fearing, dreading—but simply beautiful!

I had barely known that a "Kazan" existed until some weeks before, when the head of Radio Liberty in Munich, the brilliant Sovietologist Enders Wimbush, told me importuningly that I "must" go to Tatarstan "because the independence story is so good." Wimbush, one of the world's specialists on Central Asia, is also a wise man and knows when to let fate take over, so he did not tell me much more, except that although Tatarstan is not officially part of Central Asia, it is Islamic and is linked to the "Great Game" area by religion, by language, and by innumerable ties of history.

I suspect that, once he had me on the Train to Kazan, he knew it was better to let me discover some things for myself.

How does one describe the special—the singular—beauty of Kazan, my unknown sultana of a city? It has streets upon streets of shingled, many-colored, neat wooden houses of that Old Russia that one feared had flown away forever on the wings of the Revolution. Those stand next to nineteenth-century Parisian-style mansions of the rich bourgeoisie, who gave birth to an age of culture in Kazan when the press, arts, and theater flourished; and all stand only streets away from Ivan's savage White Kremlin, which glowers like a rooted silver hawk poised impassively over the snow-choked Volga, which for its part spreads out like the fingers of a lake into the rich steppes of the Volga region. The city has beautiful old squares, with stately buildings, and a museum that was to have been dedicated to Lenin but has now been wisely converted into a museum of Tatar culture. And, indeed, the Tatar jewelry, clothing, and artifacts are gorgeous: delicate hats intricately embroidered with pearls, hammered silver and gold bracelets and necklaces, and hand-sewn boots of many colors. (Under the implacable rule of the Soviets, in every textbook there was somewhere a sentence saying "Soviet power gave literacy to the Tatar nation." To the contrary, the Tatars were so advanced that they had an 80 percent literacy rate before the Soviets came, and the great capital city of Bulgar, even in the thirteenth century, was larger than Paris or London.)

Then there was the University of Kazan, which seemed far more European, far more French, than Russian. But then, Kazan, famous also as the city where the early Lenin lived and studied, had always been a uniquely cultured place. In the sixteenth century, the Tatar diplomats and language were considered so elegant that Ivan the Terrible himself was once given a document by the German ambassador in German and the Russian answered archly, "We accept documents only written in Latin—or Tatar."

As for Lenin, they are not so mad at him in Kazan (or so unconscious of the lovely city's potential for future tourism) that they were going to wipe out the museum housed in the lovely old wooden building where he had lived with his mother and siblings. It is a small, neat, brown frame house—very pleasant and bourgeois, actually—with immaculate little rooms, lots of perfect lace doilies, and shiny dressers and warm cozy corners. It was from that house that the strange young man, Vladimir Ilyich Ulyanov (known to the world as Lenin), then seventeen and already fixated by his brother's execution for treason, was plucked and taken to jail in 1887. (Lenin's "crime" was standing in the front row of a student meeting at the university, fists clenched, and presenting the dean with a list of demands at a time when political activity on the part of the students was forbidden.)

In short, by the end of even that first day in Kazan, I was quite breathless with the beauty of it all. Judy was, too. (We even found several little stores selling some charming locally designed and made Tatar jewelry.) I had been to Salzburg and to Machu Picchu, to Muscat and Nikko, to Novgorod and Ouro Prêto—all contenders for the prize of most romantic spot in the world—but I had never before found a treasure city that was so unknown, so new, so unexplored, and with so much promise for the future, given a little prosperity and investment.

Then you cover all of those little streets and picturesque houses with a white, sugary snow and freeze it together with bitter winds that blow through the white birch forests, and you have Old Russia anew today.

Indeed, the city was so beautiful in the snow that, despite the cold, I really did not yearn for summer—except for one reason. The ruins of Bulgar, the mother city of the Tatars, lay two short hours down the Volga, on the east side of the river, and one dared not travel there in winter.

This is the way the prominent Russian historian S. M. Solovev described the importance of Bulgar:

> For a long time, Asia, Muslim Asia, built a home here—a home not for nomadic hordes, but for its civilization; for a long time, a commercial and industrial people, the Bulgars, had been established here. When the Bulgar was already lis-

tening to the Koran on the shores of the Volga and the Kama, the Russian Slav had not yet started to build Christian churches on the Oka and had not yet conquered these places in the name of European civilization.

Indeed, the Bulgar state was one of highly developed crafts, with skilled potters, blacksmiths, coppersmiths, carpenters, stonemasons, jewelers, and tanners. Bulgar stonemasons and carpenters created splendid palaces, caravanserais, mosques, and houses as far away as Central Asia and even in Russia's beautiful cities of old churches, Vladimir and Suzdal. It arose in about the tenth century out of a mixture of the Mongols and one or more sedentary Turkic peoples who developed an urban civilization in the lands of the Oka and Kama rivers.

But Bulgar was important mainly because it so early was such a special center of Islam. "Islam became the nucleus around which the spiritual life of the Bulgar state developed after the tenth century," Crimean Tatar scholar, Azade-Ayşe Rorlich, probably the world's leading Central Asianist, and now in America, wrote. "The Arabic script that accompanied the adoption of Islam became not only the vehicle for disseminating a new religion but also the key to learning and opening the door to the cultural heritage of the Muslim East. The existence of a literary language had a profound effect on education, and in turn, that language was enriched by the fruits of education. The Muslim Bulgars had schools where secular subjects received as much attention as the teaching of the religious dogma. . . . Many Bulgar scholars of the twelfth and thirteenth centuries gained fame and recognition beyond the shores of the Volga and Kama."

But when the Mongol hordes, under Batu Khan, swept over Bulgar in 1236, they devastated its lands, just as they devastated everything in their paths. From Bulgar they swept on to Moscow, and in the winter of 1240 they reached—and destroyed—Christian Kiev, and thus all of Russia's budding links to Western Europe.

But Batu Khan then chose Bulgar as his capital, and Bulgar recovered from the Mongol conquest to become such a great trading center in the fourteenth century that it became known as the "Golden Throne of the Mongol Khans."

But the Russian czars, with their unquenchable appetite for empire and for expansion, were moving on many fronts, searching even beyond these steppes and beyond Central Asia to vast, rich Siberia and subduing the peoples on the southern edge of what was to become the Soviet/Afghan border. But when that empire fell apart in the mid-sixteenth century, the ruling Siberian khan, Ediger, turned to Ivan the Terrible, the first Russian czar. For help in keeping his crown, Ediger offered Ivan a sable skin for each male inhabitant of his region. Instead, Ivan summoned the Stroganovs, a rich merchant family, and offered them the deed to vast portions of western Siberia if they would only conquer it using their own money.

Basically, what was happening in the sixteenth and seventeenth centuries was that important Muslim territories were being conquered and then incorporated into the Russian Empire: first Kazan in 1552; then Astrakhan and western Siberia; Tashkent in 1865; Bukhara and Khiva in 1873; the rich khanate of Kokand in 1875; and, finally, in the late nineteenth century, the Turkmen territories in Central Asia were the last to be defeated.

With all this in mind, it was not surprising that once Gorbachev loosened the old bans on history, Tatar pride in their Bulgar heritage had grown so great in the post-Soviet period that there was recently a movement to change the name "Tatar" to "Bulgar." There was even a club formed, Bulgar-Al-Jadid (The New Bulgar). It was a claim not so much for ethnic pride and revival, as a reaffirmation of authenticity; it was a tie marking direct descendance from that past that the Soviets, and particularly Stalin, had tried so desperately to wipe out.

The winter before my trip to Central Asia, I had published a biography of Fidel Castro, a book called *Guerrilla Prince: The Untold Story of Fidel Castro.* I had sent a copy to President George Bush through my neighbors, who were close friends of the Bushes. Thus started an amusing little exchange. The president wrote a note thanking me for the book and saying it was "on his bedstand." Then Barbara Bush told people (on the record) that the president was reading "Georgie Anne's book on Castro." So I then wrote a funny column (at least I thought it was funny) bewailing the fact, tongue-in-cheek, that the president was so wasting his time.

He then responded by sending me a wonderful picture of him studiously reading my book aboard *Air Force One.* Below, he wrote on it: "To Georgie Anne Geyer, I go all around proudly say-ing I know the author of 'Guerrilla Prince,' Best Wishes, George Bush."

One day, on an impulse, I brought out a copy of the picture, which I carry with me in my briefcase, to show to our new Tatar friends. I didn't know if it was the right thing to do, because I did not want them to think that I was trying to impress them. As it turned out, it was quite the right thing to do: they were delighted! They studied it, and touched it; they endlessly oohed and ahhed.

Indeed, they were so happy about it that I began to show it to selected people throughout the trip.

Soon, I realized what it was that pleased them so: the picture gave them importance and underlined their hope that the world out there—the important world of leaders, journalists, and think-ers, and above all investors—would know of them. To them, I had become no less than a messenger of the American president.

Judy and I had "suites" in the hotel. A suite: read that as two small rooms, very shabby, one with two beds that somewhat resembled ship's berths. The baths were primitive, but not nearly so bad as those that would come later, when I would soberly decide I would never get clean again, ever. It was in Kazan that I started "taking a shower" wearing my wonderfully solid Hearty Okura Slippers from the gorgeous Okura in Japan. I would stand in the tub with my sturdy and unsinkable Nipponese slippers on and spray the hand-held "shower" over my shoulders. That way I never actually had to touch anything.

In Russia, the idea of learning how to look after foreigners in a hotel was about as enticing to people as military service in Afghani-stan, without a gun. So I was amazed to find the *dezhurnaya,* or "key-keeper," here to be quite charming.

"Lock your doors," the *dezhurnaya* on our floor would lecture us. "Don't go out without locking your door." (So there *were* high-waymen around!)

At first I simply assumed that these Tatar women were of that legendary band of miserable, vicious Russian Amazons who were born and bred to turn every floor of every hotel in Russia into a perfect living hell for every guest, foreign or national, male or fe-male, friendly or unfriendly, who had the temerity to dare to set foot there. But, no! The Tatar key-keepers were exceptionally nice, sweet local women, farm women perhaps, because they seemed abnormally happy to have these jobs, and even eager to please.

One becomes very grateful for small favors when one is traveling in Russia.

Tuesday we went in a tight little delegation to see the country's vice-president, one Vasily Nikolaevich Likhachev, who had been a professor at the University of Kazan. It was a perfectly beautiful day of winter, a great day of winter, a day so cold and so bright you thought you were surely onstage. His office was up in the imposing, forboding, menacing, *wonderful* White Kremlin buildings, with their watchtowers ever gazing down the Volga for the enemies that were sure to appear again. From between the pink drapes in his pleasant-enough modern office, we could see the gray sky darkening and the black crows flying and soaring. The six of us sat around a long table, drinking tea, underneath a map of Tatarstan that looked like a geopolitical Rorschach blot, the interpretation of which would only be asking for trouble.

"Our situation here is complicated and it is very important," began the vice-president, who was such a neatly dressed and kind of "square" young man that one could imagine him a football player at Iowa State. "Basically, the aim is sovereignty and independence. This means a lot of work should be done in the fields of economics and politics." Tatarstan had already declared sovereignty in August 1990, by act of the new parliament (an act that nobody in the West seemed to know about or at least focus on), but the Russian federation had not accepted such insolence and Boris Yeltsin himself had sarcastically insulted the dignity of the recalcitrant Tatars and dismissed them with a surly "Get as much independence as you *can*!"

"For this last one and a half years, we have already seen it's very easy to declare sovereignty, but very difficult to achieve it," he went on. "When people say it's very easy to cut off all relations with Russia, it seems that people don't understand the depth of the whole problem.

"In the negotiations that have been going on in Moscow, I recently sat next to the deputy prime minister, Gennadi Burbulis, the representative of the Russian republic, and I told him, and not only once, that the problem of the autonomous republics is one of the main problems of the Russian government." He paused, then looked rather pleased for a moment. "Soon we are going to sign an agreement on economic cooperation between Tatarstan and Russia. This is important because it is the first time in history that our relations with Russia are such that we can keep half of our oil. As you know, economic freedom leads to political independence— I'm sure of it. In our negotiations with Russia, I told them that I had an idea—that we should make it a unique economic area. A 'unique economic area' equals economic integration. What we need now are new laws and new documents—do it legally!—and we should also consider a common market."

The vice-president's words were indicative of the mood. Everywhere I went in those odd four days that I was in Kazan, virtually everyone I talked to in official circles was looking euphorically outward after so many years of forcible restraint and of being sacked by Moscow of its oil, trucks, and wealth. Everyone we spoke to wanted foreigners to come, come, and come.

Linar Nailyevich Latypov, the smooth and smart aide to the prime minister and the regime's leading economic advisor, received us in his busy, cramped little office, beginning in perfect English:

"Actually, the geography of our visitors is very wide . . . all the European countries . . . the United States, San Francisco Teleport, a $450 million contract for radio and telecommunications. . . . The main problem of this country is telephone communication—you can't even call your office from Kazan." At this, he looked very determined for such a small man. "By 1993, you will. Petro FAC, Inc., Texas—the extraction of oil and a refinery. Paine Webber— one of the directors is a Tatar. A huge nineteen-person delegation from Canada. Our oil: previously the bulk of the oil was taken away by Russia. Now we have signed an economic agreement with Russia in 1991 so that fifty percent of the oil extracted here will go to Tatarstan, with five million tons for export."

He paused at this. "For the first time since 1552," he went on, in a sudden and incongruous switch from showboating to wonder, "the Russians and the Tatars sat down at the table and concluded an agreement. There was no treaty on paper all these centuries. You see what is happening in Russia: there is no way out except to have an agreement with the national republics. Then the next step is political agreement, but that is very serious and complicated, that would mean independence, and it would provide the precedent for the other republics. . . ."

The manner in which Tatarstan was having to "protect" itself exposed the multiple and layered realities of the time. Because prices were only a half to a third of those in Russia proper, and because the Tatars had not gone so enthusiastically and totally into the January 2 "shock therapy" price freezing as the Russians had, they had had to put customs checks on all their roads, functioning around the clock, with all trucks going in and out of Tatarstan checked. What became apparent in my talks in Kazan was that there, as elsewhere, it was only when these dependent peoples actually felt and saw the Soviet Union going down that they jumped upon independence as the only way to save themselves. Independence became a double jeopardy: long abstractly desired but now also absolutely needed in practice if one was not to drown in the very floods of change loosed by Moscow's swift decline.

Once, I thought to ask if they had any sympathy for Moscow, for its terrible plight these days.

Latypov sniffed, as though something malodorous had assaulted his nostrils.

"If Moscow starves," he said finally, looking me straight in the eye with one of the coldest stares I had ever seen, "who will care?"

As everywhere across the trajectory of the former Soviet Union, the transformation being attempted here—from a command economy where every decision for every republic was made in "the center" and where every industry was specialized and set up to barter with industries in the other republics, to a free-market economy, where the market controls decisions, supplies, and products—was more difficult than fighting World War II. They had literally to transform the mentality of the people; they had to restructure every industry and business and discover new markets for products that were almost uniformly below world levels of acceptance; and they needed to create basic things, like telephones!

The winter I arrived in Tatarstan, for instance, foreign businessmen there could not communicate by telephone with their home offices. Nor could the Tatars call out.

The phone situation was so bad that President Mintimer Shaimiev finally ordered a phone installed in his office that was capable of direct communications with orbiting satellites—at the cost of $30,000 for installation, with the government paying $15 for every minute he used it.

Here you had Tatarstan, with 3.6 million people, studded with rich oil fields and former defense plants, a place where the Soviets had built their most sophisticated bombers. But civilian phones, when they existed at all, were 1920s rural America! For the individual, even making a call within the country was a disaster; one had to wait hours at the post office and only one household in eighteen had its own phone.

Enter the knight in shining armor fighting the biggest battle of his life, the khan on his best Mongol pony carrying messages from post to post. Enter the Hughes Aircraft Company, which was promising to drag Tatarstan out of the telephonic Dark Ages with one of the most advanced cellular and satellite telecommunications systems in the world. They were there, and they were working on it, and a lot of people had faith.

Me? I'll believe it when I see it.

The pictures of Mir-Said Sultan Galiev show him to be intelligent, gallant, romantic—and doomed. He was darkly handsome, with a square, sturdy face, long fine nose, and very heavy eyebrows. His black hair was swept dramatically back from his face like waves of that dark and turbulent sea that—in both human and in ideological terms—he inhabited.

To tell the truth, I had never heard of Sultan Galiev, even though I have always read history much like children read comic books, and in Kazan I found that there was good reason for that. Sultan Galiev was *the* hero of both the Tatar and the Islamic worlds at the time of the Bolshevik Revolution; but far from being an anti-Communist "White," he was actually a very different and fascinating kind of nationalistic "Red." He represented, in those tumultuous days in which he lived, a kind of Communism different from that of Moscow: he represented "national Communism" in Tatarstan, and he represented at the same time a secular interpretation of Islam that, had it prevailed, could have changed the history of the Middle East and very likely would have worked to save it from the regressive vagaries of Islamic extremism and politicized fundamentalism.

When I stopped in Munich en route to Moscow, Enders Wimbush shamelessly whetted my appetite for knowing more about this unknown and uniquely glamorous Sultan Galiev.

"Remember that the Tatars were the elite of the Muslim world in those centuries," this fine analyst of Islamic Central Asia said.

"They were educated in the great universities of Europe and the Middle East. They had a special philosophy, Jadidism, which would have preserved the community of believers in the faith while gradually purging the faith of its most objectionable reactionary elements.

"Then when the Soviets came, they killed all the intelligentsia and closed the mosques. Thus they stifled all the modern trends in Islam. Sultan Galiev would have married nationalism, Islam, and socialism in a unique way—and he would have united the Turkic areas of all of Central Asia. A great part of the thrust of uniting the Turkic areas—of creating the dream of one vast 'Turkestan'—came from Kazan. For seventy years, the Bolsheviks cracked down on Islam and Sultan Galievism. Then, in the mid-eighties, with perestroika, the Tatars began asserting themselves again. Gorbachev was horrified; he wanted to suppress it. Yeltsin was, too—they both wanted a big state, a powerful state—and Tatarstan was in the middle of Russia. If it blew, it could make Nagorno-Karabakh look insignificant."

The "unknown" life of the valiant Islamic revolutionary is an endlessly fascinating one. Coming of age in the 1890s, Sultan Galiev was the direct result of that long search for modernization within the Tatar and, before that, Bulgar world that spanned the nineteenth century. Tatar intellectuals became all too aware that the Moslem schools and mosques were falling behind; they began to seek new principles that would allow them to remain Muslim but at the same time to modernize. Sultan Galiev tried to bring socialism and Islam together in a "proletarian nation," as opposed to the mobilization of the traditional working classes in Marxist internationalism. After becoming a Communist party member in 1917, he "refined the Communist doctrine into a specific blueprint for revolution not only for the Turkic peoples of Russia but also for their Turkic brothers still oppressed by imperialist powers beyond its border," as one historian put it. "He had a bold vision of all Muslim peoples living together in a kind of Turkic commonwealth within the new socialist order."

Sultan Galiev called his idea of a united Turkic-Muslim state "Turan," and his conception was for a "Republic of Turan," a term still used among scholars. He of course intended it to include historic and legendary "Turkestan," which is largely confined to Central Asia but would also include Azerbaijan and a host of other Turkic-Muslim peoples in the North Caucasus and elsewhere. He even planned to codify one language for all the Turkic territories. Indeed, the concept of "Turkestan" was advanced by a number of Central Asian intellectuals, but primarily by the Bashkir soldier-scholar, Zeki Velidi Togan, who fled the Bolsheviks to Turkey, where he taught about "Turkestan" with great distinction for more than sixty years. (A tough, resilient, and remarkable man in the style of most of these Central Asian dreamers, he embarked successfully on a Greyhound bus trip of the United States when he was nearly ninety years old!) In short, the idea and dream of "Turkestan" was basically kept alive from abroad, as the Soviets outlawed the slightest mention of it. Since no one (and no oppression) is perfect, however, they incongruously named one of the largest Central Asian military districts the Turkestan Military District.

And so, "Turkestan" would have been an alliance of all the areas where the majority population or major ethnic group was of Turkic descent: Kazakhstan, with 16.5 million persons; Uzbekistan, with 19.9 million; Kyrgyzstan, with 4.3 million; Turkmenistan, with 3.5 million; and Tajikistan (the only Central Asian country whose language is not in the Turkic group but is a form of Persian), with 5.1 million.

It was these new countries that, during Soviet times, made the Soviet Union the fifth largest Muslim power in the world, with more Muslims in the U.S.S.R. than in Egypt and more Turkic peoples in Central Asia than in Turkey. Moreover, as Wimbush puts it, this ascent of Muslim/Marxist philosophy under Sultan Galiev and his comrades "constitutes more than a little-known episode of revolutionary history and more than a chapter in the formation of the Soviet state. In addition, Muslim national Communism was a skillfully elaborated revolutionary strategy for the entire colonial or semicolonial world, and herein lies its importance both for twentieth-century history and for the future. National Communism was foremost a blueprint for national liberation . . . the time was at hand when the oppressed nations of the world would rise up and cast off their oppressions. . . . Marxism must be rooted in individual nations for it to be meaningful. . . ."

But Sultan Galiev never lived to see his ideological/religious dreams realized. When Lenin died and Stalin took over the party in 1924, there were none Stalin abhorred more than these "national Communists." Even though Sultan Galiev's love for Islam was not so much religious as cultural, and with a touch of mysticism, even the small religious part made Stalin determined to wipe out these heretics. As well, Stalin began his ruthless suppression of all the histories of the national republics as a way of destroying in the public consciousness any memory of any possible alternative to the state of steel he had imposed upon these geographically unlucky peoples. Of all of those, none was more suspect and dangerous than Sultan Galiev, who was forming underground cells against the Soviets.

After being arrested several times in 1928, Sultan Galiev was arrested for the last time and disappeared into the camps. No one really knows what ultimately befell him, but surely with him died all hope of any reformist Islam, of national socialism in a secular state, and of ideas that could have served as a liberalized, education-based, central modernizing force for the entire searching Muslim world.

With Sultan Galiev's disappearance from the scene, the curtain was raised on the unspeakable horrors of the Oriental Communist Stalins on the one side and the fanatic Muslim fundamentalist Khomeinis on the other.

> *"The time will come!" they said*
> *And waited with hope.*
> *But when the time came, how many of them,*
> *How many of them, were already gone.*
> A. MINHAJEVA, TATAR POET

But the story does not end there. All reading about or knowledge of Sultan Galiev and his movement were forbidden by the Stalin regime. The Islamic revolutionary's name disappeared from the books, if not from all memory.

And, today?

There is a spacious and potentially beautiful square in front of the one really tasteful modern building in Kazan, which is a brick-and-glass design that now contains the new art museum and will eventually house the offices for the hoped-for new enterprises. It stands on the shore of the sprawling Volga, and one night I stood there in the biting cold, with whorls of ice and snow circling like gray sharks on the swollen river, while tiny lights glimmered along the shores like visiting lightning bugs of some dreamed-of summer. I thought again how beautiful it really could be.

That square had been Lenin Square. Now it has been renamed. It is Sultan Galiev Square, and soon a large monument will be created there for the black-haired romantic hero.

Trying to force people to forget is always at best an imprecise and dangerous undertaking.

One noon, as we were lunching (food not bad at all) in the government's mess in one of the official government buildings, a charming old professor, Makhmut Nigmatizianov, who introduced himself to us as a musicologist from the University of Kazan, sat down with us for a few minutes and excitedly embarked upon the story of his new passion.

"For the first time in four hundred years, I was the one who was able to give a lecture on music in one of our schools," he began. "School is the most important problem for us now, because all Soviet efforts for three or four generations have been directed at the denationalization of people—they should be cut off from their own national culture. All of our history was totally distorted, and you Americans and Europeans don't know that. Everything important was always hidden." Then he brightened considerably as he went on, saying, "I took an expedition to Siberia and to the Caspian Sea—six thousand kilometers—to put down folk songs. I met Tatars everywhere and found their songs. I published three volumes of them.

"It is commonly accepted that Tatars today are divided into Crimean, Volga, and Siberian Tatars. In fact, their roots are the same everywhere. And, you know, songs are the most stable factor in determining the ethnic factor of a nation. Language can be changed; songs cannot be changed so easily." As he continued, his broad Tatar face glowed. "Even the Hungarians have some of our songs," he went on, nearly singing himself now. "They are not only the heritage of our Tatar people, but of the whole world."

Then he seemed to think of something and asked, "Do you know what the Russians used to say? In the West there are only Germans—and in the East, there are only Tatars. That was Russian 'thought.' That," he summed up, almost giggling now with the absurdity of it, "was the Russian way of explaining peoples."

By Tuesday afternoon, after nearly two days of nonstop interviews and nonstop absorption, I could not help but notice that the three men—Rimzil, Damir, and Rimil—seemed to be trying to keep a secret. They would suddenly start talking only in Tatar and making childlike gestures among themselves like a trio of potentially very bad boys.

I considered this to be a notably bad sign, given the abundant potential for disaster in this whole little adventure. By five o'clock, there was a great bustling and moving about of our little group, and suddenly we were in the car on the highway crossing the frozen Volga, headed out to the country. My heart sank.

"Where are we going?" I first asked, then importuned, and finally demanded. "Where? Where, Rimzil? *Where?*"

He would just grin idiotically each time and say, "You wanted to take a bath, didn't you?"

A bath?

Rimzil must have been secretly studying videos of the Indianapolis 500 somewhere, because we never went under seventy-five miles an hour, and the roads were not only bad to start with, they were utterly covered with ice and snow. (Frankly, I was amazed at how well cars did stay on the roads, given the speeds at which they were driven in winter. I was told they had special snow tires—with nails in them! A typical Russian tire, perhaps?)

Then suddenly, as we sped through the night, destination unknown, Dania began to talk to Judy and me. She was our linguistic link to the men in Russian and Tatar (my Russian was serviceable, but not sufficient anymore for interviews); they could not understand English.

"My grandparents met in the traditional Muslim way," she was saying. "He saw her over her family's fence and came to them to ask for her hand. It was a very happy marriage. They loved each other very, *very* much. Then came the time for my parents to meet. It was very, *very* different. They met at a party meeting, and they decided—*she* decided—that they should get married. It was a happy marriage, too.

"But what about me? I just don't know, I just don't know." (We were still speeding through the night; Dania was talking with more and more urgency.) "I'm educated, I have had all the advantages, although"—she paused—"we live in a very poor, old house. No indoor 'facilities.' But I am too educated. None of the men want a woman like me.

"Who would I meet now?"

Judy, who is smart and quick, said, "Foreign businessmen will be coming here. You speak good English. Why don't you start a translation service for foreign businessmen? You'd be perfect, and maybe you'd marry a foreign businessman!"

Dania, who was small, thin, sweet, and shy, looked as though such a thing could surely never happen. "No one will ever marry me," she said sadly.

I was pondering the similarities between us all, and the differences: all of us women trying to figure out what these new lives offered us. But just as I was thinking about dear Dania, we zoomed off the main highway. Now we were in the pitch-black of a full winter night, we were bumping down narrow icy roads, blinded by the lights of oncoming cars. Rimzil was driving like a veritable fiend. Where in the very devil were we?

Finally, to my utter astonishment, we came to what appeared through the snow to be some kind of castle, or palace, or at least some unexpected congeries of formal grounds and gardens. Suddenly, we were driving over lawns, down sidewalks and, it seemed to me, almost over canals. Oddly, there were classical statues here and there, with incongruous hedges that almost made the area appear to be some formal French or English garden.

None of us spoke. Finally we came to a long, low house, and Rimzil stopped the car and let the motor die. I started praying. This was not the way for a foreign correspondent to die: in battle, yes, but not sunk in the snow in some pretentious backwater of the steppes of Russia, surely not!

"We're here," Rimzil said, an air of pride in his voice. I hung my head. I wanted to die, and the Train to Kazan looked good in comparison. And then he shooed us through a door into the house, which seemed totally without lights.

We were in a Tatar *bathhouse*!

It seems that the Tatars loved bathhouses like this, which were very similar to Finnish saunas. Particularly on their wedding night, it was traditional for the bride and groom to end up in a bathhouse. Well, all right, this was a helluva lot better than anything I had expected on our ride out. What's more, as the men left us to the women's section, they also left us a bottle of vodka, several glasses, and some cold beer. The entire adventure was beginning to look less and less threatening.

The dressing room was clean and neat, with two simple cots that had very clean white sheets over them. As to the bath itself, there was one big room, with a cold shower and several sinks full of cold water. The sauna room, with heated bricks that looked almost like street bricks, had plain wooden steps to lie or perch on. And, oh yes, there were the branches, which you dipped in cold water before requesting a "beating."

I had to hand it to Rimzil, Damir, and Rimil, the mischievous trio: they sure knew how to take a gal out on the town!

Judy, Dania, and I steamed for a while, and then we came out dressed, and began drinking the vodka, until the men came over, all dressed again and very, very rosy—and not only from the hot bath! It seemed that they had been imbibing rather earlier and more than we had. We drank some more, and took some absurd pictures of us clowning around like schoolchildren; and finally, finally, I got them to start back to the city.

Somehow it didn't seem so long going back, but by the time we actually headed for the table in the restaurant to get something to eat, I realized that, while I was very, very tired from the work, the cold, the heat, and the rides, the men—particularly Rimil—were very, very drunk.

And then the most extraordinary, awful, disquieting thing happened.

All the time I was in Tatarstan, I had a feeling that I tried hard to put aside, which was that just below the surface there still was lying and lurking some strain of cruelty that we could little understand, nurtured perhaps by the experience of the Mongol hordes those seven centuries ago and, in more recent eras, by the heritage of Bolshevik degradation.

Just as we were being served, and just as the men were drinking more, and more, and more vodka and champagne, with cognac on top of that, Rimil, he of the black hair and the nose pointed like a beaver's, disappeared for a few minutes.

Shortly after we arrived, a small group of people, Tatars, I thought, came in with an unusually lovely dog. The pet was a well-groomed cocker spaniel, the kind of dog one seldom saw anywhere in the Soviet Union, and it sat next to their table, wagging its short tail and looking imploringly at the plates.

Then, suddenly, Rimil reappeared. He was running across the room, dodging the edges of tables, his eyes as fierce and crazy as must have been those of Genghis Khan's horsemen, and he was holding up the beautiful cocker spaniel, far up over the floor, by its ear.

The poor animal's legs were futilely flailing back and forth, back and forth, and of course the poor creature was letting out piteous shrieks because he was obviously in great pain.

I jumped up from the table and screamed at the maniac, and he dropped the dog, which ran off in pain and fear (but safe now) to hide under its table. Rimzil did indeed look crazy but he was not at all fierce with me—particularly not when I slapped him three times in the face and shouted at him that he was the most abysmal and cruel muzhik oaf that I had ever seen in my life.

So ended the strange ride through the night, in a strange part of the world, in a strange period of time, and with stranger memories and mind-sets still.

"It's just below the surface, the savagery," Judy said to me the next day. I nodded. I think we both wondered what else was just below the surface.

One of the last people I saw was one who impressed me the most. Rimzil brought him over the morning of the day we were leaving— the Train *from* Kazan this time, no longer feared at all, because we had grown so brave and daring in this new world—and we sat and had a light breakfast together overlooking the rooftops of the old city.

Dr. Mirza I. Makhmoutov was president of their beloved Watan Society, which was surely going to bring the world to Tatarstan just as their great diplomats of those earlier centuries did. He had also been the minister of education, and he was a tall, craggy-faced, handsome man who was also, I think, close to brilliant, particularly when I brought up one of my favorite subjects, the changing (or not changing) psychology of people in Russia and its complex new environs of the body and of the mind and soul and spirit.

"The psychology of people living in a planned society . . ." he mused. "You see, they are accustomed to work by decrees, where they have the orders from above. Now, we have market relations— but nobody knows what that is. The directors of the old enterprises do not know how to establish these relations—they have no materials from the farms and they have no market—and the enterprises have stopped producing. And that is a tragedy."

"Completely stopped?" I asked. This was a savage burden on the people, if true.

"Most of them," he answered calmly. "You see, we have to learn how to prepare people to act—that is the new situation. In some ways, it is global. And if people do not know what to do, they won't do it. You know, we have no examples of what to do. The papers give the information that, in Poland, the stores are full of goods. At the same time, we see strikes and unemployment—and we are not accustomed to that. In the past here, the government guaranteed the life of the person. So now, people are only waiting. They are saying to themselves, 'I have no workplace anymore.'

"The big enterprises, one after the other, are closing. Not all at once, but every enterprise had been linked with thousands of others, from the West to the Far East. Now the country is completely divided." He paused, then issued a kind of genteel grunt of scorn. "We say that our 'horizontal linkage' is interrupted."

Then Dr. Makhmoutov began talking about what he was really concerned with, education, and his voice rose with the excitement and hope that he felt. "My idea is to establish new types of professional schools here in our country," he said, "and now I have got involved with Americans in the Community Colleges for International Development. I met Mr. Pierce and Mr. Parnell—do you know them? They sent the presidents of three colleges—an exchange of delegations. Dr. Anderson from Waukesha County Technical College in Wisconsin, Mr. Crawford from the St. Louis Community Colleges. This is a new type of thinking for us, a multipurpose institution. Our colleges prepare people for five or six things only.

"Now, my institute and the community colleges have signed an agreement to cooperate. We are going to create a Tatar-American College here. I'm starting a community college in Kazan, which will be the first in the former Soviet Union! Then we will transfer our ideas to other areas of Russia—that is the plan, that is the idea. We are now preparing the curriculum and programs, including business programs, and we are retraining between five and six hundred teachers. It is a real step toward market relations.

"The Tatar-American Community College," he finished up with ringing pride, "will open here in September." Then he thought for a moment, then asked, in what I considered a most touching gesture, "Perhaps you would come as our guest to the opening?"

I felt one of the first small bursts of happiness so far in my trip, after that talk. I felt that, yes, there *is* hope, because some people— witness this elegant man—had real, palpable, practical ideas of how to leap from the primitive forms of societal organization of Communism to the immensely complex and complicated forms of representative government and economic freedom. Some.

Napoleon, the same one who was defeated by the Russian winter, once said, doubtless in a sour mood over the Russian steppes and snows, "If you scratch a Russian, you find a Tatar." Doubtless today, if you scratch a Russian leader, you find a real Tatar problem. But as I prepared to leave lovely unknown Kazan and the plains of the legendary Volga, I realized that the problems are indeed very deep.

I asked the people if they could tell the difference—physically, in terms of mannerisms and expression—between the Russian and the Tatar. All said no. So it is very complicated, because you have the desired renaissance of an ancient culture, but you have no way to separate the peoples in order to see to whom it really belongs, if indeed to anybody anymore.

Leaving Kazan was sad: leaving nice, sad Dania who will never marry, rascal Rimzil who adored Judy, businessman Damir who talks too much, and even bad Rimil. Driving us to the train station, Rimzil suddenly became very serious. "You see us laughing, you see us drinking with you, and perhaps you think we are, really, happy," he said, almost as a soliloquy. We became silent and listened. "But the truth is that we have no idea how this is going to turn out. If there is another military coup in Moscow, we could all be killed. This whole 'thing' of transforming Tatarstan . . . it may not work out at all." He paused.

"You know, Pushkin said that there is nothing worse than a Russian riot—then, everything is swept away. That is what could happen here. The democratic government here could be swept away in a flash, giving way to the old Communist Right. Common families here want a firmer hand than we now have—that is a paradox. Chile's Augusto Pinochet is one of the examples—they used to call him a fascist. Then there are the youth gangs . . . the mafia control of so much business . . . and the breakup everywhere—some Tatars have gone to fight with the Chechen-Ingush, who also declared independence . . ."

Then suddenly he became quite angry. "Where are the Americans?" he demanded hotly. "Where is Bush? Why are you not helping us?"

Finally, he calmed down. "But we do know it has been wonderful having you here. We are sentimental people, we love strangers . . ."

Judy and I sat inside our compartment ready for the fourteen-hour overnight ride back to Moscow. It was a cinch, this Train from Kazan, a piece of cake, actually quite a fun ride, probably a potential tourist attraction.

We sat there, trying to peer out the window through the icy pane, while our four new friends clowned around outside our car. Rimil was trying to push the train back with his bare hands, so it would not carry us away. At one point, Rimzil was standing on Rimil's back in order to be able to look with theatrical lewdness through the window at us.

The Train from Kazan started. It coughed and choked. We waved, and waved, and waved; and then we threw kisses through still another window that was beginning to freeze up in this complex winter. The train was finally moving, like some struggling prehistoric creature, back across the snow-swept Russian plains. And then we were gone, and they were gone.

Judy and I sat in a kind of preternatural, serene silence for some time. This trip, we had only ourselves in the compartment and so we had the two bottom bunks. For a time, it was almost as if my mind had stopped, stopped to capture and hold the moment of my life that had been these last four days. Then I realized with a little shock that I now had to go on with the rest of the trip. The trip to Kazan—and, now, the Train from Kazan—would soon be over.

I thought about this huge and once-awesome country, in its moment of humiliating breakdown—and how decent people like these were trying to "overcome." I thought of all the liberation movements I had seen across the Third World in *its* moment of decolonialization and transformation. Was I now seeing the breakup of the Soviet Union's "colonies within"?

I thought about these Tatars, these different and attractive descendants of some of the most fearsome conquerors in the annals of man. Historians say that the very word *Tatar* came from the early Chinese word *Ta-ta-erh,* which means "barbarian," and/or that the Tatars were so frightening that they were given a name taken from the Greek word "Tartarus," the section of Hades reserved for the punishment of the wicked. Another old local saying has it that "An uninvited guest is worse than a Tatar." And, of course, as food expert Judy crisply reminded me, their real contribution to the nourishment of mankind was tartar sauce and steak tartare.

But these new Tatars were not so fierce. "They were wonderful," I murmured to Judy as the train struggled through the snow.

"They were a lot like us," she murmured back.

And before I slipped into a pleasant sleep, I was reminded for some reason of the inscription on the wall of the Kazan fortress that had been read to us, mirroring the violent trajectories of history that had swept over and across this beautiful and mournful place:

Bez kittek. Bashkalar kiler.
"We are gone. Others will come."

Chapter 3

—❦—

Kazakhstan
Rumor of the New Silk Road

*In the true sense, the history of the Kazakhs has
not yet been written. I have read the history of Russia,
America, France, and Greece. Now I want
to know the history of the Kazakhs . . .*

Olzhas Suleimenov, Kazakh writer

More than a place, Kazakhstan was a frame of mind, a pride of
ideas, and a sometimes dazzling moment of experimentation. Out
there—and I mean *way* out there—sitting atop the northern borders of the Chinese province of Xinjiang-Uygur and poised on
great plains just beyond the northern reaches of the majestic Tien
Shan mountains, Kazakhstan was trying to take its life into its own
hands. There, the traveler new to these legendary realms was to see
the most vivid and lively of the newly independent republics.

Most of the new republics were saddened at the devastation
wrought by seventy years of Soviet power, impoverished by all
those years of Moscow's voracious thirst, and exhausted by even
the thought of what they must now do if they were to survive,
much less prosper. But those qualities, though certainly present in
Kazakhstan, were not the ones that characterized the government
and outlook of this remote and fascinating republic. No, Kazakhstan was distinguished by a vibrant animal energy, by an openness
to innovation, and by an empiricism that arose out of the blending
of the relative freedom of the nomadic Kazakh with the suddenly
loosed spirits of the Russian intelligentsia who were for so many
decades exiled there.

The romantic reason for ordinarily sane people doing odd things like climbing Mount Everest has long been: "Because it's there!" The paraphrased reason for traveling to places like Kazakhstan today is: "Because it's—where?"

By the time I got to Kazakhstan in the winter of 1992, it was already Central Asia's "Wild East," where businessmen from Houston to Seoul were doing everything but riding Mongol ponies and sending the khan's couriers running up ahead to get dibs on Kazakhstan's milk and honey: read oil and gold. Nobody has enlivened a cocktail hour (or even a mare's milk break) with diverting chatter about Kazakhstan, Kyrgyzstan, Uzbekistan, or Tajikistan, not to mention the Tungans or the Karakalpaks, since Marco Polo traipsed the Silk Road in the thirteenth century. And yet today it was becoming more, far more, than only a special taste indulged in by intellectual gourmets and journalistic gourmands like me. Here you had one of the true classic backwaters of the world—one million square miles of deserts and grazing land and oil and nuclear bombs—and suddenly you had everybody in the world making his way out there. Secretary of State James Baker III was stopping by one day, Foreign Minister Roland Dumas of France, the next. In this blackness that I had so feared, I was to find even (God help us!) American missionaries.

There was a sense of excitement, a mood of opening to the world that at times was quite infectious. "We are building a railroad with China," Vice-President Erik Asanbaev told me, stretching his arms wide as he sat in his handsome office. "And we are building a transcontinental railroad from the Pacific to Istanbul. We are going to develop airlines—to Shanghai, Beijing, Tokyo, from Alma-Ata to Istanbul, Munich, and Paris." He smiled. "We will not be visiting Domodedovo or Sheretmetyevo anymore" I surely understood his excitement over that—"and we are ready to test all influences . . ."

I could not help but think that Kazakhstan reminded me a little of a wallflower suddenly transformed into a debutante.

What's more, Alma-Ata, its capital, was an amazingly livable city of elegant parks and old mansions, by far the prettiest city for a thousand miles in any direction. It had grown out of a military fortress built by the Russian czarist expansionists in 1854, and it came to be a city of bourgeois mansions, large formal parks, and modern new apartments for the intelligentsia, all overseen by snow-covered mountains. The city of apples and fountains boasted a big Russian Orthodox cathedral and a central bazaar or market where you could find the apples that were the specialty of the region, meat, mountains of peanuts, and even spices brought by road from Samarkand.

The Kazakhs were a moderate people, a kind, story-telling people. Unlike in the other republics, where resentment toward Moscow ran high, they were glad that the new government had not taken down the old Communist monuments, like those to Lenin and Dzerzhinsky. One had the feeling that those men and what they represented were so far away, the real meaning of Communism had never quite reached the Kazakhs. Indeed, there were monuments to heroes who fought *with* the czar—and monuments to those who fought *against* the czar. "You can be a hero here fighting for the czar or against him," one Kazakh man told me simply.

I would also find Alma-Ata to be a city grandly aspiring not only to the future but imaginatively to the past; they had even renamed a downtown street for the historic Silk Road, which was fine except for the fact that the real main Silk Road didn't actually go through here, although a less-traveled northern route did. But the important thing was that they believed it: they were building on the one memory of their past that held all these Turkic peoples of Central Asia together.

In reality, like all of Central Asia, the Kazakhs lived, too, with the rumor of a new Silk Road, with the hope of a new caravan route in President Nursultan A. Nazarbayev's activist economic experimenting. Kazakhstan is the biggest laboratory in the entire former Soviet Union for economic experimentation in a transition economy from Communism to capitalism.

And while Moscow's creative historians had stolen from them almost all knowledge of their recent years, they still "remembered" earlier days. "Genghis would have . . ." they would say. Or "Vasco de Gama destroyed us—we were fine until he came along . . ." (Genghis, of course, was Genghis Khan. As for Vasco de Gama, I soon learned, it was he who doomed the Silk Road and made all of Central Asia a backwater by discovering the sea route to India around Africa to Asia in 1498, thus replacing the great Central Asian caravan routes.)

Alma-Ata was also, not at all irrelevantly, the one single place in Central Asia where you could stay in a first-class hotel, and there was good reason for that. The Dostyk was the former hotel of the Communist Party Central Committee, and it had now fallen to the likes of us. It even had a reservations number in Tucson. Before, when I had come to the Soviet Union, I had always come through Intourist, that miserable creature. Now I was entering through the bedrooms of the failed apparatchiks of that empire. And how strange, too, to see that their "great hotel" was nice, yes, but really only the equivalent of a Ramada Inn in Salt Lake City!

One cannot, of course, dare to expound upon the Communists' behavior in the wood-paneled bedrooms, but one could surely appreciate the luxuries after the stinking hotels everywhere else. And the fax girl was endearing, and certainly in spirit with the new Kazakhstan, when she said brightly, "There's no problem getting faxes through to Washington. Moscow's the problem!"

Secretary of State James Baker III had come through Kazakhstan on his diplomatic wanderings about Central Asia. He came, of course, with his press corps. Later, I would hear the journalists complain bitterly about being put in one of the normal (thus awful) hotels, instead of the Dostyk. When I asked Secretary Baker about this, he only smiled a wicked smile.

It was no secret that a lot of people in Washington didn't much like the press anymore.

Some things, of course, do not change quickly. The second day I was there, I got a phone call from a Kazakh diplomat wanting to speak to "Daria Fane." I had been looking for her too, because she was our Moscow embassy's Central Asian specialist.

"How downright coincidental," I thought cynically. "How strange that they should have had us both in the same room—and surely with the same listening equipment!"

And so, having survived the Train to Kazan, I was to join an unequaled cast of the usual suspects in Kazakhstan: businessmen of fortune, swaggering adventurers, frontier oilmen, "new wave" missionaries from South Korea, and even a few serious scholars and politicians—but, sure enough, no other journalists!

Intourist's big building at Domodedovo Airport was so filthy and so crowded that even some of the tough oilmen on the plane with me to Alma-Ata said they doubted they could stand going through it again. To find one's plane, a foreigner enters that insane asylum with his luggage carried, for security, by his taxi driver. You must somehow find the Intourist office, which is far down dank halls and naturally not marked, undoubtedly because they didn't want foreigners there in the first place (most probably because we might be happy).

If they let you through after arguing with you as to whether you really *are* a tourist, you are then (eventually) transported by a rat-tletrap old bus to the "big" Intourist facility. Here one is immediately—and unrelievedly—faced with the one thing at Domodedovo that approaches truly majestic dimensions: the overpowering stench of stale urine. And here, too, the true face of the old Soviet Union lived still in the hostile, surly, and ugly characters of the Intourist guides (perestroika and glasnost presumably did not know about the Intourist terminal). It was there that I realized what a giant unregulated slum this pretentious "superpower" had become.

When we finally did take off, in a large jet that had the foreigners sitting in the front section, I pondered for the thousandth time exactly what it was that I was doing there. Then a new worry hit me: the "Turkish Airliner," that wraith of outside freedom, that reminder of joining again the real world, that magic carpet that was to carry me from Baku to Istanbul and "out" on February 10—what if it didn't come? What if I had to come back to Moscow, actually fight my way through Domodedovo again? Make my way across Moscow? Try to buy a ticket? But such ideas swiftly slipped away as I talked with the knowledgeable Houston oilman sitting across the aisle from me.

"Contracts?" he sniffed. "In Kazakhstan? They believe that protocols are the minutes of a meeting. You have heard of the Chevron 'deal,' of course. Kazakhstan—President Nazarbayev, really—signed with Chevron in 1988. To explore and go for oil in the Tenghiz range up by the Caspian Sea—northwest of the country—hard place to explore because of the rocks. Then the Kazakhs decided this year they weren't getting enough out of the gringos. So they just canceled it." He shook his head, threw up his hands in a slight, futile gesture.

"You see," he went on, "what they are doing is buying and selling—but they're still not producing." He sighed. "It's still the old Communist system, nothing more. There are things of value here, but no one owns them, so there is nothing you can do about anything."

At this point, the sour and surly "air hostess," if one can really characterize these vicious Aeroflot women by that relatively harmless description, brought us some "dinner." First we were treated to a half teacup of lukewarm sugared water, which was gray and sticky, and which I rather quickly decided I could do without (and instead took a swig from the miniature vodka bottle I had brought). This "first course" was followed by a rather large plate with one boiled and shriveled chicken leg on it with a tiny bit of vegetables. Actually, we were very lucky that was all there was.

Meanwhile, my Houston friend was trying hard to explain to me some of the more obvious ins and outs of doing business in Kazakhstan, which had all the minerals and oil and grazing land in the world but still none of the business sense or ethics to gain from it.

In the whole former Soviet Union, he went on, "there are two foreign companies that are actually pumping oil. White Nights, which is Anglo-Swiss, from Texas, and Phibro Energy, from Connecticut, is the main one in western Siberia, but they've had a time of it. Last December, the bank closed for Christmas and never opened again, so White Nights' two million dollars on deposit was gone. They took over an operation with more than twelve hundred Russians, and they soon were under attack by them for 'plundering Russia's underground riches.' Still, they are exporting between eight and nine thousand barrels a day. That's not nearly enough to even redeem their $110 million investment—but they are pumping." He paused again, shaking his head at the sheer wonder of all this madness. "We'll see," he said.

"The biggest deal being negotiated by far, though, is out in the Sakhalin Islands," he went on. "There is a huge oil field there to be developed, and they need investments of ten to fifteen billion dollars. Five groups are bidding on the project now—Exxon, Amoco, Marathon, and McDermott, Japanese Sadeco, and others. There is a big fight between the new governor of Sakhalin—who is one of the new economic 'doers'—and Moscow over whom to choose . . .

"You see," he continued, "at heart they're really parasites, as they were under Communism. They have a total misconception about capitalism—they think it's just wheeling and dealing. As I mentioned, the Central Bank in Alma-Ata has been closed since Christmas. What is striking about the whole thing is that, one, they are politically unstable; two, the Russians don't like to work; three, there is no infrastructure; and four, there is no security for cash. Really, they think that everyone should pay them for coming here."

The flight took more than six hours, for we were in truth crossing a universe of lands and peoples. For a while, as we crossed the vast steppes and plains and the Urals, I lay my head back and thought.

Thinking first about Russia itself, I wondered for a time to what degree people connive in their own oppression. Were not the Russians acting exactly as they always have in the face of repression? Instead of acting on their own and forming and crafting their lives, they wait. They "wait for winter," as they had waited for Napoleon's and Hitler's troops: not to defeat them but to devour them. They accept the whip without complaint; they are silent when well-meaning reformers offer them hope and they greet them with the suspicion and silence that doom any real change; and then they complain that nothing has changed, or will ever change, and so voluntarily they go back under the whip, saying, "You see, you see, that is the *way life is!*"

Were they now outwaiting their first real chance for freedom and human development? Was it possible they did not really want it? Perhaps the great Russian poet Yevgeny Yevtushenko put it best:

> *He who is conceived in a cage yearns for the cage.*
> *With horror I understand that I love*
> *That cage where they hide me behind a fence,*
> *And that animal farm, my native land.*

Then, looking out the window at the blackness that hung over that great expanse of land beneath me, I freed my mind to wander further. What was really going on down there? What lies beyond? They don't know themselves, so why should we travelers—we poor-man's modern Marco Polos following this new caravan trail in the sky—dare to think that *we* can know them?

Then I began thinking about all the incredible currents and crosscurrents of history that had occurred down there, below me: the Tien Shan mountains, the Silk Road, the caves of Buddha looted by the Europeans, the dying Aral Sea, the great Amur and Ob rivers of Siberia, whose melting ice in the spring smites the land like an avalanche of water, the Kazakhs, Kyrgyz, Turkmen, Afghans, Persians, Pechenegs, Kipchaks, Seljuks, Huns. "A vast shatter zone of peoples and cultures," American anthropologist Jon Anderson called it, "an unorganized world where national identities were multiple and apolycentric, with history resuming not after 50 years, or 100 years, or even 200 years, but after a half millennium . . ."

It was Central Asia—or Turkestan—or Inner Asia—or Middle Asia—or even the Heartland of Empires—but in short and at heart it was an ethnic mosaic, a Turkic world, one world, where empires briefly coalesced, then were split asunder by more conquest and war, with Mongol face blending in mating in the dark of their long nights into Turkic face, and coming out, in the Russian term, "Tatar."

At the beginning of the sixteenth century, when Europe was still emerging, Ottoman Turkey and China were the most powerful states in the world, and Central Asia was the link between them. It was a world six times larger than Ukraine, three times the size of Western Europe. Beneath me also lay the ruins of Sultan Galiev's and so many others' dream of "Turkestan." Still there remained real vestiges of it. If a fluent Turkish speaker were to set out over- land from European Turkey, with several exceptions he could communicate with everyone he met along the way from the Bal- kans to a point a thousand miles inside China, where the Turkic Uighurs still use the Arabic scripts despite concerted attempts by their Chinese masters to forcibly convert them to Pinyin.

Actually, all of these Turkic peoples in Central Asia trace their roots deep into antiquity, to the Great Wall of China, which proba- bly was built to keep them at bay. There, they mixed, and fought, and lived with the Persians, the Afghans, the Indians, and above all with those voraciously expansionist Russians of the nineteenth century. It was then that the "Great Game" began, the rush for expansion into Central Asia, largely on the part of the British and the Russians, but also even including, on the area's peripheries, the Germans.

The Russians could rule Central Asia, after finally conquering it after the 1917 Revolution, but they never really became a part of it, despite the fact that fully half of Kazakhstan alone, at the time of my visit, was of Russian stock. They never assimilated. While the czars ruled these various peoples, those autocrats deliberately for- bade any mention of nationality or ethnic origin, say, on a person's passport. Those all-powerful rulers knew full well that if they di- vided people up that way in this melange of historic groups, they would soon be faced with rival conflicts. Lenin believed in univer- salism, with German as the major language. But by the time Joseph

Stalin came to power in the twenties and thirties, he went against all of this history, and actually acted to *create* differences where there were none. When Stalin insisted they identify themselves, more than 50 percent of them did not know what ethnic group they belonged to—and so simply used the word for "human being" in their language.

In 1924, Stalin created five different republics (Kazakhstan, Kyrgyzstan, Uzbekistan, Turkmenistan, and Tajikistan) out of the confusion of peoples in Central Asia. Then he effectively created—artificially—a linguistic and territorial basis for each "nationality." Soviet ethnographers took the various dialects of the various peoples and "invented" four Turkic languages (Uzbek, Turkmen, Kazakh, and Kyrgyz) and one Persian language (Tajik). The fact that they were indeed devolved from the dialects, however, made it possible for Turks from Turkey to understand these "new" Turkic languages.

The Communists' basic idea for Central Asia, as well as for the other component parts of the Soviet Union, was that the old "nationality" was to be replaced by "modern identity." In Kazakhstan, which I was rapidly approaching, this meant trying to end Kazakh nomadism and trying to make the historically nomadic Kazakh a "citizen" of a Russian-dominated multiethnic state. To do this, to "modernize" remote Kazakhstan, the Soviets later pointedly located fifteen hundred nuclear warheads there, including more than a hundred ICBMs, which made the Central Asian arsenal larger than France's. And to Russify the Kazakh state, Moscow exiled millions of political dissidents during Khrushchev's "Virgin Lands" campaign, and in the collectivization of agriculture in Kazakhstan between 1929 and 1937, one third of the population died.

But the Kazakhs were stubborn. As Martha Olcott, the leading American scholar on Kazakh history and culture, has pointed out, the Kazakhs *did not want to become farmers*—and they did not want to be "assimilated" into the Russian state and the Communist mind-set, either. By the time I was approaching Kazakhstan, she was writing that despite Communism, the ordinary Kazakh had actually remained much the same as his ancestors, a man who "judges character much as his ancestors did, that is, by whether a man is a good father, a good son, and, most important, a good herdsman, someone with 'keen knowledge of folk meterology . . . phenological observations, signs, herbage peculiarities accumulated by the people during the centuries . . .' "

And so, amazingly, those ancient peoples "out there" did finally overcome by stubbornly remaining themselves. After the first elections of the post-Gorbachev era in 1989, every single new republic voted against the Russian language. There began an impassioned discussion about language—about the alphabet—which at heart was really about how they would or could relate to the outside world. The early Bolsheviks had forced them to use the Russian Cyrillic alphabet; now, everywhere the people talked to me excitedly about wanting to shift to the Roman alphabet as another way of opening up to the rest of the world.

Ironically, the Soviets, who had tried to impose their own dreams of a classless, even a nationless, society on the Central Asians, instead in the end unleashed these people's old and truest national feelings.

There were, now, new questions as well, questions that I would be investigating. Was there a new "Great Game"? Was it the conflict between fundamentalist Iran on the one hand and secular Turkey on the other? Was that *the* story of the revived historic conflict over the heart and soul of Central Asia?

I put my head back and tried to sleep. I was growing dizzy with the kaleidoscopic picture of all those peoples, all those passions, all those dreams and nightmares, crossing and crossing and crossing in the blackness below.

From my pleasant room in the Hotel Dostyk, I looked out upon a world that was all white. Unrelieved white mist and fog formed a white wall that seemed to break apart and re-form around me wherever I moved. Particles of water and snow hung upon every tiny movement of air. The streets, the sidewalks, and the boughs of the beautiful trees of Alma-Ata were covered with packed ice and fine snow, so that the circle of winter around you was complete. It was quite beautiful, and it was immensely peaceful. It also tended to give you a deep feeling that you were removed from the real world underneath and beyond.

How could I explore, much less understand, a place that I could not see, and that, indeed, no one could yet see?

That first night and day that I was in Alma-Ata, I was simply so relieved to be in the wonderful Hotel Dostyk, after staying in so many filthy Russian hotels, that I did not let those walls of ice and snow bother me too much. The beautiful shiny dark wood of the room, the mustard-colored silk drapes, the full and clean marble bathroom, the cantilevered window over a comfortable table and chairs to work at, the big and working TV that played *Bonnie and Clyde* for me one night, the down comforters, the pleasant dining room on the second floor with green trees growing out of a little garden in the middle of the big room and pink striped walls and cantilevered roof, the smug pleasure over the fact that President Nazarbayev's office still had to approve everyone who was allowed to stay here, the sun that did not even begin to filter through the mist and fog until nine A.M., the 800 number in Tucson where you could call to make reservations, the stocked dollar store: all made me as comfortable as a cat in a bed of catnip.

I found myself growing obsessively neat. I was creating my impeccably ordered little niche within the chaos I had until now felt around me. Whenever I took some Tums out, for instance, I stacked them carefully and artistically on a tissue. It helped. I also began here one of many little rituals that would keep me in touch with the real world—and with my old self. I had a huge rolled-up map of the world, and I stuck it up on my mirror, marking where I was at each stop. I was one hell of a way away from everything!

My first morning in snowbound Alma-Ata, I walked slowly around the dollar store off the lobby of the hotel in wonder. It seemed to me to be a store of irrelevant miracles from a strange world they will never know, except through these products of that world that they now must copy, create, exemplify: Napoleon brandy, $14; an electric knife, $36; Gillette mint foam, 45 cents; Scandinavian mineral water, 78 cents; intercom phones, $26.50; buckaroo slot machines, $51.42; a walkie-talkie, $16.90; Four Roses bourbon, $16.50; spumante champagne, $3.50.

I wondered what they must think of us, seeing us only through these products. I wondered what kind of alien creature they could splice together from these bizarre and totally unrepresentative products of the West. Was it a store of the miracles of other worlds to them—or did they realize how bizarre this display really was?

"Hopeful . . . bustling . . . rich" Kazakhstan, I soon discovered, had as many complicated faces and indigestible conflicts as did Russia.

The first noon, I sat with my two women interpreters in my pleasant room and they poured out their hearts to me.

"They say 'privatize,' but we are not allowed to do it," Dina Asip, a charming little slip of a woman with a tall fur hat and reasonable English, began. "Only the former Communists can do that. Suddenly, there are 'banks' all over the place, but we don't know who they are or what they do. This new 'company,' Krambds—they are on TV all the time. They say they 'do business,' but what? What do they do? We have no idea what is going on.

"We have had food coupons here since January," Dina went on. "They began in January, but only in one store. We get two kilograms of meat a month, one-half kilogram of sugar, one hundred grams of margarine, one hundred grams of oil—and a salary isn't enough to cover eight eggs a month."

That common type of confusion, of disbelief, of distrust—What was going on? Where should we turn next?—I found everywhere. But unlike in the other of the new Central Asian republics, one pleasant reality was the fact that it was easy to telephone officials and ask for interviews. There were several reasons for this. Many officials spoke some English, or had someone around them who did. Most had a far more energetic outlook than did their counterparts in Moscow, and welcomed—instead of tried to elude—foreigners (particularly foreigners who looked as if they might have money).

Indeed, that very first afternoon in Alma-Ata, a Friday, I was actually able to make my own appointment with Dr. Mukhtar M. Bakenov, the director of the State Committee on Geology and the Defense of Nature of Kazakhstan, and this dignified man was filled with the sense of excitement that I seemed to find everywhere there.

"We are visited every day by representatives of foreign countries and companies," he started out, with a big, friendly smile. "We are making cooperative plans and we have signed contracts with companies in Houston, in Canada . . . our policy is called the 'Policy of the Open Doors.' "

And Chevron? The Chevron deal? Was that an open or a closed door? The look on my face probably alerted him to some skepticism on my part.

"Oh, yes, there were some difficulties over the transport of oil, some details about the laws," he went on. "We became convinced that the conditions were not good for our side. The contract was signed in 'the center,' in Moscow, and that was not in the interest of Kazakhstan. Now the contract is being renegotiated." He smiled; I should know it was going to be just fine.

"But I thought you had refused the contract," I interjected.

"Oh, no, we didn't refuse, it is just being renegotiated," he responded brightly. Then he went on (still bright as a shining sun) to tick off a whole bunch of other companies with which they were "surely going to sign," as I thought of my Houston oilman and his homey wisdom.

But I could surely understand, despite everything, why the wandering oilmen of the world were indeed beating a trail to Alma-Ata and to the fickle owners of the tundra's exorbitant riches. "We have nearly one billion tons of oil," he went on, beginning to smile, or so I thought, in a strange sort of way, "and three billion cubic meters of gas. Besides oil and gas, we have gold and diamonds and rare metals . . ."

As he spoke these words of acquisitive hope, a truly beatific smile overtook his handsome face. I almost thought for a moment that I was observing a picture of Christ, but certainly a Christ of the marketplace. (And soon I would find Christians, right there in Alma-Ata, who had just that sort of Christianity in mind!)

The following day, a snowy Saturday, the Radio Liberty correspondent in Alma-Ata, a tall, dour man named Batir-Khan Darimbet, took me to a press conference with the most prominent leader of the new Central Asian republics, the favorite of Mikhail Gorbachev, and the man who would be voted on Your Hit Parade the Central-Asian-most-likely-to-succeed. He was Nursultan Nazarbayev, shepherd, former Communist party functionary, and now the first elected president of the independent republic of Kazakhstan.

But first let us consider for just a nervous moment my new "friend," the Radio Liberty correspondent. I got along with most of the Radio Liberty correspondents wonderfully. Usually local journalists or historians, most of them had long suffered under the Communists; they were now enchanted with this dream of press freedom working for the station. But Batir-Khan and I just did not get along. A tall and well-built man, he looked pleasant enough, but he had a way of never responding, instead offering this supercilious smile. It may have been just his individual, peculiar expression, but to me, that smile seemed to be laden with sarcasm. Perhaps I was overreacting, but the fact of the matter is that I had three full work days and two weekend days in Alma-Ata, and unless he had my program ready, I could have risked my very life to get here and it would all be for naught. Indeed, that was very close to what we faced on Saturday.

At eleven o'clock on Saturday, along with pretty Dina in her long tight coat and fur hat, we drove over to the big gray presidency that overlooked the city. It was in that large plaza in front of the presidency that riots took place in 1986 against Moscow, a result of the relative relief of perestroika and glasnost. Now, in the omnipresent white snow and with the gray, leaden skies, it all looked quite pretty. This was the first time that I was to notice that these Central Asian presidencies were always the center of the city. Although far from the Greek-style classical architecture that the West once so diligently copied, it was quite a handsome building, with large steps leading up to it on all sides, and it was exceedingly well appointed inside, with the Kazakh colors expressed in light robin's-egg-blue walls and deep red Oriental rugs.

We waited for a time, and then President Nazarbayev, darling of the new Central Asian order, energetically walked in accompanied by the debonair (and tired) French foreign minister, Roland Dumas. The French press corps trailing Dumas also looked a little tired; this was understandable, because they had been sidetracked the night before to Bishkek, the capital of new democratic Kyrgyzstan, where I was (uneasily) going next. Their reports were far from reassuring.

When I saw President Nazarbayev, a lightbulb went off in my mind. Who was it he looked like? I pondered for a moment, then realized that he looked almost exactly like the late Mayor Richard J. Daley, longtime mayor of my hometown of Chicago. Had Mayor Daley been part Kazakh? I wondered. Had Mayor Daley's father at some time skipped away to Kazakhstan for a few days? Was there something that we Chicagoans did not know?

Putting those silly thoughts aside, I saw before me a handsome, well-dressed, and obviously sophisticated man. He was quick and he was slick, with a blunt nose, carefully combed hair, and wily eyes. But his face, I realized, was nearly expressionless. The face was good, strong, and above all clever and unrevealing—Kazakh all the way.

When the press conference was almost over, I asked the president a very basic question: "Where do you want to see Kazakhstan five years from now?"

Nazarbayev's eyes lit up. "I will answer the lady," he cried gallantly, while the other men sniffed at this strange creature—me—in their midst. (For my part, I uncharitably wondered what they would have thought had they known I was "important enough" to stay at the Dostyk, where the president's office had to approve me.)

"Kazakhstan has many possibilities," Nazarbayev began. "I hope that in five years Kazakhstan will have entered the market economy. In those five years we will lay the foundation that will carry this country from the old philosophies on to new varieties of property . . . and then finally create a developed democratic state that is recognized by the world as a sovereign country. As for us, we will proceed according to the values of the civilized world!"

The term "civilized world" I was to hear voiced repeatedly. I was also to hear constantly—from the Kazakhs, from the Kyrgyz, even from the Uzbeks—about how they were the bridge between Europe and Asia, and that they intended to be and to be perceived as "civilized." That was why, they constantly repeated, they must now do things, not in a violent or savage or barbarian way, but always and ever in a "civilized" way. Who could fight with that?

I was at first, not surprisingly, puzzled by this impassioned and apparently sincere identification of themselves as "European." It boggled my mind until later in Uzbekistan, when I came to understand it. But at the time, I thought it the oddest of affectations. At the time, the references brought me back to "Boss" Daley of Chicago and to another possible solution to the "Daley question." Maybe, indeed, it was the other way around: perhaps Nazarbayev was part Irish?

I watched Nazarbayev and his team carefully that day, and, indeed, all the time I was there in the pressroom. The president himself was a true man for his times and even (forgive me, former Communists!) a genuine "new man." He was also a complete empiricist and, not insignificantly, a man quite willing and able to use power and to plan around it.

When Mikhail Gorbachev's hesitant and piecemeal reforms began willy-nilly transforming the Soviet Union after 1985 and weakening the Communist party's hold on the republics, Nazarbayev, virtually alone of the new leaders, rationally looked around the world to see what countries and what systems "worked." Indeed, very quietly but very deliberately, as early as 1988, he traveled to Singapore, to South Korea, and to China, and he found in this new era what he was looking for as surely as Marco Polo and the other great earlier explorers had in earlier ones.

He returned to Kazakhstan convinced that the only immediate solution for a big, woefully undeveloped and (at the same time) democratically inexperienced "country" like Kazakhstan was basically to follow the experience of Singapore's longtime prime minister, Lee Kwan Yew, who had through a strong authoritarian government and brilliant and realistic economic planning brought his country out of some of the worst poverty in the world to become one of the richest little nations in the world.

(Lee Kwan Yew gave me a good look into his thinking in 1987, when I interviewed the leathery, tough, able leader in his simple office in Singapore. We were talking about President Corazon Aquino, who had just taken office in the Philippines and had three months in order to make reforms before the "old interest" Senate took over. "She is doing it all wrong," Lee fumed. "All wrong! She should make all her reforms now, while she has the power. When the Senate comes in, it is all over." He was right; it was, and she never made any reforms at all. That was the advice that Nazarbayev was listening to—and it was good advice.)

Openly borrowing from that type of success, Nazarbayev called his policy "authoritarian modernization" or "authoritarian democracy." This meant assuming and accepting a period of time— at least five years, Nazarbayev told me—of strong presidential rule in order to transform and order the economy. Indeed, Nazarbayev exulted in coining new terms—a "social market economy" or a "Central Asian Common Market." His vice-president talked about "an economy built like that created by Ludwig Erhard in Germany after World War II—Erhard built a normal market out of a broken economy and a useless currency."

If things were not done deliberately, and on schedule, Nazarbayev believed, the new and untested "democracy" would simply divide the new country up into warring, fighting, demagogic factions, all planning not for the future but pulling the fragile new nation apart in the name of the oldest and most atavistic ethnic, religious, and tribal hatreds. It was a thoughtful analysis that would hound me all across Central Asia; and I, too, ended up believing that it was indeed the correct one.

In fact, this dichotomy—between those followers of Mikhail Gorbachev, who believed that political freedom (perestroika and glasnost) should come first and lay the groundwork needed only to modestly transform the economy, and those, like Nazarbayev, who would restructure the economy first—would come to be *the* determining question across the former Soviet Union in this winter of both waiting and decision.

"The main thing in our area and in Russia, and not only in the backwaters, is to transform the psychology, to make man master of his own destiny," Nazarbayev explained once, his words reminding me of those of so many others I was meeting. "I believe it is natural if you raise democracy from above, if you awaken people. But they must be awakened carefully, so that once awakened they will not take everything apart. This is a real problem for us."

Nazarbayev was characterized also by very, very specific economic ideas and plans that were far ahead of those of the other Central Asian leaders. He was the designer of the thinking behind the natural idea of "horizontal" linkages and associations among the new republics; in short, instead of going through Moscow, the republics would trade and plan with one another. By the time I was there, he had lifted limits on private ownership of cattle, so that meat supplies had increased fourfold. Private housing was largely in private hands, and more than 2,500 farms were independent: with only 1 percent of the arable land, they provided 30 percent of all agriculture products.

But the plan I personally liked by far the most was his idea (still in the planning stage during my visit) to open a private café in every city of Kazakhstan. He wanted the Kazakhs to see that even though such an undertaking would be 30 percent more expensive than state-run cafés, they would soon be standing in line to get in because the service would be better, they would not be barked at, they would be invited to come back. "In our conditions, we need examples."

It was when I read those words of his that I realized what Nursultan Nazarbayev would truly be in another life: not Mayor Richard J. Daley, but another fellow Chicagoan, Ray Kroc, the founder of McDonald's!

One of the many attractions of Nursultan Nazarbayev was his intrinsic hopefulness. He explained to *The New York Times* what would happen: once secure in their independence, most republics would be brought back together by basic economic instinct into his new "horizontal" association coordinated from a reconstituted but no longer dominating center. As he put it, "I'm not a prophet, and I don't know how many years it will take, but we will become a normal state, I'm certain."

. . .

Radio Moscow, morning news, nine A.M. on shortwave:

"You are listening to Radio Moscow . . . The International Monetary Fund has declared that it may take over the Russian wheat crop as insurance against loan defaults. . . . The Chechen-Ingush people have announced independence; their government has stated that it would join the C.I.S. if they were accepted as an independent country; otherwise, they will form a 'Caucasus Zone.' . . . The newly independent nation of Croatia has received its first units of United Nations troops in its war against the Serbs in Bosnia . . ."

My editor in Kansas City, Elizabeth Anderson, had been very apologetic that day in December 1991, as I was nervously planning my trip to Central Asia. Elizabeth is not only a fine editor and thinker, she is a person most sensitive about imposing upon anyone.

"You see," she began, "I have this friend in Kazakhstan, and—now, I don't want to impose upon you at all, but . . . well, I have this old friend in Alma-Ata, and . . ."

Far from feeling imposed upon, of course, I jumped at the chance of actually knowing someone ahead of time "out there." Then, when she told me who her old friend was, I was ecstatic. Elizabeth's friend Marilyn Beaney, former language teacher in Lawton, Kansas, was head of the English department at the Kazakh-American International Business Institute in Alma-Ata. Marilyn Beaney was also one of the first missionaries in the new Central Asia.

I tried to assure Elizabeth that, no, she did not have to apologize anymore: I would sacrifice myself and meet Dr. Beaney and even do a couple of columns on her—but, wow, Elizabeth, you owe me!

One of the first things I did in Alma-Ata was to telephone Dr. Beaney at her downtown institute. Thus, on the second night, a wintry Saturday, there was this handsome, diminutive American woman standing, pert hat on her head and Western raincoat on her shoulders, in the lobby of the Dostyk, waiting to take me to her nearby apartment for dinner.

"These people are so embarrassed about their country," she said, sitting in the sparsely furnished but neat and pleasant little "parlor" of her two-room, fourth-story apartment. "That is the overwhelming thing that I see. They just can't believe things could ever have gotten so bad here. They find themselves in a situation of just total humiliation."

But what was she doing here? What *was* she doing here? To tell the truth, as the evening went by I looked at her with more amazement, with more astonishment, with more wonder, than I did at the Kazakhs. It was she, not they, who seemed to me to be a creature from another world. And her whole presence there was even more astounding because, though she was there as a missionary, and the Kazakh state knew and at least contractually respected that, she was neither teaching religion, nor starting a church, but only "witnessing" for Christ in the old Baptist manner—or was it a new manner?

To do that, she was teaching young Kazakhs business English!

I wanted to construct a little court scene. "All right," I wanted to say; "Marilyn Beaney, attractive, petite, bright widow of a Sylvania International executive; mother of three grown children and grandmother of four; former professor of English and foreign languages at Cameron University, committed Southern Baptist: what are you doing in Alma-Ata, Kazakhstan? Stand up and tell the courtroom, please!"

Marilyn, who has kind of a high squeaky voice, now tried patiently to reason with this creature from afar and abroad, sent mysteriously to this end-of-the-world to flush her out.

"You see Ethiopia starving, you see they need help," she began. "But they need help here, too. They know if they want to enter the world, they need English. The citizens here seem to want very much to work with American English-speakers. Businessmen are coming here from all over the world, and English is the language of business.

"It's what we are now calling a marketplace ministry," she summed up. "It is like taking food to Ethiopia—only you bring market principles here." (It seemed to be a long road from Christ throwing the moneylenders out of the temple, but I was able to stop myself from saying that.)

Her days in Alma-Ata were, shall we say, "different" than they were in Lawton. Determined to live on the sparse Kazakh economy, she went each day from store to store and to the central market for food. She lived in a not bad but hardly prosperous walk-up apartment building that housed the academic and political elites of the Alma-Ata university and governmental society. She had prayer meetings for other Western volunteers here on Thursday nights, and if she were not such a truly unorthodox and implicitly adventurous person (she had already taught as a Fulbright professor in Mauritania), she might worry about her "salary." Funded by the Southern Baptists and by herself, its worth was plummeting by the day.

"They said we'd be paid while we're here," she explained with her accustomed good humor, "and they said the scale would be different. It was the equivalent of about thirty-two dollars a month in October, when I came here. But with the drop in the exchange rate of the ruble, I am now earning about thirteen dollars a month."

When I slipped once and called her an "evangelist," she said, with just a trace of testiness, "I am not an evangelist!" Yet under the agreement with the government, the American missionaries can certainly talk about their faith, so when several of her Kazakh colleagues came to her to suggest reading the Bible together, she of course agreed, because, as she explained to me, revealing the compulsions that drove her to come here, "It's really a privilege to come over here and join God in what he's already doing."

But Marilyn was no Goody Two-shoes. She was the kind of woman who could also pause and look around her and wonder. Once during the several times we got together, she stopped suddenly, looked at me with a worried look, and asked: "Do you think this is the right thing to do?"

How do you answer a question like that? All I could say was that I understood the logic of her imperative and of her decision—and I did. I had watched U.S. AID programs try to build schools in the Andes and help small businessmen in Panama. I had stayed in the simple houses of Papal Volunteers and in the huts of Peace Corps men and women. I had studied the effects of the other kind of aid, the military aid given by the Soviets and the United States to militaries and guerrillas across the world.

I understood that it is not a dream but the harshest of truths that "No man is an island unto himself." The alternative to genuine understanding of other cultures—and to helping people to be educated and moral, on the highest and at the same time the most practical levels—is the kind of ethnic warfare and civil war and horrors that Central Asia had known for half a millennium. Yes, I understood why she was there.

Another time in our talks, she said to me with total assurance, "I wanted to be on the cutting edge." At that moment we were walking through the light snow in the beautiful parks of Alma-Ata and Marilyn summed up, "I know I'm in the right place."

But the story grew even more engrossing, because Marilyn Beaney was far from the only missionary in Alma-Ata. To my amazement, I found that there were approximately one hundred missionaries, and not all were American. They were largely Protestant missionaries and came from a slew of countries, many from South Korea, and they liked to sketch in the new dimension by saying that they are from the "modernizing" countries. Or, as Brian Grim, another American missionary in Alma-Ata, who ran a fascinating group called Cinim, described them to me another day when I stopped at his downtown office:

"They are a new generation of missionaries looking at a holistic view of life. We can't go into countries anymore and compartmentalize life, and so we have opened up an entirely new field: it is a postcolonial missionary field based upon looking at the model of Christ in a new way. The character of our work? We are not trying to build a big empire, but we are trying to develop projects which meet local needs. I share my faith from the highest level of government to cabdrivers on the streets."

Grim was also a Southern Baptist, and he and his family had begun working in China's far northwest Urūmqi area in 1982 with the Uighur people. (His children have Uighur names.) He seemed to me to be doing quite a remarkable job, particularly given the fact that the country had really begun to shake off its old Communist patina and control only months before. Cinim is a Kazakh word meaning loosely a "community of faith," and Grim was working in a joint cultural venture with the Golden Apple Foundation, a local group formed by a former Komsomol leader. They had already brought six hundred Americans to Kazakhstan in the summer of 1991 for a big (and apparently highly successful) cultural celebration. When I spoke with him, the two groups working together were planning to send some 330 Kazakhs to the United States. They were planning a huge Marco Polo Program—"We dreamed a bit . . ."—to bring hundreds more Europeans and Americans across the entire vast Silk Road area of Central Asia.

"We want to revive the old Silk Road, the entire trans-Asian region," he mused. "And that fits right in line with the desires of people here that Kazakhstan be the center of something again."

Once again, and certainly not for the first time on this strange and arresting trip, I felt confused, but at the same time I also felt quite beguiled by the incongruities. I had come so far to be out here; this voyage had taken me to what were to us the ends of the earth, to the remote peripheries of modern (and thus, what we so arrogantly and mistakenly considered to be fully "human") life. We were the center of the world, and everybody in the world knew it, we thought, in our cultural assurance. Well, most knew it.

Meanwhile, I began to try to learn more about these "new wave" missionaries. Far from something haphazard, or even far from its being the passion of just a few believers, I found that an entirely new wave of thinking had sent the Marilyn Beaneys and the Brian Grims to the ends of the earth (or was it to the center?).

I found that the Baptists, for instance, were now using every modern tool, in particular computer networks, in a "third wave" of Christians that was determined to reach the approximately 1.3 billion people untouched by missions. The Baptist Foreign Mission Board researchers had identified as many as ten thousand ethnolinguistic groups and had precise data about each group on its computerized World Evangelization Database. This included peoples in more than one thousand cities and countries, until now closed to outside evangelization and representing that total of 1.3 billion. They were tracing "webs of relationships or networks" among these peoples, by which the word of the Gospel could "travel as surely as missionaries take the message along roadways."

Interestingly enough, the Mission Board was seeing these peoples as peoples often without modern borders; their intent was to reach not just the "open" parts of these worlds, but also the hitherto "closed" parts, and—amazingly—the mission thrust aims at completing world evangelization by the end of this century. "The 'third wave' of Christian missions could be the final one," Erich Bridges of the Foreign Mission Board contends, and he lists 3,800 missionary-sending agencies worldwide with a total force of 262,300 missionaries from two hundred countries. "Evangelization by the end of this century"—that was the cry that, directly or indirectly, brought Marilyn Beaney 10,000 miles away from her children and grandchildren to the "center" of the world.

My schedule suddenly grew awfully busy in Alma-Ata, with interviews planned right up to the moment of my leaving on Wednesday for Kyrgyzstan. So it was with special pleasure that, on Tuesday, I found myself with three full, wonderful hours to myself before my three o'clock appointment. I had a light lunch—meals tended to be a good soup, a piece of chicken with carrot salad, tea, and perhaps some fruit—and then I decided on a rare luxury.

I would take a walk. Alone. Through the snow.

It was a lovely day. The walls of mist and snow that had surrounded me and closed me off during my first two days in Alma-Ata still were there, but their diaphanous curtains were beginning to part just a bit. I could see a little further now: the tops of trees, for instance, or the monument across the road, or the president's cheerful and picturesque blue-and-white-painted house on the next corner. I found myself breathing deeply, and even childishly frolicking in the snow. It had been many years since I had actually lived and worked in full and resplendent winter, with all of her myriad caprices, and I found myself to my surprise almost giggly and playful.

It was only two blocks from the Dostyk to the big Intourist hotel, the Kazakhstan, a huge building that looked nice from the outside but was Soviet-shabby inside. And next door, there was Shaggies.

Shaggies, I should explain, was *the* cosmopolitan hamburger place of all Alma-Ata. Shaggies was South Korean. I had been biding my time, waiting for the moment when I would escape, be away by myself, and try a hamburger at Shaggies in order to savor the full fruits of Kazakhstan's potential modernization. This was my moment.

Inside Shaggies, all was meticulously clean, which for Russia and Central Asia was in itself revolutionary. The waitresses stood around in neat uniforms and smart little three-cornered hats that reminded me of Napoleon's. They actually smiled. I could get coffee and a cheeseburger for a mere 56 rubles, which in U.S. currency in January 1992 was less than 50 cents but here was a lot of money. My secret repast arrived. I sipped the coffee, and it was excellent: almost like American coffee. Then, with hope sprung afresh, I attacked the cheeseburger. It consisted of a big piece of tough sausage, a piece of heavy Swiss-style cheese, some catsup, some oats. . . . It was unquestionably the worst thing I had ever had in my life.

I drank the coffee.

Walking back in the snow, looking at the beautiful trees burdened with white, I kept thinking to myself—almost humming, really—"winter, winter, winter . . ."

Then the title of the little book of memories that I would surely write about Central Asia came to me with all the pure clarity of the ringing of a church bell on Christmas morning.

All through their history of being subsumed by the dour Russian imperium, whether of the czars or of the commissars, these people had waited for winter to solve their problems. But now things were for the first time beginning to change. Now they were waiting for winter to end. No longer only patient survivors, they were also no longer patiently waiting for progress, for justice, for presence in the world.

This was the last winter of the Soviet empire as we had known it in the twentieth century. This was the winter when they were trying, however imperfectly, to create of themselves for the first time a modern people. This time they were no longer only absorbing whatever the world chose to give them because historically absorption had been their lot in life.

No, this time they were *waiting for winter to end;* this time they were beginning to infuse into the mind-set and syndrome of their historic winter their own will and their own intention. I felt, for a moment, a breathless sense of discovering life—new life.

When Dina appeared later at the hotel to translate for me, she asked me courteously, "Well, what did you do since this morning?"

I did not know what to answer.

Radio Moscow:

"Yeltsin's economic adviser Gaidar is convinced that unless the budget is balanced, inflation will destroy the old enterprises and stop the construction of new ones. . . . The government of Ukraine announced today that two thirds of the soldiers in Ukraine have taken the oath of allegiance to the new state. . . . The Black Sea fleet, a controversial issue between Russia and Ukraine, both of which claim it, will be split between them, it was announced today . . ."

. . .

That first day, Dina and Indira, my other interpreter, had mentioned Krambds. Indeed, everybody mentioned Krambds. It was *the* example of new free enterprise at work, it was *the* hope for the future, it was banks and investments from Korea and, and, and . . .

But when I asked people what Krambds actually was, I was greeted with only blank stares and confused shrugs. No one seemed truly to know, except that "it" was on television all the time, that "it" had a lot of its own cars (which was of itself impressive), and that "it" had its own banks (which you had better be wary of, because they were remarkably cavalier about giving you your own money).

All of this, of course, made me determined to get to know Krambds, to know what it really was doing, and to know in particular who its mysterious head, Viktor Tcho, was.

This was not capricious on my part, since the single most important event in the former Soviet Union—what would make this transformation or break it—was devising and designing means of transforming the old command economy on these local levels to new free regional and national enterprise economies of scale. I figured this was the place to study it, and I was not wrong.

When I first called there, I was connected to a young Ukrainian, Sergei, who was the assistant to Mr. Tcho, and he readily agreed to see me. And so, the very next morning, I approached the Krambds offices with well-formed curiosity. Outside, the buildings were the old mansions for which Alma-Ata was rightly known in this wilderness of the world. Inside were offices that could never be charged with overspending on the niceties. Simple, cold rooms, some with burned-out lightbulbs, all with the accustomed layer upon layer of dust and soot, shabbily dressed secretaries working here and there on cluttered desks: so this was the famous Krambds. It did not, in truth, give one the feeling that this was Prosperity, Inc., of eastern Central Asia.

"We are into oil exploration, machinery, information, light industry," Sergei ticked off. "We have a lot of vice-presidents—all Russians—and already we do business with Italy, Bulgaria, Singapore, Turkey, and South Korea. We have contacts with American, English, Swedish, Italian, Indian, and Australian companies. We have our own bank. Therefore, we can say that we have a multibranched structure, and we are optimistic about the future."

Krambds fascinated me. I felt that here, in these dingy and unimpressive offices, I might find a real clue as to what was going to happen, what the new institutional economic structures out here might end up being. But for the life of me, I could not really figure out what they were doing. I talked, and talked, and talked with Sergei; I discussed the "Krambds syndrome" with others. And finally, *finally* I began to put together a very complex and interesting new way of ordering economic life that was very different from that of the capitalist world. Basically, it's like this:

As Kazakhstan began to privatize, former heads of the state enterprises (they say they are the best heads of the most successful enterprises, and they may well be) got together to form Krambds. They first took state enterprises that were up for sale and made them into stock companies. Part of the stock was given to the workers, part was bought directly by Krambds, and part was sold on the new stock exchange they created. Then they started production. Already, when I was there, they were producing two hundred different products, albeit in small quantities: bricks, for instance, 55 million of them, which is a lot of bricks for a country that doesn't have much of a functioning economy.

Krambds started in September 1988, and it went from being a kind of post-Communist consulting firm to organizing the Krambds bank. The initial capital came from the former managers themselves and then the bank accumulated capital. It leaped from 15 million rubles to 100 million rubles, and now they were aiming at 1 billion rubles. The Krambds bank, which had been open to the public a mere six months that January, had received from the National Bank of Kazakhstan a general license to operate.

At the turn of the century, many Koreans had migrated to Kazakhstan, driven by the poverty and civil wars of their homeland. Others had come after World War II and even after the Korean War. The Korean nexus was a strong and resilient one, and South Korean businessmen and investors were now pouring into Alma-Ata, as they were into parts of Siberia, Kyrgyzstan, and other formerly Soviet parts of this "new East."

I soon found my favorite story: there were so many South Koreans having dinner every night at the Dostyk with Turks, coming from the West, that I asked Batir-Khan one day what they could be talking about. He looked at me with his usual look of disdain.

"They are talking about fighting together in the Korean War," he snapped.

So it was hardly surprising that all of Krambds was being over-seen by Viktor Tcho, a descendant of one of those many Koreans who had migrated here. Tcho, I was duly informed, was the "idea man" of the outfit.

They also operated with foreign companies, and foreign capital. One firm they were creating was being organized in cooperation with an Australian firm, using Chinese technology and a German company. The future? Sergei summed it up with "You can see that Kazakhstan has a great number of conditions that permit us to be optimistic. It has a stable political situation, great industrial poten-tial, raw materials, enough progressive legislation, a highly skilled workforce, and the name of our President Nazarbayev. We can hope for the future. We can predict some difficulties. We know the difficulties that Germany and Japan suffered. But we hope for the future."

This was neither the first nor the last time I would hear the pre-sent predicament of building these new nations compared to those of defeated countries at the end of wars. In a sense, they liked to see themselves in this light, and out here it was not so bedeviling as in Russia proper, because, I fully realized, it was the Russians who had lost the cold war, not they. They had barely taken part in all those pretensions and calculations of empire, so there was no need to feel either guilty or humiliated. It had come down in the last years to what was at heart an economic war, and that war had been miserably directed by Moscow. These oppressed peoples (some-times Moscow called them "punished peoples") had not lost the war; no, they had only lost the Russians, which was a big plus. Now, not burdened by the Russians' own burden of guilt, rage, and historic loss, they could employ the war metaphor with consid-erable ease and grace, and even with some legitimacy.

As a matter of fact, the war metaphor left a lot to be desired. In war, conquerors come and take charge, for better or for worse. Here, what was so utterly draining and exhausting was the fact that there was no one to take charge; they had to do it themselves.

I thought often to myself that never before in history had such a thing happened, but never before in history had economics, that tiresome scourge that involved people's character and work ethic as much as product and planning, been the name of the interna-tional game.

I also thought about how much easier it was for Germany and Japan to rebuild and reindustrialize after World War II. For one thing, the operative words here begin with *"re"*: the defeated powers knew how to "do it"; they had just gone off the track into those recurrent abysses of national ego and human bloodlust. For another, they had the United States, which had the authority, the will, and the dollars to make them change. Can this much-heralded, self-imposed, magical "market economy" answer to their woes and do what the American occupation and American planning did to and for Germany and Japan after World War II? Can it happen without an omnipotent and generous outside force?

As we walked out of the decrepit but busy old offices, Sergei stopped me suddenly and pulled me into a side room to show me a very complicated institutional chart hanging on the wall. It was a design of power and station within Krambds. "We took this from the South Korean model," Sergei explained. "Exactly! We hold thirty percent of the stock companies of the enterprise. They hold thirty to fifty percent. That way, we can move money around, modernize, bring in foreign capital."

"You'll control a lot," I said with a knowing smile.

"What's wrong with that?" Sergei demanded, and he was not smiling at all.

As I walked back out to the snowy streets of Alma-Ata, and as they drove me back to the Dostyk in one of the famous Krambds cars, I thought with a giggle, "And the South Koreans and the Turks talk about fighting the Korean War together!"

But I still had to see the famous "idea man," and to my delight the next day Sergei duly informed me that Mr. Tcho would see me. I promised to take no more than fifteen minutes of the idea man's precious idea time, and soon there I was. Viktor Tcho may have been the president of Krambds in Alma-Ata, with a whole world of economic expansion lying in wait at his feet, but his office was no more tidy than any of the others. In truth, it did not seem to bother him. A little, intense, obviously smart and tough-minded man, Tcho got right down to business.

What did he really want? What was he doing here, that so many were so mystified?

"We want to develop our corporation, using the present economic situation in Kazakhstan to transform it into transnational corporations," he reeled right off. "With many branches. After that, we want to establish new products in the republic of Kazakhstan, including consumer goods, and to enter the world market. We believe in the kind of situation, as in Japan, where the people working in our corporation are always backed by the corporation itself."

How had they started?

"In the beginning, several people working in state structures organized themselves into a group. They knew a lot about the economic situation in the republic—and not only that. They had a lot of information, so in the first stage we were dealing with information trading. Before our incorporation, I worked at the State Planning Commission. I was the chief of machine building . . ." At this point, he drew himself up straight, which made him look about five feet tall. "I can say that few know more about it than I. I also worked on state structures. That was where our first money came from. We organized the work in such a way that we could get money from the state enterprises. We then helped them make a profit and the profit went to us. We are now working with seventy enterprises. We go in and buy the stocks of the enterprises that are going to be privatized."

I liked "idea man" Tcho. To me, he seemed the no-nonsense type of man that Kazakhstan certainly needed at this point in time. Ruthless, but . . .

And certainly, I had found at least one example of what could be done.

Kazakhstan, with its historic nomadic tribes and with horsemen who swept across the plains, was a storybook country of storytelling. In ancient times, Kazakh tribesmen sat around fires and told stories to pass down their innermost knowledge and wisdom and fears. In Soviet times, everything Kazakh was to be destroyed, but as in all the republics, sensitive and silent people hoarded and guarded their memories.

One story they told at home and in moments of safety was one from ancient times. An old man was plowing a field when he suddenly and astonishingly found a sack of gold. Knowing it did not belong to him and being an honest man, he took it to the village "wise man" and asked him what to do. The wise man told him to take it to the man who had owned the field before, but that man said, "No, it is not mine, the field no longer belongs to me."

So the first man took the sack of gold to the ruler. The ruler decided, "You have a son and daughter who are about to marry. Give the gold to them."

But when he tried to do that, they both said, "No, we should not be rewarded for our love."

Finally, someone told him to take the sack to the local sage, which he did. The sage took the gold, bought apple trees, and planted a beautiful garden that bloomed forever. And that is why the apples of Kazakhstan are so beautiful and delicious, and that is why Alma-Ata means "Father of Apples."

Hundreds of miles north of peaceful and pretty Alma-Ata lies another world, the world of the arid desert and strange site of Semipalatinsk. Across a continent, the former Soviet Union stored its nuclear arsenal, from Estonia to Moldavia, from Georgia to Kazakhstan. Next to Russia itself, Kazakhstan was the center of Soviet nuclear power, with bases for both bombers and ICBM silos.

Thus was Kazakhstan "favored," the strategic planners from Moscow assured the big, clumsy Central Asian republic. It was a great "honor" to be chosen for such a service to international solidarity.

When the Soviet Union broke up and the empire was hammered open by the winds of change, what was found in Semipalatinsk was nothing less than a vast radioactive wasteland. The nuclear site was closed in 1991, but the tragedy did not end there. The Soviets had used the area to test atomic weapons, most only several miles from the poor settlements of nomads and tribesmen. Herders with their sheep constantly entered the test site and animals grazed there; no one told them not to. Since the Soviets did not have the technology to do deep testing, the bombs simply broke open the earth and created craters that soon filled in like lakes.

Once the local Kazakhs sensed that something terrible was going on and once they found that from 20 to 40 percent of their newborns were suffering from grotesque birth defects, they became afraid even to have children. The outside world, finally able to look in at Semipalatinsk, remarked with horror that the Kazakhs had received more radiation than any people on earth; it was no wonder that 60,000 died of cancer from radiation, while the doctors were forbidden to talk about it. Moscow, having learned from Stalin, now called them not a "punished people" but an "experimental population."

"The nuclear tests stopped in Semipalatinsk and New Earth Island in October 1989. We had demonstrations and political action, protests, peace walks. Thousands gathered in the movement in Kazakhstan, where it was especially strong. We were even supported by the iron workers—by their industry—and therefore the movement could pressure the government. Tests were stopped. Then Semipalatinsk was closed by executive order in August 1991. But the danger continues to exist—it's a crime of the world against the people. The weapon was created by one but the tests were against the others—it was a genocide against the people of Kazakhstan."

The man who was speaking was Mirzahan Murzahuetovich Erumdetov, head of the International Anti-Nuclear Movement Nevada-Semipalatinsk. A tall and stocky young man of about thirty, one noted that he had his hair combed loosely down over his forehead, almost in bangs. He was sitting in big, crowded modern offices with half-unpacked boxes stacked all about in the disorder that seemed to characterize every office in the former Soviet Union. I could not help noticing that although he and the two young women in the room were working on more-or-less modern computers, all of the machinery was encrusted with grime. I wondered again why nobody would ever think of cleaning anything!

Then he told me the most amazing thing. In February 1989, when this committee was born as a protest against the testing in Semipalatinsk, the committee members, under the famous Kazakh writer Olzhas Suleimenov, noted that they were also having tests in the American state of Nevada, in the superstate of the U.S.A. "And thanks to the great idea of Suleimenov to connect the two, our movement grew fast. There is also a movement in Nevada—we have contacts."

There were indeed protest movements growing in these faraway former Soviet lands, although one might add that there was the small difference that the United States tested underground in remote areas, while the Soviet government and military tested in remote places where people happened to live.

Then, interestingly enough, the same kind of rage at the other superpower came out of this young idealist as came out of the old Communists. Suddenly his face turned dark, and bracing himself against his chair and looking accusingly at us, he demanded: "Americans are Christians. You should feel guilt. Do you feel guilt?"

Taken aback, I thought for a few seconds and then said, honestly, "No!"

Now his attitude was one of scorn. "I think the armies of the United States and the Soviet Union are brothers," he said coldly. "One body and two heads."

I replied, my voice heavy with sarcasm, "Is that why they've been fighting each other all these years?"

"They have never fought against each other at all," the idealist responded. "They supported each other—simple people die, armies do not."

Some years ago, I had decided it was not at all worthwhile to fight with these kinds of advocates, so I soon excused myself. But what was in my mind was the idea that his attitude of arrogant and xenophobic suspicion and assurance was blood brother to that of the old-line Communists.

The nuclear problem of Kazakhstan will not, of course, be settled for many years. They say they will get rid of nuclear weapons by 1994, but they are still under Moscow's control. What's more, they are still too much a symbol of power for these largely powerless people to give them up.

Perhaps the one honest man I met along these lines was an adviser to the vice-president, a charming man named Kasenov Umerserik, who told me in a low voice outside the vice-president's office, "You know, the problem is that we can't remove them in a short time. It will take maybe eight or ten years. There are physical, ecological, and strategic reasons for this—our neighbor is China." His voice lowered again. "China has territorial claims against us from the 1960s. Therefore, we need to keep them, maybe a short period, as a guarantee. China claims East Kazakhstan, including Alma-Ata. Now we have good relations, but who knows in the future?"

Indeed, who could?

The Kazakhs had seemed from a distance so different from us, and of course their history and culture were very different, but so were and are all histories and cultures different. Yet so many of the same human qualities were respected among these nomadic tribesmen, and so many people cried over the same things, and so many traditions were curiously and beautifully the same as some of ours . . .

Did I know what cats in Kazakhstan were called? Dina asked me one day. I assured her I did not.

Well, I thus discovered, the word *cat* in Kazakh is *musaqh,* and when the Kazakhs talk to a cat, they most often chirp and warble, "Mish-mish-mish."
That means "Kiss-kiss-kiss."

Since the first day I came to Alma-Ata, there was one man above all whom I wanted to see. No, I needed to see; no, I would, at all costs and through whatever means, see! I had heard about him as far away as Washington, where new economic minstrels carrying newly coined legend had carried word of his deeds to the other half of the world. His was the new adventure, I was convinced; he was the modern-day economic Marco Polo, traveling across datelines and borders to find new products somewhere over the rainbows of mankind.

But strangely enough, Dr. Chan Young Bang, the economist who was trying to put the commercial and economic Humpty Dumpty of Kazakhstan back together again, was not Kazakh. He was not Russian. He was not South Korean. The man who was overseeing all of President Nazarbayev's economic development was a Korean American, born in North Korea, now a professor at San Francisco State University!

Of course I called him immediately upon my arrival that first morning. Then I called again. He was always most pleasant and agreeable, but frightfully busy, as saviors indubitably are. In fact, I called an average of once every three hours, until Tuesday afternoon he agreed to see me at six that evening (which was a darned good thing, since I was leaving the next morning for the metropolis of Bishkek in Kyrgyzstan).

I was appropriately amazed when my taxi drove me out of the city and up the graded hill toward the big mountains that overlooked Alma-Ata. I was even more amazed when it skidded a little on the ice and then turned in to a most beautiful and even romantic park, with heaps of glorious snow, icicles hanging from the trees, and—unbelievably—the most lovely little formal, baroque, European-style villas.

"Where did this come from?" I said aloud, but of course he did not hear me.

Dr. Chan Young Bang was standing in the middle of what had been the handsome drawing room of an elegant house, and he looked as though he belonged there. A big man, with a strong chest and fine posture, he was good-looking and well dressed. And he smiled when he saw me.

"I like someone who is persistent," he said.

We sat and talked for over two hours, and with great coherence he laid out the problems of Kazakhstan before me. If anything, they were worse than one would have thought, given the surface energy.

"To be fair, Kazakhstan is way ahead of the other republics," he began, sitting back in a comfortable chair near a fireplace, "but changing people's attitudes is a tremendously difficult task. Privatization—do you know how difficult it is to privatize? There is a tremendous resistance. We have a Committee for Privatization in Alma-Ata. It was under the cabinet ministers and now it has been put under the president. There is a lot of inertia, a lot of ideological hangups."

The Magic Man from San Francisco, who would make "everything up to date in Alma-Ata," was very worried that the "shock therapy" that had started in Moscow that January 2, and which Kazakhstan had followed, simply would not work. Why? "Because unless the liberalization of prices goes hand in hand with privatization, it doesn't induce a market. How can we create a market economy when the enterprises are in the hands of government? We must distinguish carefully: it's not the lack of formula, it's the lack of mechanism under which it is to be implemented. The problem is the lack of will.

"Market economy is very hard. Our people here work hard. There is nothing wrong with the work ethic here. I come from North Korea, and the South Koreans' productivity is ten times that of the North. How to explain? It's the system. We have to find the answer in the system, not in people. The Kazakh people—I never saw such dedicated and productive people."

The youth? "The young . . ." he mused. "The situation is just devastating for them. Most of them are so cynical, they are almost amoral. All the values of this society have been destroyed. When I came, I had naive American ideas. They see business as speculation and prostitution. Right now, there is a wilderness of laws which promotes Wild West capitalism." He paused. "They are fascinated with business ethics. Why? Because they are astounded that people in the West take ethics seriously.

"A newspaper here, for instance, printed a silly article on me recently. They made up the whole thing. It was all hearsay, not even direct quotes. When the editors came here, they said, 'We are not responsible. We relied upon this graduate student.' They are saying that they are not responsible for what the journalists write, even though they agreed to do it. They divest themselves of responsibility . . ."

Dr. Bang finally admitted, rather readily, that there was no economic plan yet, that Kazakhstan was simply heading toward a new barter economy not very unlike the old Communist economy, and that "there is no market here, only a single seller. A market means many sellers and many buyers. Many world-renowned economists come here and miserably fail, because economists are not equipped to deal with the moral issue."

Before I left him at close to eight-thirty that night, Dr. Bang again expressed his hope. After all, he had escaped from North Korea in 1951, made his way to South Korea and then to the United States, and had become a prominent professor at San Francisco State. He had embarked upon many trips to Russia and to Kazakhstan, even in the hard Communist years, first to try to build bridges, and soon to advise and help them on economics. And, finally, President Nazarbayev had tapped him to be his number one man.

If all of that were possible, well, was it not possible to bring a rich area like Kazakhstan into the economic world of the twenty-first century?

Since that day in Washington when I had looked at the map of the former Soviet Union and found the place farthest from everything I knew and put my finger on Alma-Ata, I had been fascinated with Kazakhstan. It had not disappointed me. I wished the Kazakhs well, and I could foresee how even in my lifetime these Central Asian republics of the former Soviet Union would readjust themselves according to their natural geopolitical position and form a large—and very different—new East, united not with Moscow or Kiev but with Seoul, Singapore, and Tokyo. Indeed, it was already happening.

I knew I was right when, just before leaving, I learned that a Maxim's Restaurant and a Pierre Cardin store were soon to open in Alma-Ata. And so, soon, the Turks and the South Koreans would have someplace to go for dinner—and something new to wear, as well.

Chapter 4

Kyrgyzstan
The Silk Revolution,
a Democratic Buddha of a President,
and Three-Story Houses

*To disobey an order, one does not need
to be very courageous.*

General Feliks Kulov,
minister of the interior of Kyrgyzstan in 1992

No, it was all quite impossible. It was simply not plausible that in the faraway land of the Kyrgyz mountain nomads, in that tiny new country of 4.3 million people tucked way up there between China and Kazakhstan, democracy had taken hold. It was clearly preposterous to suggest that in that most backward of Central Asian republics, where the average salary was one dollar a month and barely 5 percent of the wild and snow-peaked landscape consisted of fertile valleys, the best president and the most sensible team of "modern men" in the entire area had taken over.

One could only sneer fashionably at those "impressionable" Americans who were calling the round-faced President Askar Akaev "the John F. Kennedy of Central Asia."

And yet all that was true—and more.

On my third day in the recently renamed Kyrgyz capital of Bishkek, née Frunze, Askar Akaev, the remarkable Mr. Democracy of Central Asia, leaned forward with that compelling and vibrant passion that defines him and tried to explain to me why the Kyrgyz, one of the most remote and mysterious nomadic folk on earth to us Westerners, were such a different people from those of the rest of Central Asia. "Our republic of Kyrgyzstan is favorable soil for a renaissance of democracy," he began, his black-olive Kyrgyz eyes gleaming with excitement.

Why on earth? I naturally wondered to myself, before he went on to answer my unspoken question.

"The Kyrgyz people have ancient democratic traditions," he continued. "Now, you may wonder where this comes from—and I can tell you that there are lots of reasons. We were a republic open to the whole world thousands of years ago. You see, thousands of years ago we represented an important point on the great Silk Road. In those times, we already had borrowed a mixture of Oriental and European cultures. That is why you probably had noticed that the Kyrgyz people in their mentality are of both East and West.

"So if you look attentively at all of our history, you will see people here who pray to Christ, or to Muhammad, or to Buddha. What's important here is that for many centuries all of these religions were getting along peacefully.

"Yes," he went on, in that sincere and convincing manner of his, "we Kyrgyz have always played a consolidating role. That is why I would say that, in Central Asia, Kyrgyzstan will again be the borderline between East and West."

As I watched Akaev the four times I saw him, as I sat with him for nearly three hours in his presidential office, I actually began to think of him as a displaced Muhammad (olive skin, thinning black hair, authoritative manner). Or perhaps a reincarnated Buddha (wise smile, rounded puffed cheeks) with Machiavellian eyes that had gazed into James Baker's cunning ones and immediately identified with a Texas brother.

Or could he even be some sort of Central Asian Thomas Jefferson, one who had somehow lost his way traveling home from Washington to Monticello and suddenly found himself, like so many great travelers and in similar consternation, trying to manage life while sitting atop the Tien Shan mountains and gazing out over the Silk Road?

But perhaps he was in truth only Askar Akaev, a respected physicist who had amazed a world that had hardly heard of Kyrgyzstan by returning to his native land after twenty years in Leningrad, a savvy politician who against all odds was elected president in 1990 on the new Social Democratic ticket, and even a man whom Mikhail Gorbachev had wanted as his vice-president.

And that was, after all, quite enough.

Once again, as so often on this outlandish and contradictory trip, I felt myself floating in a kind of never-never land, wondering exactly where I really was. Diplomats liked to mutter of Kyrgyzstan, "It is not the end of the world, but you can see it from here." Surely, yes, for us far away in the Western world, this was the most remote place on earth. Yet, once again, the Kyrgyz did not at all see themselves like that, any more than the Kazakhs did.

A revealing little poem has survived from the Chinese T'ang dynasty:

> *Here at the frontier, there are falling leaves.*
> *Although my neighbors are all barbarians*
> *And you, you are a thousand miles away*
> *There are always two cups on my table.*

In the car as we drove along the road from Alma-Ata to Bishkek on a cold, white, winter's day, my Radio Liberty correspondent, Tynchtikbek Tchorev, free Kyrgyzstan's finest young historian, paused once in his careful and interesting (but, to tell the truth, ceaseless) recitation of the new Kyrgyzstan's "real" history, to look at me in a pleadingly plaintive way.

"We were the original Europeans," he stated, head held high. "My grandmother was blond like you—and she had blue eyes."

I already loved Tynchtik (he allowed me to shorten his almost unpronounceable name), and I thought him one of the handsomest and most elegant young men I would meet—but, blond? He was your classic black-haired, olive-skinned, sobersided Kyrgyz type, the type that made you remember Thomas Mann's feline description of a beautiful girl at the Swiss sanatorium in *The Magic Mountain* as having those black, almond-shaped, liquid, endlessly suggestive "Kyrgyz eyes." But, I thought to myself, if he wants to think he is European, what does it really matter to me?

Back to President Akaev:

As we sat that long winter's afternoon in his attractive presidential office with its red Oriental rugs, marble walls, and large Kyrgyz flag, I had to ask, "How on earth is it that Kyrgyzstan has become, at least to date, the one new republic in Central Asia to have a democratic government?"

He seemed almost joyful as he answered me. "The Kyrgyz people have always been a freedom-loving people," he declared.

"They never invaded anyone or were conquered by anybody. And all the time, we were protected by the mountains. The Kyrgyz people were a nomadic people." At this, he smiled broadly. "Alexander the Great came by this way on his way to India," he went on. "And Genghis Khan came. Each time, the Kyrgyz fought the battle, and when the Kyrgyz saw that the opposing troops were too strong for them, they took off for the mountains. Even with the Russian Empire, the Russians didn't conquer by invading. The Kyrgyz were invited into the Russian Empire, there was a strong element of voluntary entering into the empire . . .

"For example, too, the Kyrgyz people lived in communities. They had chiefs, these were elected, and they were called *bey*. Unlike other Oriental peoples, the Kyrgyz woman played an important social and political role: she never covered her face with anything and played an important part in the culture. In the last century, we had a remarkable queen, Queen Kurmanyan Datkha. Last year we celebrated the 180th anniversary of her birthday. I want to emphasize that she did not inherit power—she was elected—and the Russians sent her a precious gift and the czar acknowledged her and included her in his court. No other woman was so honored. And when we elected our leaders, the Kyrgyz would throw stones into piles that represented the vote for the various leaders . . ."

Later, in the early spring, I was to discuss Central Asia with then Secretary of State James Baker III. It was a cozy late afternoon in his glowingly warm small private office in the State Department, and he readily acknowledged that Akaev was his favorite leader there, just as Akaev was quickly to become mine. (It did not really speak very well for our powers of discrimination, the man was so totally attractive.)

When I told Baker the story about the Kyrgyz running toward the mountains rather than fighting those good old hopeless battles that the fanatics and martyrs of the world so love, he grinned broadly.

"Akaev told me the same story," he said. Then I asked him why he had become so obviously taken with Central Asia as he had himself crossed and crisscrossed the area by American official plane that same winter (when I was crawling across the land like some poor land snail). And the American secretary of state answered, with that special, drowsy, dreamy-eyed look that comes over every potential dreamer or explorer when first faced by the likes of Samarkand, Bukhara, and Khiva, "I guess because it's a place where we can *do* something. I guess because it's all so romantic and so far away . . ."

Akaev liked many great Western figures, too, both political and literary. "I remember the words of a Professor Turner from the United States," Akaev said at one point. "He said that democracy hadn't come to the United States from Europe, but that it had come from the American woods." He smiled his broad, Buddha-like smile. "I said to him that to our place, democracy came from the Tien Shan mountains."

Another time, William Shakespeare stepped eloquently out of history to join our conversation. "We are trying to break up our collective and state farms into private farms," the president was explaining. A pregnant pause. "And so we now face Hamlet's question: 'To be or not to be.' "

Still another time, his words almost sung, perhaps in slightly misshapen song, "I hear Great Roosevelt! . . . In the 1930s, when he was trying to get America out of the Depression and he was asked whether the old guard would accept the new way, he said, 'No. In the circus, we see many kinds of miracles, but we have never seen an elephant lying on its back and doing somersaults.' "

(I thought I had heard all of Akaev's quotes, but later I heard from others that he also peppers his conversation with references to Englishmen such as Michael Faraday and John Locke. At any rate, after our conversations it was impossible for me ever to think of FDR except as "Great Roosevelt!"—or of elephants lying on their backs doing somersaults.)

And then there were the sad quotes, not from that optimistic America he dreamed of but from that ancient, ever-sorrowing Russia, which had such different realities in its contorted mind. I asked him, for instance, what pleasures he got from the presidency.

That wide, ebullient, canny smile that had danced on his lips at the very mention of "Great Roosevelt" now disappeared into a sad and resigned look. "I'd have to say that I have little pleasure and much displeasure," he admitted. "I was in the United States last year for the first time. What I could see was that America was created for pleasure. Not so, this country! I remember the great Russian poet Mayakovski saying, 'For pleasure, our planet is not equipped!' So it has been for seventy years.

"Nevertheless, I do experience the pleasure of being free, and of the brilliant opportunity to express myself. We were deprived of it absolutely. Now we make mistakes, but we have taken our own road, and certainly that gives us pleasure."

Before I left President Akaev that day, I wondered aloud at this little miracle atop the Silk Road. When Gorbachev had launched his reforms, hesitant and ultimately unconsummated yet effective enough to free all of these peoples, Akaev had returned to Kyrgyzstan. Even after he had been elected president and seemed more or less secure in power, when the Right attempted a coup in Moscow in August 1991, Kyrgyzstan was the only other republic aside from Russia to experience a parallel—and unsuccessful—attempt to overthrow its government.

It was a typical Kyrgyz drama—part serious, part farce, and completely amazing. When the local KGB chief arrived to arrest Akaev, his alert and sturdy men simply arrested the KGB chief.

I soon learned, however, that one should not make the mistake of thinking that because Akaev is so charming and intelligent, he is weak. He is not. "He is very European," his press secretary told me, "but he can be as Oriental as any Asiatic leader." He smiled knowingly as he said that.

Indeed, Akaev was at his most "Oriental" the night of the attempted Moscow coup. That defining night in Bishkek could have given the Moscow coup-makers their first success outside of Moscow and could have changed the entire outcome. But Akaev sent troops loyal to him to surround Bishkek's Communist party headquarters; he broadcast Boris Yeltsin's appeal for resistance and banned the Communist party.

"I never dreamed I would become president," he told me before we parted that first cold late afternoon. "But, far more than that, I never thought I would become a politician. I'm a scientific worker—quantum electronics. And I'd like to tell you the truth: I'm very sorry to have to abandon science. Scientific workers have great advantages—a lot of intellectual freedom, for instance—and now I have no degree of freedom."

And no pleasure, either, apparently.

This next chapter in my search for the center of the world—or, as the less romantic reader might put it, our trip to Bishkek from Alma-Ata—began on still another snowy morning in the Kazakh capital. At ten o'clock sharp, I opened my door at the Dostyk, and there stood Tynchtikbek and Nurilla, bright as little steppe puppies eager to carry me off on their sled.

At least three times, I had told Batir-Khan that I would not be ready to leave until one. I told him forcefully, I lectured him. Batir-Khan had never met Western feminism before, and he obviously could not recognize its force and strength even when it fell out of the sky upon him; in short, once again, he ignored me.

But the only effect of his rudeness this time was that poor Tynch-tik and Nurilla had had to get up at two in the morning to drive over those difficult, narrow, chopped-up, miserable icy roads to pick me up "first thing in the morning." And I should not forget to mention the chauffeur, a sweet man dressed in shabby clothes who nevertheless had that undefinable look of the decent man about him; indeed, he reminded me a great deal of our fathers and of the other men on the South Side of Chicago. He worked, he treated others fairly, he asked no favors from anyone.

Somehow, in all the talk, I never got his name. And so I came in my own mind to call him "Kenny-the-Kyrgyz." He was Every-man's driver from Kyrgyzstan.

Once on the road, it soon became clear that as long as Tynchtik was breathing the foul and polluted Kyrgyz air, he was going to be talking. He had so much to say, so much that had been hidden and thwarted all those dulled years of the cynically vaunted "Soviet power." Tynchtikbek was one of those wonders that every once in a while came out of the Soviet Union: an honest and truly intellec-tual man. Because of something noble within him, something that inexplicably emerges out of the mysterious spiritual wellsprings of certain men and women, he had been able to study (and under-stand) the perverted history taught at the university under Com-munism. He then went on to study Oriental culture at the Academy of Sciences in Tashkent. For three years, he pored over the Arabic languages of the Middle Ages; he buried himself in the history of Central Asia from the ninth to the thirteenth centuries, particularly according to the Muslim sources.

He was born in 1959 in a small village two hundred miles from Bishkek, then Frunze. In 1989, when the entire long-silent and long-closed world of Central Asia shook in unison with Gorba-chev's revolution in "the center," Tynchtik became one of the lead-ers of Kyrgyz historians who created an association of young schol-ars of the republic in opposition to traditional historiography.

They went from a small legal meeting to a bigger illegal organization called Asaba (Flag). And then began the demonstrations, when the new historians came up against the well-organized KGB militias in Frunze's Lenin Square.

By then, however, something very interesting had begun. Popular movements had sprung up in the western Soviet Union, beginning in Kiev, in Ukraine, and in the three Baltic nations of Lithuania, Latvia, and Estonia. These were fascinating movements that were to reshape the entire former Soviet Union, spontaneously organized and egalitarian groupings of the true "new men" of the emerging republics. Self-defined people and groups, they were made up of most of the true intelligentsia of these countries. Organizing, they formed parallel power groupings to the old Communist parties that used to monitor the political and intellectual life of their peoples, and, hopefully, they would soon move in and take over those functions, purifying them in the process.

These people were little less than extraordinary, for although pragmatists, many were also the most moral men and women, the only people who could form a really new society.

In 1990, a feverishly excited Tynchtik, only thirty-one years old, was sent to Kiev to take part in a Conference of Democratic Forces and to study the methods of political hunger strikes. The post-Soviet Russian officials were long afterward to become enraged at the defining role that Ukraine and the "advanced" Baltic states were to take in spreading what are basically Western civil rights techniques for responding to unjust authority and changing it. Indeed, Balts from the independence groups swarmed all over Central Asia in those months, preparing local activists for what lay ahead. ("We have the Balts to thank for *this*!" those officials grumbled over and over.)

In January 1989, for instance, the new republic of Estonia established its first language law, making Estonian the official language. Kyrgyzstan thought that was just neat and promptly appropriated the wording of Estonia's language law for itself, thus establishing the Kyrgyz language instead of Russian as its official tongue.

But Kyrgyzstan, being not only independent-minded (and plagiaristic) but also sloppy, botched up the whole printing of the law. When it was published, there were black spots all over the pages.

So instead of reprinting it, something they could not afford, the wily Kyrgyz simply illustrated once again that practical streak that had told them to run toward the mountains and away from Genghis's armies. They simply amended it, adding that "the Estonian version of the law was equally authoritative."

When the great historic strikes of Bishkek had begun in June 1990, Tynchtik was there. "On the first day of the strikes, there were only eight people," he relayed to me as we moved purposefully along the highway from Alma-Ata to Bishkek. "In seven days, there were 140 of us—and always there were 500 watching us. Then, on the sixth day, Akaev was elected president—and the first people he talked to were those on strike!" He beamed at the memory. "Then General Feliks Kulov came to us. He is now the minister of the interior."

At this, my philosopher-friend paused, then voiced again the truly compelling question: "Did you know that my grandmother was blond and blue-eyed—like you?"

Actually, I am green-eyed, but no matter. At this point in the trip Nurilla suddenly got carsick.

But wait, I have not introduced Nurilla, have I? She was to play an important part in our narrative of faraway Kyrgyzstan.

Nurilla *had* to be the girl with the "Kyrgyz eyes." She was a honey of a Kyrgyz, with arresting almond eyes that proclaimed silently that she knew just about everything in the world, and she had a pert little face that would have made her a veritable jewel of sheer prettiness anywhere. She had a well-formed petite figure that would have pleased even the aggressive, upward-striving, diet-mad young women of America.

In short, Nurilla—who was thirty-two and married to a man named Baket (which means "happiness")—was a very attractive Central Asian young woman. And she was also exceedingly petulant, as we shall soon see.

But before she lay back in the seat with a tiny suffering sigh, proclaiming the advent of *the headache,* I asked her the question that had long haunted me.

"Nurilla, did you really believe in Communism?"

Before the headache took over completely, Nurilla deigned to answer. "Never!" She paused. "When I studied in Moscow, I had been told by American girls that their system was better. I didn't believe it. Our teachers told us Americans try to give you false testimony. Our farmers believed that American farmers were exploited." She paused again. "Yes, I did believe," she went on. "You see, we couldn't imagine being in another system."

Then there occurred something deeply embarrassing to me, something humiliating to her and something that put into strange tension the entire conflict that had been between our two peoples.

I still had with me one of the big plastic bottles of bottled water from the West, one that I had been able to buy from the well-stocked foreign-currency store in the luxurious Hotel Dostyk. Nurilla was thirsty, so I offered it to her. She took it, started to drink from it directly, then drew back, as if from a poison.

She took a small glass that was in the car, poured the water into it, and drank.

The saddest look passed between us. I am convinced that Nurilla believed that her world was filled with germs, bugs, microbes, and terrible diseases arising from its physical backwardness and general ideological incoherence. She looked me in the eye with that terribly wise look of an ancient woman nearly defeated by life, and then she drank one last gulp of water—from her own glass.

I did not remonstrate with her or try to change her mind or behavior. As they too well knew, this was a time, finally, for realism and truth.

If the road from Alma-Ata to Bishkek was any example of land travel in Central Asia, the journey along the exotic-sounding Silk Road must most definitely have had its dull and tedious moments. The scenery changed very little: it was all low, barren, frozen hills that blurred into an omnipresent gray sky. We stopped only three times: once, at my request, to gaze at the spare spires of Kyrgyz Muslim burial monuments silhouetted against the pale sky; once to get gas (which Kenny-the-Kyrgyz was buying from the state, at least at this point); and once so that ever-diligent and resourceful Tynchtik could stomp off in the cold to interview new Kyrgyzstan's brand-new customs agents in an old gray house on the old gray border.

One had to understand how important this was, because it meant that Kyrghyzia, the former republic of the great U.S.S.R., was now independent Kyrgyzstan, and it could have borders and customs agents and immigration agents just as would any real country. Tynchtik, of whom I already was becoming inordinately fond, after fifteen minutes with the agents came back to us immensely pleased: Radio Liberty would just love such augurers of the new order out here.

After Nurilla put her pretty little head back against the seat to doze, leaving us with no interpreter, I, too, put my head back, half-closed my eyes, and simply lost myself in the omnipresent whiteness. Then, suddenly, as we drove silently through a low canyon, I saw them: eerie white statues of animals lining the road.

They were coarse statues, probably of cement or some similar rough material, each one several feet high and staring impassively at the road. There was one every half mile or so, and I quickly became quite fascinated with them. Later, I would learn that Kyrgyzstan was a veritable treasure-house of animals, so much so that five months of the Kyrgyz calendar were named after the animals of the nation. Kyrgyzstan had steppe turtles, wild pigs, brown bears, gray wolves, ermine, snow leopards, rock partridges, lynx, mountain goats, jackdaws, deer, large-eared hedgehogs, and even black Afghan hounds. The mesmerizing animal statues, standing upright and proud, lent a rare touch of charm to the trip.

You see, I had not known until then that only 5 percent of Kyrgyzstan's landmass was valley. The rest was gloriously but impractically high, with snow-covered mountains that were in many respects as majestic as the Alps, and which were filled with rare animals.

Why, I had not even known that two-story houses had been banned by the Communists until Nurilla pointed it out to me as we rode along. They were banned so that no one would appear to have more than anyone else.

Kirghizia is a land of majestic snowy peaks, rocky gorges, boundless valleys, turbulent rivers, glittering waterfalls, enchantingly beautiful blue lakes, wild sombre forests, and mountain meadows that are a riot of colour when the tupils [sic] are in bloom. Every people, whatever its history, begins its chronicles with the date when it acquired true freedom and became the rightful master of its own destiny. For the Kirghiz people, this turning point was the Great October Socialist Revolution. From patriarchal-feudal relations to developed socialism, from medieval backwardness to contemporary progress—such was the road travelled by the Kirghiz people during the lifetime of one generation. . . .

The present day republic is a prosperous land with a powerful multi-branch industry and a highly developed mechanized and many-sided agriculture. Formerly a neglected province that did not even have country roads before the revolution, Kirghizia is now covered with a network of asphalt highways and railways, and its skies are crossed by the routes of local and union airlines, linking the republic's capital, the city of Frunze, with Moscow, Leningrad, Sverdlovsk, Novosibirsk, Soci, Kiev and other cities in the USSR.

These were the exact words that the old U.S.S.R. used to describe its fraternal republic of Kyrghyzia, where everyone lived joyfully and nobly, and lived so forever after, and even the "tupils" were forever in bloom.

These words (as well, unfortunately, as many, *many* more) were on the official postcards, as well as on the general propaganda, and it showed just how, shall we say, "overly enthusiastic" the old Communists could be.

They could better have described new Kyrgyzstan perhaps a little differently. In fact, I found a tiny land of 4.3 million people living in miserable gray wooden houses, with a capital city of few attractive government buildings, where even the parks and streets were all gray ice and gray soil. There was a desperate tiredness about the people, but also a kind of simple decency. Kyrgyzstan, like Kazakhstan, had been a place of exile, so both the czars and Stalin had sent out here so many Russians, Ukrainians, Germans, and others that by the time I came only 52 percent of the population was native Kyrgyz and 21 percent was Russian, and 74,000 ethnic Russians had already left Kyrgyzstan since independence.

Had the Soviet historians not been so ideological, not to speak of so flagrantly dishonest, they would have found something else: the historic Kyrgyz were a most arresting people, with a nicely engrossing history.

It seems that the Kyrgyz emerged out of history a mysterious people who only very occasionally came to the attention of historians or thinkers. The fierceness of the mounted Kyrgyz warriors was described in many of the battles of the "Great Game" of the European and Russian nations in Central Asia from the seventeenth century onward, but they were always on the edges of the drama. Historians were always writing about Cossacks sweeping out of the Caucasus with 35,000 men, sent by the mad czar Paul I, against the British into the snowy Kyrgyz steppes. Meanwhile,

Kyrgyz tribesmen were always capturing Russian citizens in the 1700s and selling them into lifelong bondage in the flourishing slave markets of Khiva and Bukhara.

"The name 'Kyrgyz' was first used in 201 B.C. to describe the nomads in the south of Mongolia," Tynchtik, my patient tutor of his people's history, related to me, much like an ancient Kyrgyz shaman would relate his people's legends. "They were a tribe of Turkic peoples. In fact, in the northwest of Mongolia, there is still a lake called Kyrgyz Lake, with ancient cemeteries from the fifth century. In Manchuria today, there is a group that calls itself Kyrgyz: we have common historic roots, but we speak a different language. Our most significant period was the end of the ninth century and the beginning of the tenth, in which we have our Homeric 'Manas.' This is something sacred for us. It is an oral encyclopedia of the Kyrgyz people, and in 1995, we are going to celebrate the one thousandth anniversary of Manas."

The Kyrgyz presence came to the attention of later historians when, in the twelfth century, the first big incursion of Mongolian peoples struck into Central Asia. Indeed, the modern Kyrgyz language closely resembles the inscriptions of the Mongols.

It was in those ancient days that the Kyrgyz, along with the aboriginal Siberians and Mongolians, lived believing in the spells and incantations of their shamans—the physicians, priests, and prophets of these tribal peoples who cured ills, led the prayers and rituals, and generally communicated on behalf of man with the spirit world through the medium of various states of trance. It was a primitive but ordered nomadic world, with rituals that bound them to their society and an abiding faith in religious beliefs centered around the guardian spirits of nature. Blood sacrifice of those same animals that the Kyrgyz carved statues to propitiated these spirits.

And then came the Russians.

When the Russians swept out of their steppes in the second half of the nineteenth century, fueled by the incredible energies of czarist imperialism, all the key regions, cities, and peoples of Central Asia were, one by one, dominated and destroyed. Russian missionaries began immediately to demolish the shamanistic culture and to try to impose the Russian Orthodox Church. The natives adjusted: they blended the new with the propitiation of the ancient spirits. The nomadic Kyrgyz saw their best grazing lands go to Russian settlers; and on October 14, 1924, the Kyrgyz finally became a "glorious autonomous oblast" of the Russian Soviet Federated Socialist Republic.

Then Tynchtik went back to his favorite theme again, speaking in his poor English and smiling in the midst of such sobering history each time at the mere mention of that bewildering idea.

"You see," he said excitedly, "ever since the Asian period, we combined the Mongol and the European. Even the Chinese used to describe us as 'the Europeans.' The natural Kyrgyz had blue eyes, fair hair. My grandmother was considered to be pure. With European and Mongol features! The Turkomen had purely European features also, until the Mongol invasions . . ."

Once again, I was staggered by this idea—that the black-haired, dark-eyed, Turkic/Asiatic Kyrgyz way out there on the roof of China thought they were Europeans. But I was tired now, and I was not to learn the answer to that question just yet.

Nurilla wakened from her headachy sleep and—mercifully—Tynchtik talking about Kyrgyz history.

"Do come in summer next time," Nurilla murmured, gazing out the window. "You feel the heat of the day and the dew of the mountains. It's something that can't be expressed."

Then she shook her head and added, "My husband—he's been writing his economics dissertation for four years and he can't finish it." She paused, then asked, looking probingly at me, "How can he at a time like this?"

"A joke!" Tynchtik announced, with a stubborn playfulness. "Will there be special stores for those who survive perestroika? Like the stores for those who fought in the Great Patriotic War, or Afghanistan, for those who survived. . . . You know—"

"There—there's our department store," Nurilla added, for by now we were entering the city of Bishkek. She paused, her pretty face a mask of sadness. "There's nothing in it," she said.

As we entered the gray city of Bishkek, with its squat houses and its dull government buildings, I was thinking of the incongruity of what I was seeing, thinking of the romance of what historically lay just beyond this dreary metropolis. That, of course, was all one could see if one utilized only "today's eyes," which always so imprison us in the tiresome here and now.

The vast and massive chain of the Tien Shan mountains—those "Mountains of Heaven"—began just outside of Bishkek to the south. There, their snow-covered peaks stretched in one soaring majestic arc from the borders of Afghanistan to Persian-speaking Tajikistan to China's own Central Asian provinces. Then, south of Urūmqi, the mountains came to a halt at the Turpan Depression, a lush and unexpected oasis I had visited in 1984, seeing the other face of the Silk Road.

What touched me and what excited me more than anything was the fact that adventurers were still coming here; no more was even a forgotten corner of Central Asia like Kyrgyzstan the forbidden backwater that so many of us had for so long thought it.

The daring young American explorer, my charming friend Edwin Bernbaum, in the eighties and early nineties was one of the new modern intellectual adventurers who had set out into this wild and forbidding territory. There, in the Himalayas to the south, he had found and catalogued the great "Sacred Mountains" held sacred by the peoples of these ancient cultures. He wrote of those lands just to the south of Kyrgyzstan:

> North of the Himalayas and the Tibetan Plateau, thousands of miles from the nearest ocean, rise the remote and mysterious mountains of Central Asia, shimmering like mirages on the distant horizon. The K'un-lun, the T'ien Shan, the Pamir, the Altai, ranges whose names conjure up visions of faraway places, stretch off in long ridges of snow peaks to waver and vanish in clouds of dust swept up from two of the harshest and most forbidding deserts on earth—the Gobi and the Taklamakan. Older than the Himalayas, and nearly as high, these little-known ranges form some of the most formidable barriers in the world. . . .
>
> And then, across the middle of Central Asia, skirting the northern and southern edges of the Tarim Basin, runs the Silk Route, a system of ancient caravan tracks linking China to India and the West. For more than two thousand years, tenuous lines of oases strung along the feet of the K'un-lun and the T'ien Shan have made it possible for merchants, pilgrims, and explorers to undertake some of the longest and most difficult journeys on earth . . .

These words are breathtakingly similar to those used by the earliest explorers when they tried to describe this universe. Unforgettable early explorers like Chang Ch'ien, the indomitable envoy of the Chinese emperor Han Wu-ti, who trekked across these immense expanses early in 139 B.C. Chang Ch'ien is the man believed to have opened the Silk Road, so much so that Chinese historians speak of him as "having made the road" (a term that survived for centuries of travelers) as the Chinese emperor established settlements and constructed beacon towers along the route.

A Moroccan, Ibn-Battuta, left Tangier on June 13, 1325, with the "intention of making the Pilgrimage to Mecca . . . to leave all my friends both female and male, to abandon my home as birds abandon their nests." But a mythological "wing of a huge bird" finally took him to "the Yemen . . . to Cairo . . . to Baghdad, the Crimea, Bukhara, Samarkand, Kabul, Delhi . . ." He had been "swayed by an overwhelming impulse," and his journeys totaled 75,000 miles—from Central Asia to the far Orient—which, incidentally, was three times the distance traversed by his much more famous predecessor, Marco Polo.

Traders and pilgrims, ideas of every sort—Buddhism, Nestorian Christianity, Manicheism from Iran, and Orthodox Christianity—were passed from hand to hand and from mind to mind across these venerable—and dangerous—caravan routes.

It was out of this world that the Kyrgyz emerged in the ninth century to drive the Turkic Uighurs out of the region and into the Tarim Basin. Finally, in the tenth century, the Kyrgyz were themselves pushed out of Mongolia entirely, and they finally found their home in the poor, snug, high little country they now inhabit.

But we were in "downtown" Bishkek by now. It was gray and it was cold. As I faced the problems at hand, I put Silk Road musings momentarily to the back of my mind. Even though the Silk Road had not come directly through Kyrgyzstan, I knew two things: it influenced every people of Central Asia in ways that stretched far beyond truth or reality, and I was myself finally closing in on it.

It soon struck me in Bishkek that I was still another stranger from afar, come to them in their eyes to unearth as many secrets as had those early travelers. Different kinds, to be sure. Less romantic types, certainly. And yet there was a certain similarity: we were discovering these remote peoples and they were also discovering us.

The secrets they were to reveal to me were not secrets of the hated Mongol invasion; neither were they those of the many

Ukrainians, Germans, and Koreans who were forcibly exiled and removed to Kyrgyzstan. Both the czars and Stalin thought of this faraway land as an irrelevant place where intellectuals and politicians could do no political harm and would most likely soon die from the harshness of the land and from the sheer boredom of cultural isolation.

No, these were modern secrets, terrible secrets, diabolical secrets.

It was my second morning in Bishkek. Efficient Tynchtik had arranged for me to see (or so it seemed) just about everybody of any consequence. The big old government building downtown was pleasant enough, formal, with marble steps and wood-paneled rooms. There, for nearly four hours, Tynchtik soberly marched in person after person.

I sat at a desk, and each one sat in his or her turn around a table. I don't know if Tynchtik actually had the guts to time them, but as a matter of fact, each one sat for about fifteen minutes and then simply got up and disappeared.

It was a Kyrgyz historian, a pleasant but serious man named Begaliev Suvakun, with an unruly mustache and hair slightly over his eyes, who wanted to tell me "the story."

"At the beginning of 1989," he began, "we organized an organization called 'Memorial.' We wanted to write a progressive history of the republic, of the different nationalities: Jews, Russians, Kyrgyz, Koreans, Germans, Ukrainians. We named two cochairmen of the organization; one was Kyrgyz and one was Russian." He smiled a wan smile. "What we were doing was of course illegal. This was still the period of the Communist party in power. We dealt mostly with the repressions of 1937, and we began to publish articles with the names of the forgotten.

"Remember, in 1937 the whole country was under Stalinist repression. Our very best were murdered. The whole intelligentsia was killed. Yet until now, nothing was known about the murders. There were documents here, but they were difficult to get. Some belonged to the KGB, some to the relatives of the murdered. In Kyrgyzstan, about ten thousand were killed. It was all done at a place called Chuntash, which is about twenty kilometers out by the mountains. There was one witness who kept silent all these years. Now she has finally spoken, saying that she had seen 138 killed there. She even had a list. The best of us were killed," he went on, "and I realized that I had now heard that terrible truth many times.

The father of our great writer, Chingiz Aitmatov, was killed there. The first Kyrgyz professor who wanted to change the alphabet to Roman was shot there.

"Then, last year, I witnessed the exhumation of the bodies. There were bullets in almost all of the skulls. Nobody in the world knew. And we learned other things . . .

"In 1916, for instance, the Kyrgyz had tried to rebel against the czar. There was a mass killing, and more than fifty percent of them were killed. That sort of information had been completely hidden from us. In 1915, there was the Armenian genocide, and the whole world knew—but no one still today knows about the Kyrgyz genocide. So when democracy came, and Akaev was elected, we finally came to learn our history from real history. So the main task of the new historians is to tell all the people about the truth."

I asked the question that above all had been tormenting me for many years of covering that old Soviet Union: "What does such a repression, such a horror, do to a people?" How does a people come out of such a history, knowing not only that almost all of its leaders connived in such unspeakable brutality, but that they themselves had remained silent in the face of it?

"Well, the youth . . ." He faltered for a moment in beginning. "It is tragic for them . . . but at least at last they have been given the truth about what happened here. On the other hand, they feel enraged toward the people who killed these absolutely innocent men.

"You must realize that for seventy years, there was no such thing as a history of Kyrgyzstan, only a history of the Soviet Union. Only last year was our history finally included in the curriculum. Only since 1991, in the schools and universities. Now they read articles, papers, magazines. Remember what Santayana said, that if people don't remember the past they are condemned to repeat it. Yes, people really are depressed to know all of this, but on the other hand, for such a long period they have been in a political vacuum. And not only the Kyrgyz people, but the whole Soviet people!" Here he shook his head in mock disbelief.

"I myself thought, when I was at the university, that the United States was a country of exploitation and that only the poor lived there. Then glasnost came, and we were all quite amazed to learn that this was all hypocrisy. Thank God that the total system has been split into bits! We were a kind of experiment, they made their experiments on us . . ."

Here his voice, a serious monotone throughout our discussion, for just a moment seemed to bound through the air. "But today we're free—just like in all of the civilized world!" he added.

"But don't you feel the loss of faith?" I had to ask.

"Of course," he answered slowly, then hesitated. "But to tell the truth, I never really believed."

Had they believed or had they not? It was a difficult and complex question, not to be easily answered. Once again, one had always to take into consideration the fact that Central Asia did not spawn Communism and therefore felt little responsibility or guilt for it; it was imposed upon them by Moscow and now it was unimposed. The difference in feelings of trauma and guilt between these little lands and Moscow was riveting.

While I was pondering his last statement, another man came bustling in the front door, wrapped tightly in a warm winter coat, for his own fifteen minutes of this odd kind of "fame" provided by this new wanderer come from afar along the Silk Road.

"It was all far from reality," the new man said dourly. "From 1960 to 1970, there were lots of anecdotes about the Communist party," Suvakun interjected again. "Since then, nobody really believed. It's just that people were afraid."

"But where will the people go for a new faith?" I had to ask.

"I think the majority of the people still have faith in humanitarian ideas," Suvakun went on. "They are struggling again to find some moral order. In the West, you inherited it; here, it was destroyed, all destroyed, and we have to try to find it again. Which is very difficult. I guess that we believe in Kyrgyzstan reborn. We are trying to cure the Communist sickness.

"We do have a history of our republic that goes back thousands of years, and we have our famous epic, Manas. We have people who preserved all of this history for thousands of years. Certainly no ideology that did not even last one hundred years can replace that!"

One after the other they came, all morning long. They waited quietly around the door, then sat for fifteen, at the most twenty, minutes with me, and simply and straightforwardly told me their part of the terrible story—and of the wonder of survival. It was almost as if it were some strange court of the civilized world that perhaps I unwittingly represented to them.

Then, having proffered their testimony, with dignity each stood up, said good-bye, and left—and immediately the next one came.

Jeksheev Jipar, a handsome, very Western-looking man, was with the Democratic Movement. His group was not yet a party (and perhaps never would be) for the simple reason that, for seventy years, only the Communist party had been allowed to exist. He related to me how, as much as he hated to say it, the mafia, who are really thugs and racketeers, had great influence, particularly in the parliament, which remained under Communist control. "Whatever law is issued by the president won't be fulfilled if people in the localities are corrupted and if the parliament will not enforce it," he said. It was the one major threat to democracy—along with the menacing threat of ethnic conflict—that I was to hear everywhere.

Camilla Keuenbacka was an attractive woman, even fashionable in a draped dark dress over a slim figure, who was vice-chairman of another democratic party, Erkin Kyrgyzstan. She sat down for her turn and told me how they had studied the experiences of the United States, Japan, Singapore, and Great Britain to decide what kind of parliament to create. (They were amazed to discover such facts as that the American Congress could even reduce arms purchases!)

Another tall, pleasant man, Omurbek Abdrahmanov, for his turn, explained to me how he was organizing a Congress of Private Employers, which would serve as a go-between between new businesses in Kyrgyzstan and foreign businesses and industries outside. "We had forgotten the word *private* for seventy-four years," he said at one point. "The old structure doesn't want the word to exist, but the only way out is private ownership." He had even written a little book, which was to become a best-seller, to tell people how to do it.

The testifiers literally flocked into the little room. They were all interesting, hardworking people, attempting against what must often seem impossible human and geographical odds to finally build something decent in this faraway place.

I very much liked them, and I also felt very sorry for them, not in the usual sense of "feeling sorry" but in the sense of identifying with their sorrow and honoring their courage and dignity.

In all of the chaos and change and uncertainty around them, these people had somehow survived and might just even eventually overcome. In all of the human and spiritual devastation wrought by Communism, they had not lost their moral principles; even though during those dark years those principles were seldom publicly invoked or even spoken of. Could there really be some natural moral order in man?

I decided that day that I would leave that to the poets and the theologians, who have quite enough trouble with it!

For more than a quarter century as a foreign correspondent and as a syndicated columnist on foreign affairs, I have stayed in some of the most miserable, most filthy, most contemptible hotels in the world. I even took a kind of perverse pride in it when I was younger.

One, in the dismal little town of Santarém on the Amazon River, had what might fashionably be called today a "gender-mixed" bathroom and a distinctly irregular water flow. The Amazon adventurers, gold miners, and soldiers-of-tropical-fortune—all male then—and I would at appropriate times retreat into little wooden "showers," with high wooden barriers between them, there to wait, each one in his own stall, until the water came.

Our eyes shone and glimmered with hope as we stared at one another above the barriers, naked, gambling against time and hoping against hope that the water would soon surprise us again and come.

Eventually it would, and there would be a great splashing about, and then we would emerge from our stalls, most of us having put our clothes back on again. I will always remember it as one of the more comical moments of my life.

The Hotel Ala-Too stood in all of its mildew-gray splendor opposite Bishkek's train station. But I have to admit that the Ala-Too did not even stand up to the charms of that little hotel in the Amazon.

I have cried over wars and famines, over revolutions-gone-cruel and loves-gone-sour, but I had never before cried over a hotel.

At the downstairs desk that first evening, the woman clerk yelled at me, "You'll pay now, you'll pay right now!" (Her behavior was almost a relief to me; it proved that all the old imperial "vigor" of the Soviet Empire, which these hotel floor women always so fully and nastily embodied, was far from extinct.)

"You'll pay for two nights, or you won't get a room!" (Now I was struck by the very audacity of it all: they should have paid *me* for staying there!)

Sensitive Tynchtik looked stricken at such insolence to his American guest (and perhaps, I was beginning to sense, he perceived himself to be my "savior" of one sort or another).

"That'll be 360 rubles or 70 dollars a night!" the woman screamed again.

In that case, I soberly informed her, I ought to pay in rubles—only, of course, because I wanted to help stabilize the ruble. That made my room the equivalent of three dollars a night.

President Akaev's later words would ring all too true: nobody could mistake this country as "created for pleasure."

It was when they took me to my room that the tears nearly came. There were actually two small rooms, one with two cots in it, each bed covered with a mildew-colored quilt, and the other with a simple couch, chairs, and table. But as shabby and dirty as the rooms were, one thousand times worse was the bathroom. Everything—the sink, the toilet, the bathtub, the pipes, the floor—was simply encrusted with feces and filth. I had to keep myself from vomiting on the floor and making the entire scene even worse than it was.

I actually started to say to Tynchtik and Nurilla, "I can't stay here," and then I stopped myself. For one thing, Tynchtik was clearly filled with shame at the primitiveness of the hotel, and I didn't want to embarrass him further. But, beyond that, I had known from the beginning of this "adventure" that if I got myself out there, I would have to get myself back.

I did find a welcome place of refuge in the dining room, which was a large room with heavy drapes drawn against the cold outside, with passable broiled chicken and carrot salad and beet salad every night—and, as always in the old Soviet Union, quite reasonably good Soviet champagne at only a dollar a bottle.

Moreover, I was immediately taken with the little Kyrgyz band there, which played that appallingly bad Soviet version of rock, but which was composed of sweet young men who came over often to drink champagne with me. (The waiters invariably gave me a bottle of champagne to take to my room, apparently not yet aware that under free markets you do not give away the product as you did under Communism, when the people owned everything.)

Often men would sit around in the dining room eating while keeping their fur hats set smartly on their heads. It was a habit I found strangely charming in such a charmless place; and then, of course, there was the dancing.

On Friday night, I had settled myself in for my now more-or-less regular evening, with my usual dinner at 7:30 or 8:00. The band started up, and a little Uzbek man barely five feet two inches tall got up and started dancing around by himself. He was charming, a sweet person, almost a picture of welcome innocence, as he whirled about with his arms up in the air, his feet tapping out quick little steps. He was having himself quite a time, and I suppose it was inevitable that he would ask me to dance.

First I said no, but then, watching him, I saw genuine disappointment, so finally I got up and joined him in a formless little whirl-around dance.

This seemed to win the hearts of the band, and from that moment on, I got always the very best service in the hotel, not to speak of enough free champagne to keep me gaily skipping down the Silk Road in my dreams for many nights.

But the part of the hotel that engaged me the most was the huge clock at the end of the hallway. It was two feet in diameter, a big, black, imperious creature with bright little electric lights all around its circumference. It was always going, always moving, always nervously lit up and *tick-tick-ticckkking* along in a most peremptory and didactic manner.

For a while I thought it was the only thing in the city, much less the hotel, that worked. Every single light on it burned passionately. I could not help but wonder, in that broken society, where time had stopped for so many years, why anyone really needed to know what time it was at all.

The second day in Bishkek, I tried to "reason" with the clerks at the front desk. Did they not have a better room? Could they not find a more hospitable bath for me somewhere in the historic Bishkek of Alexander the Great, Genghis Khan, and the noble Manas? Could they not *please help me*?

The answer came, huffily, arrogantly, autocratically, that of course the Ala-Too had "suites," *if* I could pay more. Somehow I managed to stop myself from throttling the woman, but the record clearly shows that all I said was, "I shall look at them."

As we walked down the long, bleak, totally forbidding and even frightening hallway, with the dark and sloe-eyed men of the East lounging for hours against the scrofulous doors of the rooms, I noted again the extent to which the women working in the hotel

Washington Times photographer Judith Olney traveled to the lovely old Tatar city of Kazan with the author. Here she revels in Kazan's glimmering January snows. *(Judith Olney)*

This street scene in Kazan explains much of the city's Old Russian charm. Kazan is filled with aged wooden houses such as these that carry the visitor back to czarist times. They are intermingled with the elegant nineteenth-century mansions of that era's budding bourgeoisie, whose promise was destroyed by communism. *(Judith Olney)*

The Tatar city of Kazan stands at one of the broadest and most dramatic parts of the legendary Volga River. The nourishing "Mother Volga," as the Russians lovingly call it, is buried in snows from fall to late spring, reminding the visitor of the implacability of winter in Russia. *(Judith Olney)*

One of Kazan's many treasures is the Russian Orthodox Cathedral of St. Peter and St. Paul, with its fanciful decoration and Easter-egg colors. Dating from the eighteenth century, the church looks particularly lovely against the ivory coverlet of the winter snows. *(Judith Olney)*

Typical of Central Asia's new age of reaching out to the world was Kazakh president Nursultan Nazarbayev's trip to Washington in February of 1994. Here, this preeminent leader of Central Asia shares a press conference with Susan Eisenhower, the granddaughter of President Dwight D. Eisenhower and an enthusiastic scholar of Russia and Central Asia. *(The Center for Post-Soviet Studies/MH Photography)*

Looking at Central Asia from neighboring Sinkiang Province in China, the onlooker can only be awed by the shimmering cold majesty of the great Tien Shan mountain range that for centuries had sealed off Central Asia from the outside. During the long winters, great peaks and frozen lakes like these locked Central Asians inside their long-forgotten lands. *(Aramco World)*

Kyrgyzstan is a little country of gray and unnotable cities and towns, but the fanciful folk-art patterns of the ancient Kyrgyz horsemen are still found in bus stops such as this one. It is in a village near the beautiful Lake Issyk-Kul, where the Kyrgyz had hoped American president George Bush would visit. *(Hermine Dreyfuss)*

Kyrgyz president Askar Akaev, for thirty years a physicist in St. Petersburg, is noted as the only genuinely democratic leader in Central Asia, so it was not surprising that he would be invited to visit the United States. Here, in the spring of 1993, he is speaking at The Freedom Forum in Arlington, Virginia. *(The Freedom Forum)*

Tynchtikbek, the wise Kyrgyz philosopher, and Nurilla, the petulant and ambitious translator, pose proudly in front of the brand-new American embassy in Bishkek the day it opened in February 1992. The building was formerly the headquarters of the Komosomol, the Communist youth organization.

In contrast to the dreary, tiresomely uniform Soviet-age urban centers, the legendary city of Samarkand is one of the most charming in all of the former Soviet Union. This mellow street scene is typical, with its tree-lined streets and relaxed people. *(Hermine Dreyfuss)*

The imposition of cotton monoculture upon Uzbekistan was Moscow's major curse upon its Central Asian peoples, but this pretty young Uzbek woman *(left)* also personifies the "romance" that the Soviets tried to attach to cotton farming during the Soviet years. *(Hermine Dreyfuss)*

Uzbek tribal and city women *(bottom left)*, like these in the ancient Silk Road city of Bukhara, can be seen daily on the streets of the old cities in dress of every possible era. *(Aramco World)*

The long and dramatic staircase to the entrance of the Timurid royal cemetery at Samarkand *(bottom right)*, where members of Tamerlane's family and other royal notables are buried, is one of the many glorious architectural and spiritual monuments of historic Samarkand. *(Aramco World)*

Devout Muslims pray in the Mestchit Khanaka Mosque in the southeastern Uzbekistan city of Margelan. The location of the holy place, near the troubled Uzbek border with Kyrgyzstan, is near the cities of both Osh and Fergana, which in recent years have seen the most bitter and bloody ethnic conflicts between the two peoples. *(Aramco World)*

Baku's elegant Lenin Square became the agitated center of violent Azeri demonstrations against neighboring Armenia in the early 1990s, when the bitter war between Armenia and Azerbaijan over the disputed enclave of Nagorno-Karabakh set the region aflame. Demonstrations such as this one often ended in murderous pogroms against those Armenians who stayed behind in Baku. *(Armaco World)*

The author peruses one of the charming streets of Old Baku. Though scabrous and poor, this neighborhood dates to the fifteenth century, and its sinuous streets surround the palace of the Shirvan shahs.

were always busy-busy-busy, washing, ironing, and folding sheets and towels.

In fact, they were quite enthusiastic about it, which in truth I thought a little strange, since they were remarkably indifferent about cleaning up anything else. But it was something I was to see elsewhere across the face of the former Soviet Union: people could be quite determined about laundry and bed linens, but about nothing else at all.

"You won't want those rooms," one of the key-keepers said in Russian, cupping her hand to warn me, in a hoarse whisper, about "those rooms" even as she led me down the hall to show me one of the famous Ala-Too "suites." "They are *very* cold," she insisted, probably thinking because I was blond I was sickly. "You won't like them."

But she was wrong. The "suite" was so much better than my first two little rooms that there was no choice; besides, the very coldness of the rooms gave me the feeling, perhaps imaginary but nevertheless real to me, that the rooms were cleaner. (It also gave me a certain reassurance that the Bugs of Summer were frozen stiff somewhere in those old walls.)

But it was one strange suite. There was a long entrance hall and three rather large rooms: one, a dining room, with a big table and television; and the other two, bedrooms, with cots in the corners. The one I chose to sleep in had only one cot and a small rug. There was no other furniture.

From the cot, I could keep my eyes open part of the time and peruse the front door. And the bath, while not aiming at anything as foolish as clean, was not nearly so bad as the other one.

The clerk at the front desk still gave me the fisheye of the seasoned fiscal thinker who knows a person who can't pay when she sees one. "That will be 750 rubles, you know!" she said when I returned to the lobby, arching her old brows. "And you'll have to pay the first night now!"

I shook my head in mock humility. Then I gave her the equivalent in rubles of seven dollars and went up to my suite.

It was good that I was in those new rooms, because that very night I awoke at three in the morning—truly one of those three A.M.s of the soul—with the eerie and terrifying feeling that I had been totally abandoned there, in Kyrgyzstan, in this strange place of nomadic tribesmen riding Mongol ponies atop the Tien Shan mountains.

As I awoke and stirred under the two comforting feather quilts, I felt, somehow, that God was lost—or, since we might suppose that God does not easily get lost in his universe, and since I was already in enough trouble without getting into any problems with heresy—that he had simply abandoned me.

It was very cold that night, and my suite was at least as cold as the outside and perhaps colder, and I had never felt so lonely in my entire life.

God was gone, I thought to myself, and I would never find him again. I then felt—very strongly—that I probably would die soon. I began to wonder where. Would it be here in Kyrgyzstan? Or perhaps in Samarkand? Or Baku? Or would I make it to Istanbul, thinking I had actually escaped these godforsaken places, and then perish in some ludicrous fashion, perhaps in an automobile accident in front of the Istanbul Hilton? That would indeed be an ignominious end, the kind that fate often chose for those who lived by stealing away on night flights and climbing sacred and forbidden mountains.

In retrospect, I can see that I was suffering a kind of classic cultural deprivation. There was really almost no sensory input for Westerners here. I was beginning to feel that I was floating alone, untethered to any culture or history that I could identify with. My sensory capacity was withering just as people's cells become dried out from lack of water.

And if I died? That would indeed mark a strange end to this entire adventure. I, who had always wanted to see all of the world, finally laid to rest in faraway Kyrgyzstan, where on a clear day you can see the end of the world.

It was then, as I lay there in the dark and the cold, clinging only to myself under those two warming quilts, that I felt myself identifying with all those hundreds of thousands of poor souls—Germans and Jews and Ukrainians, Koreans and Russians, Mennonites and Tungans—who had been so cruelly exiled to the Kazakhstans and Kyrgyzstans of that "prisonhouse of peoples."

By the time the sun had staggered up atop another high-winter morning, I found that I had dozed after all and was feeling somewhat better. I looked, but I did not see God anywhere around in those unhappy corridors of the hotel, or outside on the corner, but I didn't see the devil either. Now I thought that perhaps God was simply in the dining room, eating with the agreeable little Uzbek dancer or taking a nice stroll down a snowy park path with Nurilla.

Just as I was relieved of one obsession, a second little obsession took over.

I had been trying—gamely, I really do think—to deal not only with the lack of familiar sensory input, but also to deal with the omnipresent filth.

That morning, I simply decided something: I would never get clean again. I could bathe in a marble bathtub for fifteen years, I could sponge myself with Wash 'n Dris for a generation, I could wash with Vitabath coconut until Genghis Khan returned from the dead and Alexander the Great was resurrected—and I would never be clean again.

But while realizing this, I determined to face the immediate problem squarely, forthrightly, with clarity of intent and dignity of manner. I devised a way to simply shoot out from under the two down comforters, run crazily across the bedroom and into the bathroom, and leap into the dirty tub with only my indomitable old Hearty Okura Slippers on—*without touching anything*. I would then hold up the nozzle of the "shower," which is a rough translation for what it was, quickly splash some water over me, and jump out and run crazily back to the bedroom. It was certainly an invigorating way to start one's day.

Nurilla was filled with ambition, with yearnings, with desires. Thomas Mann's character incarnate was a veritable bundle of emotions. Or let me put it more directly in the plain words we used on the South Side of Chicago: Nurilla was filled with greed.

On the third day—three days after our initial ride from Alma-Ata—she decided to talk to me about money. We were walking out of the world-famous Hotel Ala-Too, near the beautiful Kyrgyz Alps (as any world traveler would know), and pretty Nurilla, in her fur hat, high-heeled boots, and long Anna Karenina coat, suddenly stopped in her tracks. There was a look of alarm on her face, but it did not escape me that it was also a look of wonderfully controlled, Kirgiz-eyes alarm. I knew I was in for trouble.

"I know I should have done it," she began. "My husband told

me last night—again—that I should have talked to you about money right away!"

Immediately, I became as distrusting as any girl from the South Side of Chicago, taught at birth to watch out for charlatans and crooks lurking on every street corner, could possibly be in the presence of an obviously ambitious Kyrgyz woman.

"I should have . . ." she began again.

She shouldn't have.

"Nurilla," I began, in my best and most imperious and impatient Mother Superior tone, "I pay my own expenses, but what you or the chauffeur are to be paid is negotiated by the Radio Liberty correspondents. What was it that Tynchtik told you?"

She drew her little self up, in her high-heeled boots and her long coat. "Fifty dollars a day," she announced defiantly.

Once again, I was awestruck at the audacity of a person.

With an average salary of one hundred rubles a month—or less than a dollar—Nurilla was asking for payment from me, for five days, of an equivalent salary of four years!

Momentarily I ruminated over the curious idea that I must have stumbled upon one of those rare Kyrgyz who did *not* run away to the mountains to hide when faced by the likes of Genghis Khan or Alexander the Great. For an instant, I found myself even sustaining a kind of grudging admiration for this shameless Kyrgyz beauty who dared so impudently to try to face down a representative of the rich West (acknowledging all the while that she may well have also thought that we were peripheral, since they, of course, were central).

And then I just got mad.

In fact, I got strikingly, impatiently, furiously mad! As it happened, at this point in our little drama we happened to be getting into the car with Tynchtik and Kenny-the-Kyrgyz. The explosion of voices rocked poor, sensitive Tynchtik, so much so that at one point he actually put both mittened hands over his ears, like some sleepy cat trying to hide his eyes and ears from the sun.

"Fifty dollars a day!" I cried. "Are you crazy? Don't you know where you are?"

Nurilla was still defiant. "That's what the translators make at the United Nations!" she cried in turn. "Why shouldn't we be paid what we're worth?"

I noted that remark with only a cold, stony, superior silence. "Indeed!" I said, mostly to myself. Then I turned to Tynchtik, who by now was looking so absolutely terrified at this female imbroglio that his eyes were almost closed shut. "How much did you agree to pay her?" I asked.

But, of course, Nurilla had to translate the question, and he just looked more and more terrified—and disgusted.

But Nurilla was being worn down. "Well, how much will you pay me then?" she demanded. "I'm worth two dollars an hour, at least . . ."

I quickly figured it out. For, say, a ten-hour day, that would mean Nurilla was making twenty dollars a day. Even that was twenty months' salary in Kyrgyzstan. So, even at that price, for five days of work, she would have made a hundred months of salary! (I was pleased at my math.)

At this point, Tynchtik was walking away to the agricultural ministry, where we were to talk with a deputy minister of agriculture. Nurilla had started to cry, and I wanted to go home to Washington and end this crazy trip. So I left her crying in the car, with Kenny-the-Kyrgyz sitting behind the wheel, looking helpless, and I went into the interview with Tynchtik. He scared up a nice-looking, well-dressed young official who translated quite well enough; and by the time we got back to the car, Nurilla had composed herself and apologized.

For my part, I agreed to the two dollars an hour, and she ended up red-eyed but looking for all the world like a woman who had got rich despite herself.

It was then that I chose—devilishly, you say, and you may be right—to show them the famous picture of George Bush, president of the faraway and powerful United States of America, reading my book! Nurilla's face fell. Her color changed. She began to chirp instead of talk. After this, a new respect for the American president's emissary effused her very being.

Over and over she apologized. She "didn't know, didn't understand." I finally told her to quit apologizing and just get on with her work.

One of her good qualities, however, was that she was endlessly curious. She told me that afternoon that she had just read in their newspaper that the Japanese had bought the American Empire State Building.

I said that I didn't know but that, yes, I suspected they might have.

A time later, she looked at me with a look of true puzzlement and asked, "Georgie Anne, how are they going to take the Empire State Building to Japan?"

In my five days in Bishkek, it seemed that every hour or so we were returning to the big presidential palace for interviews or meetings. This was actually a rather handsome big gray building that stood on a small hillock right in the center of downtown Bishkek. Inside, it was nicely appointed, with marble hallways, pleasantly modern offices, and heavy drapes. It was surrounded by small parks, which soon enough gave way to other, grayer public buildings, and finally to the endless shabby mildew-gray neighborhoods of small wooden houses that characterized the city.

But the most amusing thing about the presidential palace was that every one of its seven or eight entrances was exactly alike, so we kept going in one or another entrance, losing our way, and having to tramp around and around and around in endless circles. Dear Tynchtik was a better guide to history than to that diabolical building, and perhaps the building should have been taken as a symbol of just about everything that was so confusingly unreal and unworkable about Communism.

The second afternoon, late in the day when the sun was sinking into another imprecise dusk, we had just emerged from the labyrinthine building and were walking down one of many identical sets of steps when Tynchtik suddenly—and with great joy—stopped the uniformed military man who was just then walking up. They hugged each other, obviously not so much friends as real comrades. Tynchtik spoke excitedly, like a chirping magpie, in Kyrgyz, before turning to me.

"This is People's General Feliks Kulov," he said, his voice soft and filled with something akin to awe. "He has agreed to see you tomorrow."

I soon heard the wondrous stories about the "People's General" who amazingly enough was the new democracy's minister of the interior. And the whole story was indeed amazing. Much less than a year ago, the minister of the interior of Kyrgyzstan would have been the worst and probably the most cruel KGB hack; but then, even less than a year ago, I as a foreign journalist would not have been in Kyrgyzstan.

Now I was actually to have an interview with the man who was the minister of the interior! Not only that, he was the military leader who had stopped the old-line Communist party hacks' attempted coup in Moscow on August 19, 1991, by arresting the parallel coupsters in Bishkek. (In his enthusiasm, he even mistakenly locked them in the many-sided and mazelike presidential palace, along with President Akaev.) Stopping a parallel coup in Bishkek was no small thing, because Kyrgyzstan was the only other place where a sympathy coup could have taken place; his acts most probably changed history. Once again, I had to pinch myself.

The next day, at twelve sharp, we drove up to the People's General's interior ministry, another pleasant-enough modern building, and were escorted into his office, which boasted a huge stuffed eagle, a long shiny table, and the best coffee I had anywhere in Central Asia. He was a charming—no, a captivating—man, and it was no wonder that many were already saying that he must be the next president after Akaev. The People's General was a handsome man, small and erect, with rugged good looks, a very square-jawed face, and a smile so pleasing that one found it hard to constantly remember he was a military man at all. "I wonder if he's married," Nurilla whispered to me before the interview began.

"Who are we today?" the general mused with that slightly devilish big smile, as we sat down around the long table. "Look at the buttons on my uniform! They still say 'U.S.S.R.' We can't even change the buttons!" He smiled. "A military man should have special buttons on his uniform, don't you agree?" He smiled again, but this time a more ambivalent smile. "But our republic doesn't have insignia yet . . ."

Why had he himself personally changed, left Communism? What had changed him, brought him to this new world of attempted democracy and free enterprise?

"Twenty years ago, I began to think it all over," he said. "I had studied at the Institute of Internal Affairs, and I remember even now how our teachers there were talking about the reasons for crime. In the official texts, the reasons were that people couldn't overcome the past and they couldn't overcome capitalism. In our texts, they said crime was typical in capitalism because of private ownership. So under socialism, there shouldn't be any crime at all.

"I became interested in crime in the capitalist world, but at the time I couldn't develop any of my ideas. Then, when Gorbachev came, we had more information and could begin to discuss things openly. I still think there isn't a system without crime, but it is different in different countries. As for socialism, it is very easy to have economic crimes because of public ownership: everybody wants to take something with him into his private life. Our men were under the power of the Communist party and they could not check the party itself. It became kind of a state mafia."

In the hour and a half or so that we sat there with Kulov, he explained well what was happening. Former Communist party leaders were taking up "business," becoming monopolists: "What we are afraid of now is the corrupt former Communist leaders privatizing important state assets for themselves." Crime was increasing: "To tell the truth, if you don't keep things hidden, they're gone." People were too used to public ownership, so everybody wanted everything given to them, and that is why private ownership was so urgent. Most people only understood democracy "in some vulgar way." And then, again, "The biggest task is not to let monopolists buy—when an enterprise is being sold, twenty-five percent of the income is taken by the state, so it will not all go into one hand . . ."

Tynchtik, who was gazing at our People's General with more than a touch of adoration, then inserted, his voice rising to a crescendo, "Until 1992, in Kyrgyzstan the militiamen did not break up demonstrations—because of Feliks Kulov!"

Tynchtik and Kulov, I soon discovered, had met during the first hunger strike in the park, when Kulov was the "cop" and Tynchtik was one of the first "dissidents" against Communism.

"If they were peaceful demonstrations, we did not break them up," Kulov said, with a touch of sternness, explaining how he could be a modern policeman but also do his job. "But if hooligans were there, we would do it. Of course, this became complicated because the Communist Party insisted upon our breaking up these demonstrations. They really insisted and swore at us, but we did what we thought right."

Where, I asked, did he get his admirable but rare stubbornness and spirit?

He laughed heartily. "That is not stubbornness," he answered. "It is simply that, because of perestroika, I changed my conscience. My understanding of my responsibility before the law is that you can't make people think the way you want them to think with guns . . ."

"That was courageous, what you did," I told him.

For the first time, he shook his head strongly. "No," he said. "To disobey an order, one does not need to be very courageous."

Before we left, he gave me a charming little archaeological figure. It is a small carved stone, about two inches high and rounded at the top. He has stylized eyes, a long nose, and a long and incongruous beard. He is a genuine artifact from some unknown early Kyrgyz culture—and I love him dearly.

After we had said good-bye and were walking out of the ministry, Nurilla focused her Kyrgyz eyes on Tynchtik and demanded to know, "Is he married? What is his wife like? What does she look like?"

But my story of the People's General did not end there.

My story of Feliks Kulov came to a stirring end in "the saga of the lost glasses," which of course and not surprisingly involved the pretty, officious, and ever-watchful Nurilla.

You see, the very first night I was in Bishkek, I lost my glasses. Actually, it was at that memorable moment of checking in at the elegant front desk of the Hotel Ala-Too, when for reasons that have already been explained I was at my very lowest ebb. I remember taking them off at the front desk; perhaps that busybody woman there took them, hiding them away in a drawer until she could sell them on the black market (not, of course, that I would want to accuse anyone unfairly . . .). Nurilla, however, was utterly convinced that the glasses had been stolen; for the next morning, when I informed her, she began snooping up and down the miserable hallways like a Sherlock Holmes of the Tien Shan. She went from door to door, like one of those black Afghan hounds they boasted about, trying to sniff out the glasses.

"Probably someone entered your room during the night and snatched them," she decided almost immediately.

"No, Nurilla, no one came in," I responded. How was I to tell her that I had barely slept a wink in that miserable room—and that I would almost have welcomed a stranger?

"Let us put tape over the door," she said, "and then, when we return, we can see if anyone has entered the room."

I just shook my head, and we were off for our interviews.

Nothing more was said about "the great story of the *Amerikanka*'s glasses," which in remote Bishkek was beginning to rank with the great odysseys of Kyrgyz legend. Nothing was said until we were leaving the People's General's office, when I noticed that our little detective stopped to talk to several of Kulov's men who were standing in the outer office. Then, as we walked out, Nurilla was shaking her head knowingly. "I told General Kulov's men about your glasses," she told me, head held high.

I simply grimaced—and forgot the whole thing.

That night, after a full twelve hours of interviews, of walking through the snow and ice, and of constantly getting lost in the crazy octagonal presidential palace, we returned to the hotel at eight-thirty. I was ready for my usual and sustaining chicken, carrot salad, and champagne, and I was bone tired. Tynchtik and Nurilla accompanied me to my suite, saw me in, and checked the rooms for any problems.

It was then that I noticed the two big, hefty men standing suspiciously out in the hall.

They were very big, very dark, very intimidating. They reminded me of the South Side Mafioso enforcers of my youth in Chicago, and they were literally leaning against the wall outside my door staring . . . at my door. Sensing my "discomfort," both Tynchtik and Nurilla immediately went out to talk to them; indeed, they talked with them for quite a while.

"They are Kulov's men," Nurilla announced, looking very proud of herself when she returned. "They have questioned everyone in the hotel about your glasses." She smiled, and so did Tynchtik. "You are very safe here now," she added. "Nobody will give you any trouble now."

In fact I *did* feel very safe there now—and nobody so much as looked at me after that. I slept better that night than at any night on the trip. But the saga of the lost glasses, which will surely go down in legend as a modern-day counterpart of Manas, was not yet over.

Saturday, February 1, 1992, dawned white and gray. Since I was attempting to leave the next day for Tashkent, we proceeded early, at eight o'clock, to be exact, to the "city airport" to get my plane ticket. The airport turned out to be what could have been a rather attractive stone building—if someone had only stooped, now and then, to clean it. (What little air traffic there was used a larger airport outside of town, and this facility was more or less abandoned.) Whatever action there was revolved around little rows of ticket sellers, whose presence in itself marked an exercise of the creative spirit, since both airports were generally closed and only an occasional plane lumbered in.

Not surprisingly, despite this (shall we say) lack of urgent traffic, the entire transaction took forever.

Dear Tynchtik had to reason with the woman clerk—no easy task, that!—for there were many and profound questions to deal with: Should the ticket to Tashkent be paid for in rubles or dollars? When did I need to go? Why was I going? What was my purpose? And, finally, the most problematic question—and something I had not had to deal with as yet—where was my visa for Uzbekistan? In fact, where was my visa for Kyrgyzstan?

I smiled. Of course I had no visa. People do not understand what happens when an empire collapses. Republics, regions, ethnic enclaves—what should we really at that stage of the saga call the Kazakhstans and Kyrgyzstans of the world?—overnight announce that they are now republics, that they are "independent" and "sovereign."

But while this rhetoric is easy, and while most of them even immediately proclaim borders of one sort or another, in those early days of self-determination when I was there, most still did not have diplomatic missions or laws about such bothersome bureaucratic niceties as visas. I had the five-week visa from Moscow, but that was supposedly for *Russia,* and did not indicate these new republics, which of course nobody quite knew existed.

I accepted that the validity of the Russian visa depended wholly on the mood, on the health, and probably on the sex life the night before of the man or woman wielding this new bureacratic Power of the Visa! So here we encountered a problem: I was clearly in Kyrgyzstan "illegally"—except that there was no longer any truly applicable law.

We had to go downtown, and hang around several offices interminably, to get a stamp, all of which proved to me that the hated Soviet bureaucratic mentality was not yet dead. On our way, just outside the Foreign Ministry, Tynchtik met one of the ministers, who laughed derisively at his government. "We are the 'new men,' " the man said, making a joke on the old Soviet idea of the socialist "new man." "But underneath that, we still have these old men." He virtually giggled as he said it. Then, with that, he wished us luck, tipped his hat, and jogged off and away through the snow, amusing us but not really helping us very much.

In the end, after an appropriate period of waiting and waiting and waiting for the little bureaucrat, we did get the stamp, and it cost me the equivalent of $1.79 in rubles to fly from Bishkek to

Tashkent—which, believe me, turned out to be far more than the "flight" was worth.

At two o'clock we proceeded to the single most touching event I was to experience on my entire trip: the opening of the very first American embassy in Central Asia. After all those years of isolation from the world, Kyrgyzstan was overcoming America! And even I was not prepared for the emotions that would evoke in most of us, and particularly in me.

When we arrived an hour early for the three o'clock ceremony that historic afternoon, several hundred Kyrgyz had already gathered. They were standing without speaking in a long line and, in their neat fur hats, looked for all the world like a group of early Central Asian or Siberian nomadic trappers. The embassy itself was a small gray building, and it had new windows, and even new bushes, which had just been planted and already had tiny green leaves sprouting in hope and perhaps in promise.

The first American envoy had arrived on January 20. It had not been exactly easy to find an "appropriate" building in Bishkek. When the Americans and the Kyrgyz did find one, President Akaev had said forcefully that he would have the building ready for its opening on February 1—and the townspeople watched in amazement at how workmen who usually barely worked at all now worked around the clock.

But that was not all: the little house had been the Komsomol (Young Communists) headquarters; it was situated two buildings down from the local KGB; and it was on Dzerzhinsky Boulevard, the street named for the founder of the KGB. In recognition and in honor of the street's new tenants, the government had renamed the street "Liberty Boulevard."

The three of us entered the building. There, to my amazement, I found staring at us an old friend, a diplomat I had known in Islamabad, Pakistan, and whom I had seen a bare three months before in the embassy in Nicaragua, where he was then serving. Now Ed McWilliams, the new American chargé d'affaires and a respected scholar of Central Asia and of Russian and Central Asian languages, was opening the first American embassy in Central Asia!

"You're following me!" he exclaimed, and we were both just delighted with what Antoine de Saint-Exupéry would have called one of those wonderful "accidents of journeying." We hugged each other, to the great delight of Tynchtik and particularly Nurilla, who was now appropriately impressed that I knew not only President Bush but the embassy chief in Bishkek. Indeed, both her and Tynchtik's eyes shone at the distinct professional possibilities now opened to them.

The ceremony started at 3:10 P.M. President Akaev had just arrived, looking robust and happy, greeting everyone with his radiant smile and looking for just a moment as though there could indeed be pleasure in Kyrgyzstan. The Kyrgyz leaders and the five Americans who had journeyed to Central Asia to bring it back into the world of nations stood in a neat little line in front of the microphone, while the American flag still hung limp beside the building, waiting.

"This is not only a ceremonial event, it is an event that is far from ordinary," President Akaev began, speaking in Kyrgyz, which was then patiently translated by interpreters into Russian and English. "This day marks the opening of an entirely new foreign policy for Kyrgyzstan. The national independence of Kyrgyzstan has been recognized by eighty countries, but the opening of a mission has so far been done only by the United States. We are all aware of a new geopolitics in the world—and we possess the same values today: private property, and political freedom."

Then Ed McWilliams stepped up to the microphone. "This ceremony marks the end of a historical process," he said. "We are establishing the first diplomatic mission in this part of the world, while President Akaev has built an international reputation as a builder of democracy, of interethnic peace, and of a market economy. Kyrgyzstan shows that democracy can bloom anywhere. They do not want aid; they want the opportunity to help themselves develop their great new country! And so we open a new era of friendly ties. Long live the democratic republic of Kyrgyzstan!"

At that moment, the sound truck that was standing by played the American and the Kyrgyz national anthems. As "The Star-Spangled Banner" was played, the limp and drooping American flag, hidden by the side of the little building, began to rise. In the biting cold, cutting through the omnipresent grayness of Central Asia, the flag began to flutter over the sad and needy city as it was raised—and the colors were dazzling, cutting through all the pain and dirt. And it was then that the tears of joy for them and for us came, uninvited, to my cheeks.

Sunday morning, before leaving, I walked over to Ed McWilliams's hotel, which was just down the block and seemed quite definitely better than mine. We had a light breakfast and talked, and talked, and talked.

"I was very impressed that President Akaev showed up," Ed mused, as we paused over a rare cup of decent coffee. "He has clearly caught the imagination of his people—and he has caught ours. He reminds me a little of JFK—he is young, and good with people, and fascinated with ideas.

"There is a lot of interest in the State Department in the Kyrgyz experiment, and in the Akaev experiment. The whole problem of making a multiethnic state work—it's very tricky, it means showing respect to everyone."

Why was Central Asia—so far away from us, so remote from our immediate interests, so alien to our cultural memories and patterns—important at all to us? Or, indeed, was it?

"Yes," Ed answered, slowly but positively, "it is important. We go back to the heartland theory: if the heartland is unstable, the rest of the area will be unstable."

Thus was I introduced to one of the major—and controversial—theories about the importance of Central Asia: the "heartland theory." This idea that Central Asia would be of great importance to the world again—for the first time since the untimely demise of the Silk Road as a result of Vasco da Gama's treacherous compass—was first put forward by the British explorer Sir Halford Mackinder when he introduced the theory in a 1904 paper to London's Royal Geographic Society. In his book, *The Geographical Pivot of History,* he envisioned Russian control of the Eurasian landmass as the "pivot of world politics."

Gerald Robbins, a business consultant and writer specializing in Turkish and Central Asian affairs, wrote in *Global Affairs, The American Journal of Geopolitics,* in the fall of 1993, that Mackinder "saw Eurasia as a gigantic natural fortress impenetrable to seaborne empires and abounding with natural resources. . . . Whoever fully commanded and developed Eurasia's vast wealth would inevitably dominate the world."

Ed paused, then picked up again. "It could be the balance between fundamentalism and progressive Islam, for instance. As you know, secular Islam in many places is under siege by the extremists and fundamentalists. Certainly by the end of the decade, we will see the 'Great Game' revisited here."

It all sounded potentially grand but also dangerous—and all I could think about was how grand it had been the day before, when the American flag had been raised by the fresh winds over the old Komsomol headquarters.

"Yes," he said, pondering, "you see these new embassies that we're opening in the area; but the problem is that no new money has been appropriated. Congress gave us a list as to where we should go, but the money has to be taken out of other posts, essentially from the European bureau. That's just the way we are structured." Then Ed looked at me and shook his head. "The Kyrgyz expect so much from us," he said. "What they don't know is that I came here with $7,500 to establish an embassy."

"For how much time?" I asked.

"Into the foreseeable future," he answered.

Now it was I who shook my head. And, I thought, how disappointed Nurilla will be.

I remembered at this point, however, that President Akaev had also been remarkably and even painfully realistic about Kyrgyzstan's possibilities. When I had asked him, for instance, whether his new little country could really constitute any kind of market, he shook his head and said, "I'd have to say no. Our money doesn't work—it's just a sheet of paper—you can paper the walls with it. We can be swept away by the hurricane. We are just an island in this great sea. All we can really do is give concessions to foreign companies to look for minerals."

And what problems he had! All at the same time, he was trying to initiate market-oriented reforms, stave off the collapse of the economy, attract foreign investment, and desperately try to set up new rules of trading between the new republics. But his consummate and overwhelming potential nightmare came in the fear that ethnic hatreds—or even the fight for their miserable little gray houses and for space—would erupt again and overwhelm his hopes. "My greatest fear," he had told me, "is that ethnic conflict will be revived as a result of one republic gouging the other. The gas we get from Turkmenistan is so expensive, I have suggested we just burn the rubles for heat. I am so afraid we will become like animals fighting one another over prices."

In 1989, months of what was essentially a little civil war had broken out in the southern Kyrgyz province of Osh between Kyrgyz and Uzbeks, with probably one thousand left dead. And there were many other areas of potential ethnic conflict, like the Fergana Valley.

At the same time, Akaev had the enormous problem of the ecological devastation that raged across the entire landmass of Central Asia. The climate of Kyrgyzstan has changed in the last few years, largely because of the death of the Aral Sea in the north of Uzbekistan and because of what the destruction of that huge body of water has done to the winds and sands. When I was there, one third of the population was getting its drinking water from streams, rivers, and primitive wells; it is not surprising that more than 1,500 people die annually from gastrointestinal illnesses.

Despite all these problems, Akaev always seemed to remain an optimist. "My optimism is based upon the democratic traditions of our people, the ones we have already spoken of," he told me. "We have rich mineral resources. We hope we can create a healthy market economy and live in peace and see our country integrated into the world economy. Japan and South Korea had economic miracles. Who knows? Maybe you will come back in five or ten years and you will find a Kyrgyz miracle!"

Again, one could hear the faint but persistent strains of memory. "Many, many years ago, we were already a republic with an open gate," he had said. "For the Kyrgyz people, confinement in our own shell is not the proper way of life . . ."

And, besides, they were Europeans.

It was my last full day in Bishkek. I was beginning to leave the hotel, my two bags all packed, the picture of George Bush and my Hearty Okura Slippers all duly tucked away, when Nurilla stopped me in the hotel lobby.

She had been pacing up and down, back and forth, her sharp little heels *rat-a-tatting* on the dirty marble floor. "The hotel is very worried," she said suddenly, looking rather worried herself. "They are afraid their reputation will be hurt because people now think that your glasses were stolen here."

Once again, I was to be filled with awe at the very audacity of the young woman. Had I perhaps missed something? Did this hotel actually have a reputation?

Then she brightened. An idea! "Maybe," she summed up, "you should tell them that they weren't stolen!"

Nobly, I put behind me the thoughts that were really surging through my head at this suggestion. Nor was I angry anymore at Nurilla; in fact I had grown rather to like her, for she did work hard and she was clearly trying to do her best (and earn her best). So my noble self only replied, "Nurilla, I never said they were stolen!"

"Why, that's right!" she responded brightly. "*I* said they were stolen!"

When we finally did leave that last Sunday morning for the optimistically termed "flight" to Tashkent, I realized that, despite everything, I had found my favorite Central Asian republic. The Kyrgyz were one of those precious nonfanatic peoples. President Akaev was one of those rare national leaders who thought things through, was cognizant of his people's weaknesses as well as their strengths, and then acted in accordance with reality instead of acting irrationally in accordance with impossible utopian dreams. One mark of their good sense was when, during Gorbachev's often misguided efforts at reform—when he waged his famous "anti-alcohol" campaign—the Kyrgyz had been forced to cut down all their vineyards, which were something precious in this part of the world, they at least understood how crazy that was.

But I wondered, too, what would become of Kyrgyzstan? When spring came? When the next winter came?

En route to the airport, Nurilla suddenly pointed out the window with great excitement. "Look, look," she said. I looked but could see nothing special.

"Look, look, a *three-story house*!"

And, indeed, there before us on a miserable little gray road stood a three-story house! What were things coming to?

Nurilla was thinking. The picture of President Bush reading my book—the picture whose presence there was a sign that America cared about Kyrgyzstan—must have somehow flashed before her eyes.

She suddenly mentioned Kyrgyzstan's huge and gorgeous mountain lake, the country's major natural attraction, Lake Issyk-Kul'. "We'll invite President Bush to see the lake," she announced, as if she were asking him to a cocktail party in Georgetown.

Then again, why not? James Baker had been here—and so had I.

. . .

Much later, when I was home again, I would discover many more things about the Kyrgyz, although all my searches never quite totally explained their vaunted "Europeanness." Columbia University professor Edward Allworth, one of the world's specialists on Central Asia, mused with me one day about this phenomenon, but admittedly without resolution: "There is a legend among them that they trace their lineage to Alexander the Great. There is something there, for in the original Kyrgyz writings of the eighth and ninth centuries, they are described by contemporary sources as blue-eyed and red-haired. It is probably evidence of what happens when Mongol and other physical characteristics are introduced into a people." There are even blonds in Afghanistan, I discovered, in Nuristan, and some scholars claim with authority that these Nuristanis are descendants of Swedes!

The other Bishkek airport, like its near-abandoned annex, could have been a nice building if someone had dared to employ a dust-rag and a pail of soapy water. It was a huge structure, now nearly empty, but it was covered by a conservatively measured one-inch layer of dust and grime.

Tynchtik insisted upon buying me some coffee (amazing) and some rather tasty beef in aspic (even more amazing) at the little coffee bar that (amazingly) was open.

They wrapped my two bags in rough brown butcher's paper and tied them securely with rope. That cost me twelve rubles a bag. At first, I could not understand what they were doing, but finally they got through to me that, this way, nobody could break into my bags without such a heinous crime not being rather easily noticed. It seemed logical at first, except that, if they did break in, all we would be able to do *was* notice it.

Kenny-the-Kyrgyz gave me a little pen as a farewell present; I was touched beyond belief, and have it to this day.

And, when I powdered my nose with a little compact that I had bought in the Ala-Too's foreign-currency shop, Kenny-the-K's whole face lit up. "You bought that *here*?" he said, beaming like the very springtime that was surely coming. I knew why he was so deeply moved; it was because I was actually using something that I had bought in Bishkek!

I gave Tynchtik an envelope with a heartfelt thank-you note and one hundred dollars, for I knew he would not take money directly because he would be too proud. I paid Nurilla, who now became a veritable reverse-virago, endlessly and tiresomely apologizing for her greed (which allowed me, with grand noblesse oblige, to forgive her repeatedly). And when I gave Kenny the dollars that were his rightful pay for five days of travel, work, and gasoline, he just kept turning the bills over in his hands. "I have never seen dollars before," he said, and then he looked up so gratefully at me. It all came close to breaking my heart.

And then came my plane across Central Asia.

Chapter 5

Uzbekistan
Voyage to the Center of the World

How can people find me,
if I do not discover myself?

Mir Ali Shir Nava'i,
fifteenth-century Uzbek poet

Flying from Bishkek to Tashkent, those winter worlds-within-worlds beneath me changed constantly before my eyes. Halfway into the two-hour flight, the snows of those immense blurred plains of northern Central Asia began to fall away; very gradually, they were displaced by the dreary tan sands of the milder south. From the air, it seemed only a shabby and strangely ragged place.

I looked out the window as much as I could, a pastime predicated not only upon purposes of curiosity but on the very deliberate attempt to try to forget the sheer terror that these air trips were evoking in me. Forty of us were jammed into a small plane seemingly made of rough canvas, which this strange winter had transformed into a kind of shaking and shuddering public toilet. Ice carried in on the passengers' shoes or boots mixed with urine overflowing from the toilet, which together served to create an appallingly rancid and sickening smell that never for a single moment left us.

No one talked, as though the sheer exhaustion of this new era had tired their tongues, too. It was as impossible to expect food or drink as it was to expect Marxism's "new man" to meet us at the Tashkent airport (that was assuming, of course, that we ever got to the Tashkent airport).

Later, when the trip was over, I discovered that Aeroflot had had no fewer than thirty-six unannounced crashes during that last year—and I was not surprised. But I was once again painfully grateful merely for having survived an "airline" with no ground crews, no maintenance, and no schedules. Nor was even the pedigree of the planes any longer clear. Originally part of the reasonably effective Aeroflot fleet, they had now been taken over by the new Uzbek state and had been painted outside, with crossed-fingers boldness, UZBEKISTAN AIRWAYS. Long after I was home again, I was not really surprised to read in the *Financial Times* that a country in Southwest Asia had leased several of them to see its way through an airline strike, and one of the planes had simply dissolved into bits, killing everybody.

Alma-Ata had been exciting, with its dreams of linking Europe and Asia, Istanbul and Seoul. Little Bishkek had been oddly nourishing, if only through the welcome and refreshing childlike quality of its unlikely democratic daydreams and of its innocent hopes for a railroad over the Tien Shan mountains to China.

But it was Uzbekistan that was to be the most historically exciting stop, for it was in that dusty capital city—laid out by the Russians in the 1870s and '80s in the style of the garrison towns of British India to be the capital of the recently conquered province of Turkestan and the seat of the Russian governor-general—that I would begin to see that there were new Silk Roads arising right before my eyes. Even as I struggled to cross winter's vast plains and deserts, new commercial explorers were battering down the walls of these closed economies, journalists were just beginning to come, and diplomats, oilmen, and even some (thank God for them always) "purposeless" adventurers were starting to wander in, adding some welcome of sheer romance to the mix.

It was in Uzbekistan, too, that I would finally discover the clue to the riddle, where I would come, finally and unbidden, upon the real reasons for Central Asia's eternal sense of center.

Radio Liberty correspondent Tahir Umarov was at the ready at the gate to the airport, and I immediately found him to be an effervescent and most agreeably comical companion. Small and portly, with very black hair, he looked at the insane world around him out of quizzical, popping black eyes that seemed to be eternally amazed by one thing or another in this, mankind's brief voyage through life. He always wore a formal suit—and a perky, nifty, thoroughly bourgeois little hat. I remember always laughing a lot with Tahir, for he was one of those rare men who was always doing humorous and self-deprecating things and then laughing at himself.

One day, for instance, he came running out of the president's palace and suddenly realized that he had left his hat inside. He threw me and the driver, his brother-in-law, a perfectly devilish look, and then went racing back inside at top speed, his short fat legs bobbing up and down like some Eastern Charlie Chaplin being chased by a hungry tiger, only to emerge in minutes again absurdly and appropriately hatted—and walking with regal formality.

I had been in Tashkent in 1967, and how different that era was! That fated fall, the U.S.S.R. was celebrating the fiftieth anniversary of a Soviet power that evoked fear and trembling across the trajectory of the globe. The Soviets were secure at home; they were as obnoxious as a paranoid people suddenly come to total power could possibly be; they were a military world power, the inspiration of the striving and searching new countries of the Third World; they thought they constituted no less than a millennial empire.

Now Moscow, so long "the center" and so hated for so long, could no more impose its corrupt cotton quotas even on a remote and disdained Muslim republic like Uzbekistan. Now, indeed, Moscow could do virtually nothing in this new and independent republic. Instead, the Uzbeks were keen on getting the 10.8 percent of Uzbekistan's population that was Russian *out,* and they could take their language and ideology with them!

And how Tashkent itself had changed! In 1967, it was a languid, desert town of low buildings, eternally dusty, with dark back alleys and "native quarters," mosques and minarets, a world of labyrinths overlain by a liquid blue sky that seemed to go on forever. Sturdy Uzbek elders, called *aksakal* (white beard), shuffled about the old streets in their four-sided embroidered velvet *tyubeteyka* hats and their long flowing *chupan* coats, their long mustaches gleaming in the sun, their masked eyes and faces reminding the stranger that this was still the eternal Orient and that Russia would always be an unwelcome transient wayfarer here. Visitors stayed at only one old hotel specially reserved for the tourists who were forced to overnight there on their dogged and determined way to historic Samarkand, Bukhara, Khiva, or Khokand, or perhaps even to set out nostalgically along the Silk Road toward China.

Now, instead, I found Tashkent to be a thriving city, with well-planted squares and heroic statues honoring not Soviet heroes-of-production but rather fabled Uzbek poets like Nava'i. I found pleasant public buildings and a subway that challenged Moscow's for gleaming marble, crystal chandeliers, and sheer glossy elegance. Good God, Tashkent even had a decent hotel, named (how surprising!) the Uzbekistan.

Yet Tashkent was still different. Until recently, the city had a famous statue of Karl Marx in the middle of one of the parks surrounded and crisscrossed by *aryks* or irrigation canals, but his sculpted features might have more likely been mistaken for Genghis Khan than the famous German-Jewish economic philosopher. Despite the severe earthquake damage of 1966, in which much of old Tashkent was destroyed, the city still has an old area near the famous Chigotai Gate that was once a part of the original Silk Road. Like much of the Silk Road, this sounds romantic (and surely is in historical terms) but today, alas, there is little to see there; the road is only a sad dusty track.

Almost immediately upon checking into the Uzbekistan, however, I realized that the trip was getting to me in ways I had not expected. The World-Famous Lodencloth Cape-Coat and red checkered Babushka that I had chosen so carefully as a security measure so as not to look obviously American were turning out to be rather too much of a protection; indeed, treacherous traveling companions.

Now, with attentiveness to my grooming necessarily "lessened" by the difficulties of travel in the former Soviet Union, I tried the first morning to walk into the *valuta* (foreign-currency store) of the hotel, and the woman snapped at me:

"This is a *dollar* store! Only foreigners, you!"

Was it time, perhaps, to be heading homeward?

That first morning, too, at the very first hour, I launched again into still another of my heroic searches for bottled water.

During those first euphoric and then exhausting years of Revolution, the Soviet Union had gradually ceased to be a country: it had become a kind of huge and sinister aquarium. That murky and suffocating vessel was filled to the brim with oozing germs and poison-bellied tadpoles and voracious pop-eyed bugs whose entire lives were lived waiting for the chance to bore right into the gut of some unsuspecting traveler and adventurer (thinking all the while that he was actually drinking safe bottled water!) who once again in history dared to traverse its modern caravan routes.

Successful, they would gorge on the very blood that was supposed to sustain you, much as Ivan the Terrible had satiated his bestiality with the blood of his victims.

Translated into English: the water was deadly.

Until Alma-Ata, the solution had been easy enough. You could still buy foreign bottled waters in their nice, neat, *clean,* Scandinavian plastic bottles, and that was all I drank. But after I figuratively fell off the world from Kazakhstan to all these remote beyonds, I was really not surprised to find that there was no more foreign water to be had.

Invariably at the hotels, the waiters would say brightly, "Oh, yes, we have bottled water!" But their version of such a product consisted of something that was most assuredly only the poisoned tap water in bare disguise. The purveyors of this treachery simply put the aquarium into dark green Russian bottles, then smashed some dirty old caps smartly down upon them.

"Where is the bottled water?" I asked in the big, rather fancy restaurant at the Uzbekistan.

"*Nyet,*" the waiter said.

So I moved my search to the little "buffets" that were scattered around these hotels. These were the myriad counters that the Russians somehow just loved to throw about. The "salespeople" there were even more indignant that I should make such an errant request, and they shooed me off impatiently.

Finally, an attractive young Ukrainian man standing behind me at one of the buffets whispered, "You get it in the buffet at the end of the corridor on the fourteenth floor."

I made the mistake of asking "Why?" and he made a face at me as if to say, "How could you ask 'why' to any of the idiotic things they do here?"

So I took off for the fourteenth floor. There was indeed a buffet there. Naturally, it was at the farthest end of the long corridor; that was so no one would ever easily find it and only the most valiant would achieve victory. It was a busy little place nonetheless, with tiny tables and a lot of wilted and sad-looking sandwiches and warm beer—but no bottled water.

"You get that from the *dezhurnaya* on the tenth floor," a Russian man whispered to me, looking as though he were somehow peeved that I hadn't known that; then he stuffed his limp chicken sandwich into his mouth all at once.

Sure enough, the floor woman on the tenth floor had the water. "How many?" she asked: sober businesswoman, she!

"Four."

Quickly she got out four bottles, and I was quickly back in my small but pleasant-enough corner room.

I got water from her every day. As with so many things in the former Soviet Union, I never knew why.

Uzbekistan's most famous and serious intellectual, Jamal Kamal, spread his arms wide—symbolically—as he talked about Central Asia's new "space" in the world. How eloquently he spoke about all the dreams, old and new, that these new frontiers had awakened! "Before, to go to Kabul, we had to go through Moscow," this intense and cultivated man was saying, "and many times we even had to stay inside the plane in Moscow. Now we can go from Tashkent to Istanbul. We have embassies here from India, Turkey, Mongolia, Libya, Cuba, and China. Our president is at this very minute in Geneva . . . and he *went there directly*!"

(Ah-hah, I thought to myself. I knew it! They had declared independence because basically they did not want to go through Domodedovo anymore!)

"I want to give you one example," he went on. "First of all, Uzbekistan now belongs to *me*. You see, every people must have its own space, its own room—after that, we deal with the other questions. We deal with parties, with an opposition, with human rights. We were a colony, and you know what the situation of a colony is . . ."

At that, he paused, leaned back in his attractive office in the Writers' Union, and shook his head slightly, as if in wonderment over some change in the ionosphere that he had never dreamed would come to pass. "We will have an army—our own army," he said. "We have declared our independence, and we shall have our army. Without an army, what is independence? Our students are being trained to go abroad for study, some to the United States, more than a thousand to Turkey. Then they can compare conditions of life everywhere. Such experiences will provide a stimulation for development. This is all something fantastic for us," he said. "It is our achievement, to have our own way to the countries of the world. The whole area is awakening, we are shaking hands with one another . . ."

. . .

The Writers' Union of Uzbekistan, where I met Jamal Kamal, is one of the most beautiful buildings in all of Central Asia. A historic and formal mansion that was built in czarist times, it is the pale yellow and pure white of a young girl's summer dress. It has high, crenellated white ceilings and an aura of royalty about it. And elegant Jamal Kamal seemed to fit there.

Like others in those small and determined little bands of intellectuals in Central Asia who had persevered, who had been politically defeated by the Communist authorities but who had survived to enter into this new era, he had given in neither to the restraints of Uzbekistan's czarist past nor to the ideological nonsense and persecutory predilections of the Communists. Jamal Kamal himself had even translated Shakespeare into Uzbek, and how proudly he drew volume after heavy volume off his shelves for me as evidence of his truly international intellectual searchings!

At this point in the conversation, a neatly dressed, polite young man walked into the room and the two men embraced and shook hands. It was clearly an emotional meeting; there was even a sort of rarefied passion about it that left me curious indeed.

After the man had left, Jamal Kamal explained, "He is a Crimean Tatar writer—he came in to say 'Good-bye, thank you all for your Uzbek hospitality all these years . . .' They are all going back, yes, every one of them."

At that, I found myself a little breathless, as I contemplated the ways that history could change before our very eyes.

Separate from the Kazan Tatars by language and culture, these other Tatars had lived in the Crimea for centuries and, in 1921, Moscow actually recognized the presence of this ancient people on their historic lands. At that time, there were probably about 300,000 of them. But after the Germans occupied the area during World War II, Stalin put them on his sinister list of "collaborator nations," accusing them of collaborating with the Nazis. Thus, Stalin gave collective responsibility for putative "guilt"—something rejected by the civilized world—to entire nations and introduced the concept of "punished people." Within six days of liberation, the entire Crimean Tatar "nation" was deported—within hours—to the Urals, Siberia, and Uzbekistan.

Meanwhile, all traces of them were destroyed by Stalin in their homeland.

Now, because of Mikhail Gorbachev's reforms, the Crimean Tatars were actually going home. It was a saga of peoples that I was to encounter across these long-blighted and long-punished lands.

But then Jamal Kamal suddenly stopped his enthusiastic talk about reaching out and opening to the world, and became more realistic, more restrained. "Things are not good, not bad," he summed up. "Middle: like life."

It was an optimistic appraisal.

The next day, I walked in on a scene that could have come right out of a Hemingway novel. There was the slim, elegant hero, languid somehow, with a distinctly tragic sense about him. He should have been sipping Bacardis and Cuba libres at Sloppy Joe's in Key West and Havana or walking across the river and into the trees or listening to hear whether the bell really does toll for any of us. I almost looked around me for the swishing sound of a tropical ceiling fan . . .

Mohammed Salikh, the other most-respected man in Uzbekistan—journalist and poet, author of twelve books, member of parliament and of the parliament's committee on international affairs—was also founder and leader of a democratic party called Erk (Freedom), which was the major opposition party to the old Communists who were still in power here.

The first thing that struck me about Salikh, as Tahir and I walked into his big, spacious office in another old czarist-era building, was how tall, youthful, and Hemingwayesque-handsome he was. In a land of generally small and suspicious-eyed people, here before me was this long, lithe figure with fashionably sallow cheeks and elegant fashion-magazine cheekbones. With his all-white suit and midnight-black hair, and with his insouciant posture, Salikh looked more as though he had walked out of the bar at the Palace Hotel in Madrid—or perhaps had just slid down a dangerous hillside in Spain in *For Whom the Bell Tolls*—than out of Uzbekistan's stolidly tormented and drearily complicated city-state mafioso-style politics. But it turned out that this Central Asian romantic was painfully realistic.

"The situation is not good," he started out, smoking Marlboro cigarettes nonstop, as his figure seemed to form and re-form like a liquid presence behind his desk. "There are political and economic problems that enormously affect the standard of living. After the reforms, the standard of living sank to a very low level. It is lower than that of the population of the Russian republic. The political situation is also tense. The balance of political power is still held by the National Democratic Party of Uzbekistan—they were the Communists. So power didn't change but is still situated in the same place."

The situation was this: despite his own personal popularity, Salikh's party, Erk, lost the elections of December 29, 1991—most Uzbeks would say it was because of a thoroughly corrupt election, and they're probably right—and the corrupt but reasonably effective old-line Communist Islam Karimov remained in power as president in the new name of that National Democratic Party. Karimov had warned his susceptible and long-suffering people against political liberalization, predicting it would lead to popular unrest because of the catastrophic condition of the economy and because of the terrible difficulties of marketization, while Salikh argued the opposite. But Karimov, like many of these figures, was not simple—he was a transitional thug who was holding the country together.

And, yes, "Our program would have totally changed the old structures," Salikh went on. "We offered and offer new structures of power from the village soviet to the presidency. We believe that we must give power to local officials. In order to reform, we must have three powers—executive, judicial, and legislative. Now all those powers are in the hands of the president, and not of the law."

Actually, what I was seeing in Uzbekistan—as in virtually everywhere in the former Soviet Union—was a classic "gray area." Gray areas involved at least two levels of authority instead of one. These are the official and the unofficial, and most often one can barely see the dividing line (although one can nearly always feel or sense it). It means that nothing is ever clear, that power is uncertain and diffused, and that ordinary human beings know not where their loyalties—or even their more simple interests—lie.

In Uzbekistan, I found layer upon layer upon layer of grays. There were the president and the old Communists, of course; there were Mohammed Salikh and Erk, his popular official opposition party; and there was Birlik (Unity), the movement that formed outside of the political structure in response to perestroika, which came late to Central Asia but which did come. Like the other informal organizations of intellectuals, journalists, and freer-thinkers in general, Birlik began after Gorbachev's reforms were well under way, and its goal gradually became to achieve economic and political sovereignty while restoring the cultural values of the people of Uzbekistan. Despite the deep sociopolitical sleep of Uzbekistan and the people's traditional subservience to those in positions of authority, Birlik soon gained a considerable following; and when James Baker toured Central Asia in February 1992, he met with its leaders, as well as with government officials.

This process of historic transformation—one group of educated "modern" worldly men and women trying to transform a feudal society without violence—was most interesting. The most clever and relatively moral people in these new states that were forming before our eyes saw that, despite all, the hated center was not holding. So they first organized not parties, exactly, but inchoate movements of deeply concerned people.

The idea was to form a new power to move in and finally *over* the old Communist power—monitoring the Communists, presenting an alternative set of governing ideas and principles, and perhaps finally actually forming a political party to move directly to take power. The idea was good, and they'd had some remarkable successes, but they were still far from reaching the third stage.

"Is anything changing?" Tashmuhamedov Bek, the number two man in the movement, asked, shaking his head slowly. "There is practically nothing but cosmetic changes. The Communist structures have not changed and the grip on power in the system still lies in the hands of the Communist elite. This is a big danger because the standard of living is rapidly going down and there will be upheavals and crises. So we are faced with two options: either those in power will be swept away or they will repress the popular movement."

We are now back with Mohammed Salikh again, and he is talking about the economic picture, which is also dreary. "The monoculture of cotton must end in Uzbekistan. It has been here for seventy years, but it will not be in the future. Eighty percent of the land was given to cotton; now it is down to sixty percent. We must lease this land. At least it is in our hands now, not Moscow's. The problem is that it is very spoiled with chemicals. This land is perfect for everything—for melons, watermelons, peas, fruits, vegetables. It is subtropical. Our first problem is to establish an agrarian reform in order to raise the standard of living. Then we can begin to build small plants, small industries, here. That will give work to people and prepare us for better products. These must go in a parallel manner.

"Foreign investment: is there any? No. All foreign governments have for so long been connected with Moscow. Foreign countries know Moscow, even Alma-Ata, but they do not know Uzbekistan, Turkmenistan, Tajikistan. Americans, Germans, and others . . . should look closely at Uzbekistan."

But there were many other good reasons why foreigners would hesitate to come into Uzbekistan—and, in particular, there were reasons why foreigners would hesitate even to touch the land of Uzbekistan or eat the products of Uzbekistan. And these reasons are far more frightening than the obvious one of simply losing one's investment money.

The major threat to this crossroad of Central Asia used to come only from Moscow. It came palpably, in the form of autocratic orders, officious party bureacrats, and brutal security forces. They, at least for the most part, had blown away on the cleansing winds of perestroika and glasnost.

But by the time of my visit, unquestionably the greatest threat to Uzbekistan's tentative new independence was a hauntingly amorphous one. It did not shout out orders; it chose no dissidents and no Crimean Tatars to execute; it did not persecute the press, close free-thinking radio stations, or purge the intelligentsia. No, it moved silently, on the winds, carrying salt and poisoned dust as far south as the ancient city of Samarkand and even to Kyrgyzstan and to the mountains of its Chinese borders—and all because the unscientific Russian "planners" had used up the water in their hunger for cotton.

You can still see the great Aral Sea on most of the maps of the world. And until ten years ago, it was indeed a vast, shallow, 25,659-square-mile oval-shaped sea, the world's fourth-largest inland body of water. But maps, too, can lie; today, the great Aral barely exists. It is only a raw wound in the earth.

Formerly underwater mounds of salt and pesticides are now laid open to the sun and air; like bedeviled dervishes they toss their poisons out on the wind to wreak diabolical havoc in every direction. What was the sea, meanwhile, has become a grotesque Central Asian "Sahara," with ships marooned upon great, lifeless dunes in what had been the center of a body of water that had provided fully one tenth of the fish catch of the entire Soviet Union. Rusted, hollow, empty hulls stand, beached and moored on the peaks of the poisoned dunes.

Thirty years ago, the sea was more than the combined size of the states of Massachusetts, Connecticut, Rhode Island, and New Hampshire. It teemed with fish. By 1991, the Aral had lost 60 percent of its former size and 75 percent of its water volume. By the time I was in Uzbekistan, Karalski, which had been the Urals' main fishing port, sat nearly forty miles from the "shore."

Today, the Aral Sea may still be on the maps—as a matter of fact, even the most responsible cartographers do not know how to deal with such strange "disappearances"—but it does not exist. We might simply consider it a dinosaur, but it is a dinosaur that does not sit passively in museums but is instead raging its destruction across the world that killed it.

"The most dangerous thing, as the Aral disappears, is the dust and the wind," related Professor Pirmat Shermuhamedov, who is president of the Aral Sea Committee, which is trying to ameliorate the effects of the sea's destruction. We talked in Tashkent in his office in the Writers' Union. "Its dust rises to a height of three miles and it spreads to more than three thousand miles around. They have found the dust of the Aral in the tea plantations in Georgia and on the territory of India. The weather now is very hot in Tashkent and in Uzbekistan. The scientists say that if we totally lose the Aral, there could be snow in summer . . ."

But the devastation in the Uzbeks' very heartland threatens far worse to come. The landmass of Uzbekistan, so traditionally rich agriculturally that it has been for centuries the stuff of Central Asian legend, is now widely chemically poisoned. Excess minerals from fertilizers and chemically polluted water have caused soil conditions to deteriorate across Central Asia. What happens is this: the earth becomes more saline, so that ever-greater amounts of water are needed to leach and irrigate it. The result—heavily salted land—means that crops do not grow and that the underground water fields are silently poisoned. Already, the shrinking of the Aral Sea has had a decisive influence on the climate of all of Central Asia. The growing season has been cut short; frosts have occurred in Tashkent and in Kazakhstan in May, with the resulting subsequent loss of crops on thousands and thousands of hectares of land.

As for the human beings, the Karakalpaks, a historic Turkic people who had the lousy luck to settle centuries ago around the Aral Sea, are now dying "unnaturally," larger and larger percentages of their children born with mental retardation. Two thirds of the population of the Karakalpak area suffers from hepatitis, typhoid, or cancer of the esophagus—and this according to the Russian press, which hardly takes great pleasure in pointing all of this out. The infant mortality rate in some areas of this region, which was an autonomous region under the Soviet Union, is 111 deaths per thousand live births, more than four times the official all-Union 1987 average. By 1989, fully 83.2 percent of the drinking water, which comes from the toxic chemical–poisoned Amu-Darya River, was deemed by Karakalpakstan's immunological service as unfit for human consumption.

Journalists who have traveled to what is left of the Aral Sea have found the human debris remaining there to be dazed, sick, and often nearly incapable even of moving. "Where else would we go?" they asked the visitors. "I don't think people would welcome us anywhere else."

Doubtless they are right. And, ironically, the Karakalpaks are now called one of the new "punished peoples." Unlike previous victims—the Crimean Tatars, for instance, who were isolated and shunned because of supposed political heresy—the Karakalpaks are being shunned because of ecological catastrophe. They were the new "fish" in the poisoned aquarium that had been so deliberately built for them.

No question about it, what happened in the Aral Sea area now stands as *the* example of the ecological irresponsibility, bureaucratic arrogance, and self-destructive tendencies of the entire seventy years of Soviet power. In what was in truth a colonial quest for King Cotton, Moscow diverted not only the ancient waters of the Aral Sea, but also the waters of the two great rivers of Central Asia, the Syr-Darya and the Amu-Darya—all to irrigate cotton because it was Uzbekistan's "internationalist duty" to mass-produce in order to allow the Soviets to bring the Third World into the Communist camp.

But even as the Aral waters began to recede, the rigid bureaucrats in Moscow refused to acknowledge the changes. Arrogantly, the masters of the Kremlin simply imposed whatever cotton quota they dreamed up, thus bleeding the rich soils and, not accidentally, making Uzbekistan into the most appalling example of total corruption (which was, of course, really saying something!) in the entire Soviet Union.

Soviet specialist Hedrick Smith tells a characteristic story:

Moscow had imposed upon Uzbekistan incredibly high yearly quotas of cotton. The quotas were plucked out of the air, frivolously, which meant criminally. At the party plenum at which the corrupt and feudal Communist leader Sharaf Rashidov was promising to produce 5.5 million tons of cotton, Leonid Brezhnev whispered his nickname, then said, "Please round it off. Add half a million more."

Rashidov, the "political prostitute," immediately answered, "Yes, yes, Comrade General Secretary. We in Uzbekistan will produce six million tons of cotton." All voluntary!

And in that dark economic Disney World, half a million was duly added on the spot!

Another story: In Tashkent in 1976 at harvest time, the figure "5,200,000" was painted on walls all over town; it referred to the "final victory" of 5,200,000 tons of cotton. But when it became clear that the harvesters would not reach anywhere near that amount, in the dead of night painters were dispatched across the city to paint over the "2" with a "0." But with true socialist efficiency, the painters-of-the-night missed a few. The next morning, when victory in the harvest was duly declared at 5,000,000 tons, some people could still look at the building next door and see that the target had really been 5,200,000!

But this, remember, was the world where the central planning commission sent out a book as large as the Manhattan phone book every year detailing exact numbers of what every plant must produce!

In the end, it is the apocalyptic problem of the Aral Sea that hangs over this period of transition and waiting, like a wraith of what could and will happen elsewhere—and everywhere in this poisoned land. But when world-famous American environmentalist Lester Brown traveled to Karakalpak and to the remaining lakes of the Aral at the end of the 1980s, what finally struck him nearly dumb was the fact that the local leaders were just doing more of the same, and wouldn't consider doing otherwise. Despite the considered serious advice of men like Brown and the other environmentalists who traveled there at risk of their lives on tiny single-engine planes, local leaders would talk only about diverting still more Siberian rivers to raise the Aral's pathetic water level. (Mind-sets change very slowly.)

Today on the eerie "shores" of the Aral, from which men hauled 160 tons of fish each day thirty years ago, the old "sailors" now find tin for cans by walking out on the seabed to savage the ships they once sailed. At Muynak, which used to be the scene of the Aral's fishing fleet, there is still a cannery. And it still works. It packs fish brought more than two thousand miles—from the Baltic Sea—frozen! (Mind-sets change *very* slowly.)

Here I was facing still another winter. I was seeing how the winters of these peoples today have changed. The threat to them is no longer the historic invasions, nor the bloody conquests, nor the ludicrous rigid ideologies that were earlier thrust upon them.

Today, instead, they face the winter of frozen minds. Upon changing that mentality everything depends, including, because of the economy and its interlocking ties to the ecology, their—and very likely our own, as well—continued survival on this planet.

A sunny morning in Tashkent—sitting on the simple couch in my little room in the Hotel Uzbekistan—listening to Radio Moscow:

"The truth is becoming known about the army and police attacks in Lithuania last year. Even police are testifying . . .

"The meeting in Turkey of the Black Sea foreign ministers opened this morning. It was the first time in history that the new Central Asian republics that abut the Black Sea were present at such a meeting. Their presence was enthusiastically accepted and praised in Turkey. The countries are expected to sign an economic treaty of cooperation . . .

"Russian officials announced today that Russia has no potential adversaries . . .

"Radio Nagorno-Karabakh has been sending out desperate signals to the world . . .

"Mikhail Gorbachev declared today that he lost the chance in late 1990 and early 1991 to go with the democratic forces . . .

"Russian President Boris Yeltsin has returned from his trip to Washington, D.C., after stopping in Paris . . .

"The Republic of Georgia has declared that there are now forty thousand mercenaries from the Armenian diaspora fighting in Nagorno-Karabakh . . ."

Problems on the local scene: en route to Uzbekistan, I had heard the startling news that there had been massive food riots in Tashkent. Thousands of university students had demonstrated against price increases (a classic reason in revolutionary situations for bloody riots, one might add), several were killed, and the Karimov government finally gave in, slashing prices. (My political sources believed that the riots were organized, planned, because new prices were announced that very morning: a loaf of bread that had cost ninety kopecks was suddenly thirty kopecks. They believed it was old, dependably evil Moscow that had "organized" them; Russian wanted chaos in these new countries, so they could clamp down.)

Then there was the crime. The Russian mafia was something I had carefully watched, always fearful that these organized, well-financed, ruthless criminals would dominate not just some aspects of society, but *all* of society. Once the Communist party fell, there was a real chance of this, and in Moscow, the mafia, which bore no resemblance to the notorious Italian crime families except in its ruthlessness, indeed had all the spare rubles to dominate trade. By 1992, it was doing this.

Meanwhile, in Uzbekistan, the Ministry of the Interior reported that, since 1985, some seven hundred "organized criminal groups and armed formations and bands" had been put out of action there. Nevertheless, they said that "the poisonous tentacles of the mafia reach out to more than 500 businessmen and about 160 underground millionaires in the jurisdiction." The gangsters were keeping up with perestroika by preying on newly organized cooperatives and making them pay protection money. The genuine crime-fighters were already weary and suffering from a kind of Central Asian weltschmerz, articles said.

It could get somewhat depressing thinking about the problems right outside my window in Tashkent. I returned to Radio Moscow . . .

These were days to think. Days to ponder all the astonishing things I was seeing in this different part of the world. Nights to try to put things together in my mind.

One morning, I was sitting in my room at the Uzbekistan, which after the hotel in Bishkek seemed so very pleasant, and I found myself writing in my ever-present notebook:

"How strange this now is! Particularly from the first time I came here in 1967! It is no longer that old riddle wrapped in an enigma. It is no longer that bleak prisonhouse of nations. Russia and Uzbekistan have reached the point at which all the protections and presumptions have overnight been stripped off—all the mystery, all the calculation, all the deceit. And now, what is there? It is in many ways a terrible moment: the worst invasion and conquest of all. For they must now remake themselves in their former enemy's image—and the most terrible thing of all may well be that they may find themselves not able to do it."

Already I realized fully that there were several reasons why the Central Asians might not be able to "do it"; by doing it, I meant opening themselves to the world from that "center" that they now subliminally sensed not in Moscow but in themselves. By doing it, I meant modernizing their societies, not in accordance with others' expectations, but in profound accordance with whatever was left of their inner historic and cultural selves. They had had all those horrific, wasteful, destructive years of Communism, wiping out their culture and their very honor as human beings. They had always lived with the sheer terror of their geography, with all that had meant in terms of their huge landmass and of being forever separated from those oceans, lakes, and rivers that so free men. They had always those enemies all around them.

But the strongest danger to their opening up by far was that of religion. From Washington to Moscow to Bishkek, foreign diplomats and businessmen and journalists remembered the Ayatollah Khomeini's politicized and violent Islam and whispered obsessively, "Is Islamic fundamentalism going to take over Central Asia?"

The political side of that question was "Will Iran 'win' or will Turkey 'win'?" These speculators were, of course, whispering about the possibility of another "Great Game" in Central Asia, son of the original "Great Game" that pitted the British, the Russians, and even the Germans against one another in the nineteenth century to sack the wealth of Afghanistan and much of southern Central Asia. This time the new game was to be played around Islam.

But was it there? In truth, I was having a hard time out there trying to find any new games that were any fun at all.

One afternoon, seeking this new Islamic "Great Game" (did the players of this new one perhaps greet one another with "Allah

Akhbar," or "God is great"?), I went out to see the imam of the most important mosque in Tashkent. On the outskirts of the city at the end of long, dusty, bumpy roads, past houses that seemed patted together with the same tan mud and dust, stood the madrasah. And, surprisingly, it was a beauty! It was built in the same style as most of the caravansarais along the Silk Road, with a large square patio and the "offices" of the clergy and seekers-after-faith all around it, their open-walled little cubicles opening like expectant eyes upon the central patio.

But it was down the road that we found something truly wondrous. In a small and very, very ancient and tiny mosquelike building, whose hoary mud bricks seemed gravely pitted with time, we found (if legend was to be believed) the grave of the great teacher Abu Bakr. He had lived in the ninth and tenth centuries and is credited by many with personally carrying Islam to Central Asia from Arabia.

"Pilgrims come here. They say that they can feel the energy of his person," Tahir whispered hoarsely. Strangely enough, I could believe it.

As the late-afternoon wind whistled around the ancient ruins, and as the sky turned from winter's blurred gray-blue of the day to the ominous dark gray of the evening, for a moment I believed that I, too, could feel a dim energy pulsating from the grave of that ancient pilgrim and from the victory of his quest. It even seemed to me for a moment that a slight but real throbbing came out from the ruins and reached my innermost being. For that moment, it seemed to me very strongly that I had reached a breathless moment of pure peace.

Or was it, I thought afterward, merely the wind?

Al-Hadji Zahudhan Kagurob, the white-haired imam of the mosque, sat in his beautiful little office in one of the graceful niches around the central patio. He wore a solid black suit and did not look unlike those priests of the Roman Catholic church from our neighborhood on the South Side of Chicago, where most residents belonged to a faith that, like Islam, believed in a borderless world united by that faith. My surprise, frankly, was that he seemed so "normal," so relaxed, so very noticeably lacking in fanaticism and in Khomeini's dark passions.

Seventy years of Communism: what had it been like?

"Seventy years of Communism," he repeated, as though chewing on the phrase. "It was bad. In those seventy years, they wanted to kill religion in all of our whole land. Not only Islam, but other religions too. After the 1930s, they killed religious people, they changed our alphabet to Cyrillic." He paused. "Now in our schools we are teaching Arabic in special classes. Until 1989, only two men a year went on the Haj. Then perestroika came to religion in 1989; since then, we have built many religious buildings, and many madrasahs, and we have taught many students. The next year after 1990, two hundred and fifty went on the Haj; and in 1991, twelve hundred went. This year, we will see . . ."

Influence? All that "Great Game" influence from outside? "None at all," he said briskly. "With Turkey, the influence is only in business. The Saudis have helped only with books. Two years ago, they gave us one million Korans and four hundred thousand of them are in Central Asia . . ."

Food? Does the mosque help the people? He shook his head unsympathetically. "We ourselves need help . . ." he answered.

Before we left, one of his young men insisted upon taking us into the library of the Institute of Islam. This mud-colored building abutted the madrasah. At first, I did not want to go; it had been a long day. But I was terribly glad he insisted, because I was simply breathless at the beauty of this library in the midst of so gray a world.

Outside, all the earth was mud-colored; even the houses could fall into tan piles of dust. Even the women dressed in the colors either of dust or of the night. Outside, it was an undifferentiated world, a world that seemed perpetually dirty because there were no striking colors and nothing shiny or reflecting.

But inside . . .

Intricate pale blue and white Islamic designs lined the ceilings, with great whorls of gold swirling about the most austere of Muslim geometric stars, all of it reminding one of the very complexities that must be heaven itself. The building's central atrium soared three stories high, which seemed terribly, unnaturally high in this city of low, mud-colored houses, with their high fences pulled tightly about them, protection from history. Around the second floor stretched a beautifully carved balcony that was so pure in its whiteness that it could have represented all the sins of man erased in some galactic explosion. The furniture, mostly chairs and a lovely desk, were exquisitely carved with intricate Islamic motifs.

Once I was in that library—once I was standing in that beauteous and sacred aerie in the midst of all that dour ocher desert world—I wanted never to leave again, wanted only to lose myself in its serenity of intellect and in its comforting marriage of faith and of feeling. I experienced a rare moment of total joy.

"There is something more," my guide whispered to me, his voice respectfully low and filled with awe. "They have an original copy of the Koran here."

An "original" copy? At first, I did not understand. Then the men led me to a small room where tinted glass set in a wall shielded what looked like a box carved into the wall, much like a safe open on the side. Through the thick glass, one could see no less a sight than one of six copies of the original Koran, brought here sometime after the Prophet Muhammad taught the entire Middle East the truths of Islam in the seventh century. Like the great travelers of the Silk Road, this awesome book of life traveled from Arabia, where the Prophet Muhammad lived and taught, to low, white Somalia on the Horn of Africa, to elegant Petrograd in the icy north of Russia, to the old Bashkiri Muslim city of Ufa near Kazan, and finally here to the unlikely plains of Uzbekistan, the center of those plebeian Russian hopes for a cotton empire.

Finally, home!

In 1978, I had interviewed the Ayatollah Khomeini outside of Paris. For an hour, while I sat on a Persian rug in one of his little French summerhouses, enveloped in a chador. I had stared at his brooding sinister black eyes. His fanaticism, his punishing patriarchy, the violence of his teachings: all were palpable. I was never surprised at his sending hundreds of thousands of Iranian boys across the Iraqi minefields to clear them.

But this Islam was nothing like his. This Islam was peaceful, rational, and civilized.

For a girl raised in a Baptist storefront church in a Roman Catholic neighborhood who was always the little blond angel in the Sunday-school plays, I found myself profoundly surprised at my unexpected responses to Islam that day in Tashkent. Indeed, I felt a little as I had when I saw the grave of Abu Bakr. A strange and unaccustomed feeling of awe and, yes, of holiness, came over me.

Once again, I did not want to leave this very special place.

. . .

I was finally approaching the center of Central Asia. I was approaching it warily but with a small, tremulous sense of excitement. I was at the same time also approaching the new "Great Game," the new conflict between the Turks and the Iranians over the pocketbook and soul of Central Asia. I could feel that I was coming ever closer to the core of this special place—like a Catholic finally entering St. Peter's, like a Muslim arriving in Mecca, like a Jew finally seeing Jerusalem.

I realized, that dark, cool early morning that I left Tashkent for Samarkand, that I was also leaving behind me the historic peripheries of Central Asia—the open plains of Kazakhstan, the secrets of the Kyrgyz hidden in their few valleys, the little renaissance of the Tatars—and that I was approaching its own historic heart and soul.

That Wednesday, February 5, 1992, at about six o'clock, I made my way downstairs in the pitch-dark and soon found Tahir, his brother-in-law-the-chauffeur, and our interpreter outside on the broad patio in front of the hotel. We had decided to drive that day to blue Samarkand, lying between the Kyzyl-Kum (Red Sands) and the Kara-Kum (Black Sands) deserts; there, among rather a good many other things, Tamerlane (Timur the Lame) built an exquisite city, lived in golden tents, and left behind on his conquered lands towers built of human skulls that were lighted at night by spirit beacons.

But Samarkand was not simply any historic city, nor merely some forgotten old emperor's capital. For centuries, for a few great travelers and for many doomed ones, Samarkand had become *the* symbol of mystery, of romance, and of the final search for the end of the world—or for the center of the world, depending upon how you thought of it. Legendary Samarkand was the golden city of its times, in which science and knowledge flowered; and one *Economist* writer opined that the "spicy enchantments of Samarkand have enticed megalomaniacs for centuries."

British diplomat, writer, and soldier-adventurer Fitzroy Maclean approached Samarkand in 1958 and found himself also unnaturally breathless. "For five or ten minutes, we drove across the dusty, barren expanse . . ." he wrote. "On either side of the road, a wilderness of crumbling ruins and ancient graveyards stretched away into the distance. This was once the site of the city of Maracanda, founded, it was said, by Alexander the Great. Then suddenly, we topped a rise and came all at once in sight of the minarets and glittering turquoise domes of Samarkand, spread out before us against a background of brilliantly green gardens and trees. Away on the horizon above the blue heat haze rose a range of distant snow-capped mountains . . ."

Another British writer, James Elroy Flesker, once wrote an evocative little quatrain about the mysterious lure of the city:

> *We travel not for trafficking alone,*
> *By hotter winds our fiery hearts are fanned*
> *For lust of knowledge which should not be known,*
> *We take the golden road to Samarkand.*

Golden road?
Well, not exactly.

We left Tashkent as the sun came up, and we rode in silence for some time through the dust-colored Oriental backstreets of the city, with their walled gardens so like the veils of the religious women. Once outside the city, Tahir looked out at the flat, sand-colored landscape, with nothing on the horizon and only a few bleak little houses here and there, and declared suddenly:

"Look! There is a horse running."

There was so little to see that I looked quickly out across those vast plains to try to catch the horse before he disappeared. But I saw no horses running; indeed, I saw nothing running at all.

Then there came into view the incongruous sight of what was obviously a small and primitive horse-racing track, and a pleased Tahir was pointing to it.

I realized then that our interpreter was getting tired.

"There we grow cotton," Tahir began. "Our production is not very big, but when our farmers have their own fields, they will be like America . . ."

Millions of years ago, this entire area had been a desert called Mirzacho, which not surprisingly meant "Great Desert." There was nothing here then: no people and no animals. But gradually people came and, being people, carved little canals out of the earth to provide some primitive irrigation for farming. Indeed, the entire area was desert until as late as 1950.

Every once in a while, the adventurers and travelers who were drawn to Central Asia, as a thirsty man is to water, would find fruit-laden oases, which broke the boredom and danger of the end-less sands.

"Until the fifteenth century," Tahir went on, "when the water-ways to India and the Orient were opened, Uzbekistan was the only passageway between Europe and Asia, between Turkestan and Arabestan . . ." His voice suddenly turned dreamy.

As we drove down the "golden road," barren golden mountains seemed to move out to meet us. We crossed the Zarafsha River. The mountains were not friendly ones, with ragged patches of snow in the highlands. These were lonely places, without a blade of grass or the hope of ever having one. An occasional black and white bird—even the birds seemed starkly colored—flew by us. I tried hard to recognize them, but could not.

"There used to be a train that went from Tashkent to Samar-kand," Tahir went on, "and then it went on from there to Du-shanbe and Afghanistan." He sighed. "No more."

"Where are the old city baths that I have heard of?" I asked.

"Yes, I know him," Tahir answered.

It was then that I realized that our interpreter was *really* growing tired.

But our young Uzbek interpreter did snap back, as we drove past cotton field after cotton field. He was able to explain to me in relatively hopeful terms that some of the farms were now being bought and sold. Already in 1991, the old collective farms, which still existed in one form or another, were allowed to sell 5 percent of their cotton privately, with the rest still going to the state; by 1992, that percentage was up to 15 percent, and farmers were free to sell 50 percent of their vegetables, fruits, and grains. The farmers were making more than twice as much money on cotton sold pri-vately as they did with the fixed price set by the state. Farmers were taking better care of their land, diversifying crops and using far less of the dangerous pesticides, with organic methods being sub-stituted. Irrigation was being made more efficient, with more ditches being lined with concrete to prevent runoff.

So there was indeed some hope.

When we arrived in Samarkand four hours later, I found that the small and pleasant city reminded me agreeably of Urūmqi in Xin-jiang Uygur province in northwest China. It had the same languid streets lined with tall and straight poplars; it had similar pleasant villas and some formal mansions that had belonged to the early Russian settlers from czarist times. It reminded me, too, of the incredible scope of the Russian conquests in the nineteenth century. Urūmqi, whose majority population is Turkic, was roughly 1,200 miles from Samarkand—yet they both had existed historically in almost the same exact world.

The streets were surprisingly pretty, and clean, and the answer to that puzzle was money. Samarkand had something to sell. The rich historic lures and "monuments" of this ancient city, not to speak of nearby Bukhara and Khiva, beguiled the West and, not incidentally, brought in the monied planeloads of the new Marco Polo tourist-adventurers of the "civilized" world. There was even a joint venture with India to build a beautiful modern hotel!

Now I am going to complain. I had been working fourteen to sixteen hours a day, every day, on this trip. The whole adventure was fascinating, but it was also endlessly difficult. Almost everything except conversations in English and light conversation in Russian (or an occasional exchange in German or Spanish) had to be translated. (And now the interpreter himself was tired and would have taken us to the running horse instead of the horse race, had we let him!) Then, and almost at the same time, I had to translate in my head, according to cultural sense, what the interpreter translated—not only what the person said but what he meant!

Which translated means, I was tired!

Thus I had enormously looked forward to this rare day of not working but of just absorbing feelings, beauty, history—of not fighting language and cultural differences and of trying desperately to break through—and so I was more than a little crabby when I discovered that Tahir had dutifully made still more arrangements for some interviews. I was downright cranky.

"This is our stock exchange and its name is Turkestan."

By now, we were sitting in this tall, modern building that ironically had formerly been the State Planning Board, and it was quite nice and even (God forbid!) clean for what had been the Soviet Empire, and this attractive and courteous man was sitting there explaining to me how the new stock exchanges work. His name was Ahsham Razukob, he had been (not surprisingly) a Communist official, and now he was a loyal member of Mohammed Salikh's democratic party, Erk.

"It started only in September 1991, and now we have one hundred and fifty brokers working here," he told us, as businesslike as any businessman in Sioux City or oilman from Tulsa, "and they are very experienced brokers. We are also starting classes for students—in marketing—in the tenth year now, there is a class in marketing . . ." He had his notes written out, and it was all most efficient in the new Central Asia. "We also have a special school for the English language. The students in the school learn English for business, and for selling. After a while, we want to be in the international stock exchanges."

A big smile!

"And eventually we want to open a special institute here . . ."

It all sounded so perfect, it all rang so true and right, that I was beginning to be tentatively hopeful.

Now he was insisting that Americans should come—must come, *needed* to come. Why? He made it sound as though he were Calvin and this was a case of the very salvation of our souls. Mr. Samarkand-Stock-Market then looked at me very seriously.

"The Americans should come," he said, looking me square in the eye.

And so I stared right back. "Why?" I asked in solemn tones that tried to equal his.

"The first ones who come . . . will win!" Mr. Stock-Market intoned, ending on a glorious note.

It was not only a great challenge, it was a great moment! We would win, if only we would come—we should come, so that we could win! The logic was impeccable. Momentarily, I found myself appropriately breathless at the possibilities. But then I pulled myself up and thought to ask:

"What will we win?"

Suddenly the great challenger of Uncle Sam, the lineal descendant of the artistic beast Tamerlane, the would-be economic savior of Central Asia, faltered. He paused. His face reddened slightly, and he said nothing.

Emboldened at the same time that I was confused, I pressed my own case now, asking, "What do you have to sell?"

It was as if I had hit him with an old Soviet production quota, it seemed to be such a mysterious question.

"Ummm," he said. "Ummm . . . products . . . land, buildings, shops, big plants . . . ummm . . ."

Minerals?

He brightened. "Oh, surely. Oh, yes, ummm, minerals," he said, "Surely . . ."

(I wasn't so sure.)

What kind? Where? How would we get them out?

Only that blank and slightly frightened look again.

Did he have any handicrafts?

"What is that?"

They are important.

"What do you want?"

I want to get out of here.

Again I realized that our interpreter was getting tired. It was time to quit, but I had known that before we came here.

Finally, it all ended. It ended when he admitted to me that he had no idea at all what legendary Samarkand had to sell to the world market. He didn't know the products, he didn't know the minerals, he only knew that the Americans should come—or they would surely lose.

And finally I understood, too. I understood that these men were not a stock exchange at all ("Turkestan, that is our name!") but a commodity brokerage. They were exchanging commodities in much the same style as the Soviet Empire had bartered commodities—between republics, between enterprises, between entities. This was quite all right with me, because it may just be that for many years they will have to work out some original intermediate forms of the old barter relationships. But please don't tell me this is a "stock market" so the West will come and bail you out with all kinds of investments, because, my friend, those "investment opportunities" do not exist!

Once again I realized that there was still very little sense, if any at all, of what Western capitalism really means in terms of informed individual ownership of stock and, most important, in terms of the extraordinary creation of wealth through savings and deferred gratification.

There is a story that goes around Samarkand that occurs to me even now when I think about "Stock Market Turkestan." It goes like this: "For you Westerners, French is the language of love, English is the language of orders. For us, Tajik is the language of love, Uzbek is the language of business, and we don't need to tell you what the language of orders is!"

I certainly understood that Russian was the language of orders, but Uzbek, the "language of business"?

. . .

When Marco Polo lay on his deathbed in 1324 in his beloved Venice, he raised his head slightly at the end and whispered, "I have not told the half of what I saw."

It was the grandest way to die for the man who is unquestionably the Western world's greatest traveler and discoverer. He had exemplified in his very being the life of valiant adventure, of avid scholarship, and of joyful discovery that the best and most romantic of men gladly lay down their lives for. He died having immeasurably enriched the body of knowledge of a skeptical Europe, but, knowing the Europeans' skepticism, he held some secrets within his own heart. He passed from the world having traversed "impassable" deserts and "impossible" mountain ranges.

When Marco Polo set out to explore the world in the thirteenth century, medieval Europe's "map" of the world was a Christian conception; it was of one's religious "neighborhood"—the church, the castle, one's coreligionists. Feudal law was still the rule across Europe and, in the throes of religious passion, the Crusaders took Constantinople. Houses in London were still made of thatched straw and did not even have chimneys.

In comparison, contemporary Arab conceptions of life were much more complex and sophisticated. The great universities at Alexandria and Baghdad actually helped save the works of Aristotle and Plato when Greek civilization and learning entered its twilight years.

It was not surprising, then, that Marco Polo's writings and descriptions of what he saw traveling those many thousands of miles to China and Central Asia should have been made fun of in the Europe of his time, which overestimated its own culture and refused to know of others. So it was that the "civilized" Europeans shook their heads and thought of his remembrances as tales of fable and legend.

What could the wandering Venetian merchant have seen anywhere that was possibly greater than the magnificent cities of cultured Europe?

And those stories! Marco Polo insisted upon telling them such nonsensical tales as finding in a place called "China" a "sort of black stone dug out of the earth which could be ignited and was more inflammable and durable than wood." (They had no idea that in China people had burned coal a millennium earlier in the Han dynasty.) He said that he had found still another kind of stone, one that could be spun into fine hair and would never catch fire. (His stories about asbestos were even more outrageous to the "educated" Europeans than were his stories about coal!)

Marco Polo only nodded at such provincialism and, smiling, went on telling people only half of what he had seen "far beyond the sea."

It was the exploits of two other extraordinary men, Marco Polo's father and uncle, as well as that famous and beguiling city of Samarkand, that lured the great adventurer to set out for Central Asia and the Orient. Father Niccolò and Uncle Maffeo had set out in 1260, when Marco was still a boy, to travel to Constantinople for trade and commerce. Civil wars along the way made it impossible for them to return to Europe, and they found themselves 3,000 miles away from home, in Samarkand and Bukhara.

When they finally returned to Venice in 1269, exhausted and painfully thin but jubilant over their voyages of the body and of the soul, Marco was a seventeen-year-old young man enraptured with their exploits.

But in the end, it was Marco Polo's peregrinations that changed the world and changed worlds. Christopher Columbus was enormously influenced by Marco Polo's book, *The Travels of Marco Polo,* which no doubt helped create the desire in his mind to sail west to reach India and the mysterious East. The Portuguese navigator Vasco da Gama, equally inspired by the open roads and open seas of Marco Polo, was also probably inspired by his *Travels.* It caused him to set out in 1497 on a journey in search of the Khitan Kingdom, which was the medieval kingdom of a conquering Tatar people in the north of China. Instead, he found a new sea route to India around the Cape of Good Hope.

In Central Asia even today, people tell you that Vasco da Gama's discovery of the sea route to India and China doomed the Silk Road—and partially this is true. But equally important was its gradual deterioration for other reasons. Bandits had for many decades become such a scourge of the Silk Road that its use declined. Then, when the Americas were discovered, Europe got up, stretched, and faced itself in a different direction entirely for nearly five hundred years.

With sad irony, then, it can be said that the very discoveries of such men as Marco Polo doomed to inconsequence the very cities and regions they had with such wonder originally opened to the world.

But while the road lasted, beginning with Chang Ch'ien's expedition in 139 B.C., it had, over the centuries, developed into a coherent system of 8,000 miles of caravan tracks that linked the recesses of China and India to the West. Its routes were not so much roads as we understand them today—there were no asphalt surface and no bridges—but consisted rather of paths that the caravans themselves had created in the earth. The Silk Road constituted the "Main Street" of the known world.

Travelers depended for their survival upon strategically situated oases, each one no more than a few days' march from the next, and they depended upon water from the glacier-fed rivers from the vast mountain ranges to the north. Actually, too, there was more than one Silk Road: "making the road" meant following either the "Road North of the Heavenly Mountains" through modern-day Kazakhstan, or on the major "Royal Road" south along the terrifying Taklamakan desert, with its three-hundred-foot-tall sand dunes and with its understandably evil reputation for travelers. In many eras, the Chinese policed the route with garrisons and watchtowers.

The caravans of the Silk Road carried not only silk, but gold, metals, woolens, linen, ivory, coral, amber, precious stones, asbestos, furs, ceramics, iron, lacquerware, cinnamon, rhubarb, bronze objects, weapons, mirrors, and jade. But silk, luxurious silk, was what captured the imagination of Europe as the soul of the East. Indeed, as early as A.D. 14, the Emperor Tiberius banned men from wearing it, calling it an "instrument of decadence." And the historian Pliny wrote disapprovingly of it as making garments that "render women naked" and drained the economy as well!

Royal messengers were often sent on the Silk Road for their rulers. Riding fresh steeds, they sped from one to another of a hundred fortified stations, covering the road in only nine days. Herodotus wrote that "these couriers were stayed neither by snow nor rain nor heat nor darkness from accomplishing their appointed course."

If those words sound familiar, it is because they are: some years after Herodotus, they were adopted as the motto of the United States Postal Service!

The Silk Road also carried modern ideas and religious faith. As early as the first century A.D., the compassionate religion of Buddhism entered China over the road and through the oases of Central Asia. Later, Nestorian Christianity, which denied that Christ could simultaneously be human and divine and in 432 was outlawed by the Catholic Church at the Council of Ephesus, passed that way. So did Manicheism, born in Persia in the third century and based upon the "Two Principles of Light," the spirit and the flesh.

Indeed, the road was veritably pulsating with myths, legends, and faith. According to Chinese Taoist texts, one could find, hidden in the awe-inspiring heights of the K'un-lun mountains along the Silk Road, a paradise ruled by a goddess of immortality.

But it was when Islam swept over the entire Taklamakan region by the fifteenth century that the Silk Road was finally abandoned. China had shut herself off from contact to the West, and of course the devious Vasco da Gama had by then quietly carried through his evil watery work.

As the Baghdad-born specialist on the Middle East, Elie Kedourie, put it: "There was no science or industry to speak of in medieval Europe. It became a dynamic society after the discovery of the Americas, and it was then that the decline set in in the Muslim world. The trade routes became diverted from the Middle East to the Atlantic. Thus began a period of stagnation in the whole of the Middle East . . ."

But it was Ibn Khaldun, the fourteenth-century Arab philosopher of history, who best characterized the historic patterns of Central Asia, which were repeated over and over: urban peoples gradually developed, with their own Chinese, Persian, Arabic, Turkic, or Parthian cultures; mounted nomads, primitive next to the urbanized peoples but highly developed in the arts of war, periodically assaulted the city centers; finally the nomad-warriors adopted the civilized ways of the peoples they conquered; and soon they themselves had become decadent and were then open to attack by new waves of nomadic invaders.

Due to our lingering over lunch, it was very nearly dusk when we went to see what they call "the monuments" but which are really the great works of art of the reign of Tamerlane in the city of Samarkand.

We started in the Gur Emir (Ruler's Tomb), the turquoise-domed mausoleum of Tamerlane himself, where he is buried under the world's largest piece of dark green jade, from Chinese Turkestan. From there we walked to the Registan, the principal square and the one that even the finicky Lord Curzon would write in 1888 was the "noblest public square in the world." These treasures of mosaic and tile, with their intricate arabesques and scrolls, were no direct copy of Persian art, although they were inspired by Persian culture. No, they were built according to Tamerlane's fancy, they were Tatar in conception, and, as one writer said, "even the ruins have an imperishable beauty." No kinder to buildings he disliked than he was to peoples he did not fancy, Tamerlane at least twice ordered a completed work torn down and erected again. He loved color, his biographer Harold Lamb wrote; he had "the poetic sense of the nomad, and the desert dweller's pleasure in foliage and running water." His cities were gardens, gardens built on towers of skulls of the people he conquered.

The Registan was a place for prayer and talk, a concourse for politics and news, a rendezvous for the great lords, and an exchange for the merchants. It was where Tamerlane ventured first when the "Lord of Samarkand" returned home, having conquered the Mongols, India, Khorezm, Persia, Media, Tabriz, the City of the Sultan, the Land of Silk, the Land of the Gates, Armenia the Less, Erzerum, the Land of the Kurds, Damascus, Aleppo, Babylon, Baghdad . . .

Today's visitors are tourists who sit in the square on many a balmy summer evening watching the sound-and-light show that begins with "I am the Registan, the heart of Samarkand . . ." It was indicative of the style of Russian imperialism that, even in the relatively liberalized Gorbachev years, these popular shows were given in Russian, German, French, and English, but never in Uzbek, which only happened to be the language of 20 million people.

Alexander the Great had been the son of a king and had his Macedonian people behind him. Genghis Khan was the heir of a chieftain and had his Mongol horsemen supporting him. But Tamerlane had been a boy of lesser importance, only a child herding cattle and caring for the land. In the end, as Harold Lamb summed up, he overcame the armies of more than half the world, tore down cities and rebuilt them in his way, saw the caravan trade of two continents pass over his roads, fathered the wealth of empires, and constructed sumptuous palaces in Oriental gardens for his own pleasure.

He died on the march toward the last power strong enough to oppose him: China. He was addressed then with the reverence due a god, but, strangely enough, his favored title was not too different from what many called Marco Polo—Amir Ma-vara'na'nahr (Lord of Beyond the River).

We walked silently through the ruins for nearly two hours. No one spoke. Certainly I did not. I was awed by their barbaric splendor and by the sheer beauty of their design and color. I thought at first that all they represented was power and conquest, that all Tamerlane and Samarkand celebrated was suzerainty over their neighbors and oppression of the rebellions. I thought about how empty of ideas the monuments were—and they were and are. I thought about how different they and that age were from our world; about how Tamerlane and his successors "created" wealth by seizing it, while Americans, acting originally out of the Protestant ethic, created wealth by the magic of actually enlarging it. I was right, but I was somewhat wrong, too. If they seemed strange thoughts to be having there and then, they certainly were!

Before we were forced to leave by the onset of darkness and the necessity of having to travel four hours in the blackness back to Tashkent on those horrible roads, we climbed up to see the Shah-i-Zinda complex of mausoleums. This necropolis, where so many of Tamerlane's family and following were buried in the fourteenth and fifteenth centuries, is exquisite. We walked down long outside pathways, over ancient cobbled little streets, with mausoleums on all sides, each breathtakingly decorated with mosaic, brick, and tile. Finally we climbed into a tiny dusty room. Here, Tahir whispered to me, was the tomb of the Muslim holy man, Qasim ibn Abbas, descendant of the Prophet Muhammad and the man who had brought Islam to this part of Central Asia.

Without warning, suddenly one of the two Samarkand "stockbrokers" who were still with us fell to his knees. His head dropped down on his chest. I was not afraid, because something about it made me realize that this was an action that must be respectfully observed. Then from his mouth flowed a torrent of strange chattering and chanting that, had I not somehow been aware of the holiness of this moment, would have deeply frightened me.

Instead, I closed my eyes and listened. I actually began to tremble. The sounds were alternately like an agitated bird chattering and like a monk chanting. It was one of the most extraordinary things I had ever heard. It went on for about five minutes before our colleague stood up, dusted himself off, and climbed out through the same little window through which we had climbed in.

No one had to tell me that he was talking to the holy man.

Jamal Kamal, my friend at the Writers' Union in Tashkent who had translated Shakespeare into Uzbek, once wrote a popular poem that seemed to me to capture the awe of that moment:

> *My cradle was the territory of Great Asia,*
> *The cradle that rocked Ulughbek and Avicenna,*
> *The light in whose eyes has spanned a thousand years,*
> *This is the world that led the caravan of history,*
> *This Samarkand, this Bukhara—these two universes.*
> *This is the cradle of Communism in the bosom of the East!*

Before Communism came to Central Asia, came the "Great Game," which was the impassioned game of the English, Germans, and Russians to influence, civilize, and take the khanates, the emirs, and the tribes of Central Asia. Once again, this Inner Asia was being discussed in terms of what outsiders were doing there; the "Great Game" was always a ball pushed around by other peoples. The Central Asians were "discovered" anew—by others; ruled anew—by others; fought over anew—by others.

By the middle of the nineteenth century, Central Asia was rarely off the front pages of the European newspapers. It was romantic, it was fascinating, it bespoke the magnificent luxuriousness of the East, and it was immortalized by Kipling's "Kim," in which the boy-hero says, "Now I shall go far and far into the North, playing the Great Game." But now, instead of the British and the Germans winning, the Russian armies under the czars were taking one by one the ancient caravan towns and khanates of the former Silk Road. In 1865, the walled city of Tashkent fell to the czar. Three years later, Samarkand and Bukhara; and five years still later, Khiva.

For four hundred years, the Russian Empire had expanded at the rate of nearly 56 square miles a day, or 20,000 square miles a year. By the late nineteenth century, czarist Russia was indeed fulfilling its imperial destiny. It ruled its vast continent from the borders of Europe to the Pacific.

It was no longer merely the dream of Russia's expansionist finance minister, Count Sergey Yulyevich Witte, to open up Russia to the whole of the Far East, with its vast resources and markets; the imperial armies had now made that a reality. Moreover, he was building the greatest railway the world had ever seen. The Trans-

Siberian Railroad would run for 4,500 miles across Russia: from Moscow in the west to Vladivostok and Port Arthur in the east.

T. E. Lawrence once wrote: "All men dream, but not equally. Those who dream by night in the dusty recesses of their mind, wake in the day to find that it was vanity. But the dreamers of the day are dangerous men for they may act their dreams with open eyes. This I did." The Russians were the quintessential dreamers of their day; they had dreamed of empire with their eyes open, and they would pay the price for such wakeful dreams.

Imperial Japan watched with anger and with apprehension as the Russian armies approached the Pacific coasts, infiltrated Korea, finished their glorious railroad. Czar Nicholas II had a powerful Pacific fleet and a million-strong regular army supported by double that number of reservists. They unflatteringly called the Japanese "yellow apes," and after their victories across Central Asia over similar Oriental peoples, they were utterly confident of victory—and itching for a "good little war."

For their part, the Japanese had 270,000 regulars and 530,000 reservists. But they attacked brilliantly, without warning, at the Russian naval base at Port Arthur. The Russo-Japanese war had begun, and its denouement would end Russian dreams of expansion, lead to the end of the reign of Nicholas II and indeed to the end of the monarchy, and finally to Soviet Communism itself.

Far from being over, the "Great Game" was destined to begin again, only now in a new ideological costume and on different but equally dangerous playing fields. The voice of the new era could be heard as Lenin vowed to "set the East ablaze" with the purifying gospel of Marxism. Once again, Central Asia was one of the battle-grounds; once again, Central Asia was the object of others and still far from the subject of its own desperately weakened will.

"The East," Lenin had proclaimed, "will help us to conquer the West."

It was with those words and in their spirit that the Bolsheviks from 1917 onward began their own version of the czarist conquest of Central Asia. From city to city, from town to town, and from khanate to khanate, the Bolsheviks or Reds fought other Russians across the face of the heartland of empires.

In Tashkent, four days of bloody fighting left hundreds dead and a strange brand of new ruler: the Bolsheviks in Tashkent were poorly educated and with no experience of government or of administration. Before the Revolution, Peter Hopkirk points out in *Setting the East Ablaze,* many had been drivers or oilers on the railway. In addition, they were virtually all European Russians and they looked down upon the local population; when the mud-walled caravan town of Kokand, one hundred miles to the southeast of Tashkent, fell, the number of Muslims slain was put at anywhere between 5,000 and 14,000. The towns and villages of the Silk Road were indeed ablaze.

Meanwhile, under the command of Mikhail Frunze, the Kyrgyz-born, Russian-nationality general whose name was given to the Kyrgyz capital, the oasis towns of Turkestan were also tumbling to the power of the Red Army. When the ancient khanate of Khiva was declared a "People's Republic," Hopkirk's story is that the emir, who was not too intellectually swift, had fled to Afghanistan "dropping favorite dancing boy after favorite dancing boy in his flight in the hope of thus retarding the advance of the pursuing Red Army."

These men were then followed by the courageous anti-Bolshevik Muslim freedom fighters of the famous but doomed Basmachi movement. Across Central Asia between 1916 and 1928, the Basmachis swore on the Koran to rid their homeland of the miserable pagan infidels, the Russian Bolsheviks. But in the late 1920s, they were put down by Moscow, only to be spiritually revived by the war in Afghanistan in the 1980s, when many of the Afghan mujahideen fighting the Soviet invaders identified themselves with the Basmachi movement.

By the time we left Samarkand it was dark, and we drove rather crazily through the blackness.

But I felt a certain new, agreeable peace. Finally I understood; I had seen, felt, and begun to understand the "center."

Samarkand is not simply a "fascinating historic population center." Samarkand was once a world capital, and even today people there have never forgotten that; it lives in their spirits, in the way they carry themselves, in their inner confidence. Indeed, Tamerlane, that dreamer of his day, planned to make it the capital of the world. In addition, in nearby Mesopotamia, the early peoples believed that they were the site of the Garden of Eden; in China, the ancient "Yellow Emperor" was believed to be the earth's original man; and in Siberia, the shamans say that just north of Lake Baikal one still finds the oldest place on earth!

"You see," Professor Edward Allworth, Columbia University's preeminent Central Asian specialist, explains, "the reason we call it 'Central Asia' is because it's between those great powers—China, India, Russia, and the Middle East. But there's a lot more to it than geography. The people have a sense that they are *central*: that is, they see themselves as the center of the civilized world, and there's some reason for that.

"Those people had a marvelous civilization which believed in justice, which created wonderful poetry, and which affected all of their relations with the rest of the world. They had the feeling that not only did civilization start there but that it was better there than anywhere else. They have that great security about how civilized and learned they all were back then. Haven't you noticed that the Uzbeks are very self-confident in their behavior? They don't feel that anybody is better than they are. There is also the sense that they are surrounded by great powers who look at them as the intersection of the world . . .

"Why is the area so beguiling to the West? Because the Brits who came here in the 1920s were enamored of the East; they described it in the most romantic terms, in fantasies about the luscious opulence of the East and of the golden peaches of Samarkand . . ."

I have thought about this a great deal, if only because it is such a serious inversion of what perhaps all of us think, especially in America and in the West in general, about remote and forgotten places like Central Asia.

We believe that *we* are central; *we* are civilization; *we* are learning and progress and beauty and virtue. I needed to overcome the shock I felt when I discovered that these impoverished and long-oppressed peoples "out there" still thought of themselves as the center; and it brought a certain strange joy. And by focusing with me on their history and upon their "centrality," they were saying to us: "We exist again—and we existed before, long before you."

My last day in Tashkent, a Thursday, had been a long one. Tahir Umarov invited the three of us to his home for a gala dinner, and it turned out to be a charming afternoon. His house was small and square, stuccoed on the outside. Gray, of course! But it had a small patio inside, and a low building at the back where his wife cooked.

His wife, a slim, handsome, gentle woman, greeted us—and then served us. This was still typical of Central Asia, with its male domination. She was a health worker, a college graduate, yet when it came to her husband's friends, she was as subdued and nearly as subservient as would be the wife (woman) of an Uzbek tribesman. She even wore a white dress as she served us plate after plate of Uzbek sliced meats, salads, wine . . .

I knew that the life and lot of women in Uzbekistan was a hard one. Indeed, many women become so desperate that they commit suicide—by self-immolation, which has become a national scandal.

We joked a lot, and I persisted in showing Tahir's brother-in-law, who was an intelligent chap, the pictures of my sweet new cat, Nikko, the little gray-and-white Japanese Bobtail from the Shinto shrines of Japan. We were able to speak quite a bit of Russian together, so we could speak directly.

He still couldn't understand why I wasn't married, and finally he said, comparing the pet to a man, "But the cat doesn't talk."

"All the better," I said in Russian—and everybody dissolved into laughter.

But it was sad; I had grown to like this funny little group, as together we traversed these historic worlds, dreams, and nightmares. We drank a good deal of cognac before I decided it was time to face the next step of my voyage.

My Aeroflot flight to Baku, if, of course, it arrived in Tashkent on schedule, was to leave at four A.M. That meant leaving the hotel at 2:30 A.M. In any country and in any situation, that is, of course, absolutely the worst time a plane can leave. It means you cannot go to sleep early and get up early, because the time is too short. It means, too, that you will not sleep at all at the other end. It is one perfect hell of a time to have to leave.

So, after leaving the others at about six o'clock with the genuine intention of sleeping a few hours, I drank some of the cheap dollar-a-bottle Soviet champagne (left over from the great U.S.S.R., which could disperse its champagne everywhere across its eleven time zones). I tried to rest in my little room, rest but not go to sleep, which is tricky! I watched television, and there was a beautiful tale of two lovers in a beautiful garden and forest; I thought for a moment that it must be something inspired by those romantic legends of Tamerlane in his gardens, or from the early "glory days" of Communist passion . . .

Finally, I just waited, and they picked me up in the pitch-black night at 2:30 A.M. and we zoomed to the airport, through ominously empty streets, only to find that the plane was late—but of course! It was then, after bidding them farewell so they could get some sleep, that I saw *the scene*.

The middle-aged woman, dressed in gray work clothes, unsmiling, marched in through the front door of the grim and grimy little terminal. Perhaps she was an old "Heroine of Socialist Labor," one of those good Stakhanovites whose good labor was to inspire other good socialist workers in the good old socialist days. Perhaps she was just determined, or committed, or even enthralled with her work.

At any rate, it swiftly became clear that she was about to take on the floor of the terminal—and that her personal war would make Tamerlane's battles look like child's play. The floor looked like a kind of granite—gray, what else?—and it was filthy. Filthy? So filthy, I hated to have my snow boots touch it, and that, friends, is dirty!

She began her life's work, and I was fascinated, watching her.

The gray bucket she carried was filled with gray water. Obviously, it had been used somewhere before. She dipped the dirty gray mop (the old kind that our grandmothers had, with lots of little curly cotton creatures on it) into the water and kerplunked it on the floor. *Schllwitsch!*

I could not take my eyes from this typical scene of Mother Russia and her now grown-up children. Certainly there was no "washing" in, say, the rigid northern European sense of the word. No, she just took that mop and went around, and around, and around. In ever-widening circles, like the Russian Empire expanding so many times in the nineteenth century! Like a whirling dervish in very slow motion, around and around she went!

At one point, she insisted, with that old Soviet peremptoriness, on slopping the dirty water under my feet.

It went on for quite a while, probably a full hour in that single room alone, with the handful of people there with me dutifully raising their feet and lowering them so that she and her swirling dirty water could make a shiny little paradise of the Tashkent airport.

Suddenly it ended, and she gamely moved on, neither smiling nor frowning, with her mop and her rags, to "clean up" still another room.

It was with hypnotic fascination (that plus having nothing else to do) that I duly observed that the floor was beginning to dry, and that it was drying with even more dirt on it than it had before.

There was, however, one ameliorating factor to the entire scene: the dirt was now swirled in graceful circles. Later, I saw her marching resolutely out the front door with a babushka tied tightly around her gray head; she had done her work and was going home to a well-deserved sleep.

The plane droned in out of nowhere in Central Asia at seven o'clock. The Aeroflot "hostess"—yes, there were still hostesses—was grumpy and nasty as always. But this one did at least take me, the foreigner, out first. She guided me as though my life depended upon it through a side door, so I would not be trampled by the driving hordes of men waiting for the plane.

In fact, she got me up into the plane just as the mob sprang as one out of the airport and, with a kind of muffled roar, ran like veritable lemmings to the plane. I was seated in my chair, if you can call it that, when they overtook the plane like a horde of modern Mongols without their trusty ponies.

We left at about eight o'clock. The flight was utterly terrifying. It was a large plane, in contrast to the small one that had carried me so precariously from Bishkek.

But this time it was the seats that hypnotized me. Every single seat, I'd say about eighty, had something loose. It was either an arm, or a seat, or, sometimes, the entire chair. So when we started moving and even flying (a little task that I was not at all sure this creature could accomplish), everything and everyone began to bump, circle about, churn, move, and heave, so that the inside of the entire plane seemed like one grotesque mechanical toy whose system and machinery had gone mad-hatter crazy!

I sat upright, sure that we were going to crash, and wondering, given everything, whether that was really the worst thing that could happen.

Besides, I was getting nervous about something else. It was the Turkish Airliner. I was now closing in on it, for Baku was the next and last stop.

Would it come? Or would I have to stay out here forever, to dig my grave in Bukhara or Samarkand, like so many who had played that earlier "Great Game" and had more protections than I?

These suddenly seemed to me to be rather apt questions.

Chapter 6

Baku
City of Roses and Death,
Bitten by the Wind

Self-determination was made very fashionable by the Fourteen Points
and enshrined by the League of Nations and in the charter
of the United Nations. But it is a visionary idea and there is no way
that it can be made into a pillar of international order.
It is a pillar of international disorder . . .

Elie Kedourie, Middle East scholar

I had been fooled by Tashkent and Samarkand, by the calm faces and stolid manner of its Oriental tribesmen. I had also been fooled by its pleasurably clement weather.

Moscow had been one vast stage of ice, with few skaters but with a curtain of cold that never opened. Kazan had seemed all whipped-cream snow on its lovely wooden buildings that seemed to spring right out of the Old Russia of Dostoevsky and Turgenev. Alma-Ata had enchanted the visitor and adventurer who traveled to the ends of the earth and was so pleased to find that city's sheer prettiness. My Bishkek, I am saddened to say, was unrelieved gray, white-gray, occasionally brown-gray—still, I loved her.

Only when I was in Tashkent did I feel for the first time, resting comfortingly on my arm, the pleasingly gentle hand of this spring's kinder and unique promise.

So Azerbaijan, in the figure of its great city of Baku, marked for me a tremendous—indeed, a stunning—surprise. My immediate impression was that I must have landed among the most violent people in the world. Almost without exception, their coal-black eyes blazed like their own vast lakes of oil, about to ignite. Their sour, dour expressions greeted you with a mien of perpetual accusation, as though you were their oldest enemy from the wild mountains of the Caucasus incarnate. Their rickety cars and mad driving, pitting them against the pitted roads, reminded me of the bloodlust of soldiers finally attacking to the death some antagonist despised for hundreds of years. And, indeed, they were also doing exactly that in nearby Nagorno-Karabakh.

All of these thoughts, which assaulted me within barely ten minutes of arriving at the dirty, chaotic, ramshackle Baku airport (as you can see, the place admittedly brings out in me too many adjectives, yet I can assure you that they are all legitimate), served to convince me quickly that, despite the earlier and so-welcome Uzbek portents of spring, I must now have entered some border hell at this entrepôt between Russia and Central Asia. Or, as *The New York Times* characterized Azerbaijan's first two years of "freedom" from the Soviet Union, they were two years of "war, elections, coups, pogroms, corruption, Islamic revival, resurgent Communists, international intrigue, economic chaos and the promise of wealth."

What I had entered was the Transcaucasus, in earlier times alternately called Transcaucasia, Zakavkaz, or even Farther Caucasia. Actually, it is the southern part of the historic Caucasus, that wildly gorgeous and compelling mountainous area between the Caspian and Black seas, where Georgians, Armenians, Ossetians North and South, too many groups of mountaineers to mention, and the Russians of the southern part of Russia around Stavropol have with an amazingly rare persistence eschewed living together with even a modicum of civility. These talented peoples have murderously battled and rampaged against one another for century upon century. The Bolsheviks, being still more ruthless than these "neighboring" peoples, held them in check with sheer terror from 1917—until now.

Historically, the original culture of this fascinating but bloody area is thought to have come from the ancient Greeks, who made the mysterious Caucasus the scene of the mythical sufferings of Prometheus and of the Argonauts who sought the Golden Fleece in the wondrous land of Colchis on the shores of the Black Sea. Some historians say that because of its location in the very middle of the great migrations from all sides, the Caucasus areas were so subject to Asian influences that one might even consider the Caucasus part of southwestern Asia.

Nothing in Central Asia—or the Caucasus—was simple.

But I was not thinking of the area's beguiling history at this point: I was thinking about the cold.

In Baku, I found none of the mellifluous portents of spring of gentle Tashkent, but instead found only the most bitterly cold weather I had encountered anywhere on my voyage. Indeed, Baku's howling winter winds reminded me of my hometown of Chicago, where, in January and February (and sometimes even in March, April, and May), the shrill gales from the Canadian Arctic roar down the length of Lake Michigan, shrieking with evil glee, to smite Chicago as though wielding some Biblical punishment against the city of Cain. On Chicago's Michigan Avenue, the police put up ropes for struggling citizens to hold on to, lest the population of Chicago be blown away.

Baku was similarly smitten by those equally unforgiving banshee winds from the Russian steppes, their ferocious power gleaned from travel over the similar length of the Caspian Sea. But in Baku, there were no ropes to hold you up, although perhaps some skewed justice was to be found in the fact that there were many drivers ready to knock you down.

And those, one must reasonably suppose, are some of the reasons why Baku's name means "City Bitten by the Wind."

For the first time on my trip, no one from Radio Liberty was waiting for me at the airport—something had, not surprisingly, finally gone wrong with messages between Munich and Baku—and in the midst of the total chaos and tumult there, I suddenly felt quite afraid for the first time since hesitantly abandoning my little phobia over the Train to Kazan. The mood was what one might find in a city under siege, with everyone shouting, screaming, and pushing. Finally, one burly taxi driver grabbed my bags and carted me off in one of the oldest and most disgraceful taxicabs I had ever yet seen. Innumerable people had regaled me with such terrible stories of crime (everywhere) that, as we careened (not drove) at ninety miles an hour past the gigantic oil wells along the Caspian and into the city, I closed my eyes (tightly) and began to whisper (hoarsely) the Lord's Prayer over and over, like some chattering (and helpless) cricket.

I realized, of course, that the terrifying violence of the spirit of cosmopolitan Baku and of the cultured Azeris was similar to the violence I had felt on other trips, always just beneath the surface, in nearby Iran, in Iraq, and on the ever-dangerous borders of Afghanistan. And, indeed, the Azeris were closely related to the Iranians and had been historically divided between their own state and Iran. The Azeris were the only people in Central Asia who were not Sunni but Shi'a Muslims, like the Iranians, but they were far less fanatical in their religious beliefs. There remained fully 20 million Azeris inside Iran in the northwest sections, and they were always restless under the rule of the radical Islamic theocracy of the Ayatollah Khomeini's Teheran. As to Central Asia, because they are culturally Persian and Shi'a but ethnically and linguistically Turkic, the Azeris have always been a peripheral people to the true spiritual centers of the area, like Samarkand, but they were and are always considered part of that universe of peoples that we still call Central Asia.

With instructions given in my bad but amazingly usable Russian, we did arrive "safely," if you can use that word for any drive in Baku, at the big, shabby, gray marble Hotel Azerbaijan. As dark-spirited crowds of locals milled about the front desk, many of them screaming for whatever they could think of at the moment, one English-speaking clerk snatched me from the crowd, took hold of me, and immediately gave me a dollar room—for forty dollars a night, to be exact.

I was tremendously relieved to be there, and now I had to figure out how to contact the Radio Liberty correspondents, not to mention where to check on the Turkish Airliner!

Truthfully, I was quite happy. After four weeks of this journey in Central Asia, I felt at times as though Marco Polo must have had it easier; the trips of the great Venetian, after all, were a movable feast (was it not perhaps better, more edifying to the soul, more healthy to the body, to go by foot, to travel outside, in the fresh air, than in the shuddering hold of Uzbekistan Airways?). No, I decided firmly, Marco Polo would never have gone Aeroflot, and neither would the Mongol khans have invaded if they'd had to depend on it instead of their trusty ponies.

I had now sunk to living with the relative joy of making relative judgments: this room in Baku was clearly a better room than Bishkek's, but less good than Tashkent's . . . the food was richer than Alma-Ata's but not so good as Moscow's . . .

Finally, I looked around my little room and asked myself how best to describe such stubborn mediocrity. Two cotlike beds, a long coffee table, a cabinet, heavy drapes. . . . One searches endlessly for some different—for some defining—characteristic to note. But there was none, really none at all. Every hotel was basically the same: the same design, the same bad furniture, the same dirty bathrooms.

But the Hotel Azerbaijan did have two relatively handsome, big dining rooms, replete with sticky, mediocre caviar (but, still, caviar!) that I soon discovered, with delicious deception, could be bought from the waiters for five dollars a can. He would simply nod, almost imperceptibly, when I asked him *"Yest ikra?"* And soon I would have a little package wrapped in a brown bag—and he would have twenty-five U.S. dollars.

One afternoon while I was in Baku, the waiter suddenly whispered to me after lunch, glancing around us nervously all the while, "We have some steaks today."

When I protested that I had, after all, just eaten an entire rich lunch, he looked at me as though I were quite mad. Though lacking a single pang of hunger, I nevertheless obediently ordered—and ate—the steak. That was the way things were in this "spontaneous" society.

But my room did have a splendid view of the back of the city, which was part Oriental palace, with some beautifully designed buildings paid for by the merchants of the last century, and part booming, dirty-white oil city, with endless cement Soviet tenaments. To my amazement, from my window, again I faced still another of those enormous omnipresent clocks that seemed to keep perfect tick-tock time over all of Central Asia. It was big and round, with huge black numbers. As in the hotel in Bishkek, it was one of the few things that worked, although its job was relatively irrelevant to anything real.

I sighed. Four more days, and the Turkish Airliner would come and spirit me from this suffering and long-traumatized world back to my world of prosperity and privilege—Haji Baba Geyer on her Magic Carpet.

Then the doubts began to assail me from all sides.

What if the Turkish Airliner did not come?

What if the rumor of this unlikely plane were only a huge falsehood, some grim joke cooked up by jealous post-Communists to be played on weary wayfarers from the Center of the World who were struggling to find their way home again? Indeed, what if there *were* no Turkish Airliner? Or what if it existed and yet would for any number of reasons not come this one particular Monday?

And what would happen if the Turkish Airliner did not come at all? Well, then I would have to plot to find a way to get back to Moscow. Even supposing there was a plane from Baku to Moscow, and even supposing I could get on it, I would then need to brook hated Domodedovo Airport, to make my way back to the Slavyanskaya Hotel, to buy another ticket to Europe (did I even have enough cash left?), and perhaps eventually, sometime in some unknowable future, finally leave and enter the world again.

I frankly was not sure I could survive all that.

Almost as soon as I had checked into the Azerbaijan, I made my little nest, like some animal needing solace.

Then, having accomplished that once again, how swiftly I made my way down the four blocks to the Azeri national travel office.

There is little question that my face clearly showed my skepticism, and even my inner fear, as I proffered my ticket to the amazingly pleasant and amazingly efficient agent. The young woman looked up at me and handed the ticket back. "Monday," she said, with a strange assurance. "It always comes Monday at five o'clock and it leaves at seven-thirty that same evening."

"But, *next* Monday?"

"It's expected," she said crisply.

The wind was howling down upon us, ripping and bounding off the Caspian Sea like some Transcaucasian banshee and literally lifting the breath out of me, as I walked back to the hotel. I knew that her confidence was simply another Central Asian con game.

I harrumphed.

What did she know?

Without knowing it, I was approaching still another "center."

As impossible as it might seem, this violent, traumatized, and beautiful Azerbaijan before me had once been the center of one of the most daring and hopeful experiments in all of Central Asia and in all of the Caucasus. In 1918, it had become the first democratic republic in this part of the world. On May 28 of that year, the Azerbaijani Democratic Republic proclaimed independence, as one Azeri historian recently put it in appropriately glorious words, demonstrating "to world public opinion that the Azerbaijani nation has the right to live freely within its own frontiers as do the other free nations of the world!" The people of the "new Azerbaijan" were even then filled with buoyant hope, forgetting, as men and women in moments of overwhelming passion are wont to do, what their address is.

Much like Tatarstan centuries ago when it had a kind of independence and took such noble pride in having elegant diplomatic relations with the nations of the world, the infant Azeri republic boasted it had diplomatic relations with twenty-seven states and sent students abroad to study (even, as with the proud Tatars, to Paris). The democrats opened Baku University and declared the Azerbaijani language the official language of the state. They actually began to create, for the first time, a parliamentary system. As with so much of Central Asia today, its leaders then had started changing the alphabet from Arabic to Roman, hoping to allow democratic Azerbaijan to join the Western world.

It was the son of a mullah, Mehmet Emin Rasulzade, born in 1884 in Baku, who was to become the leader of this grand experiment, having started as one of the founders of the first Muslim social democratic organization. In still more striking ways, the hopes of these progressive Muslims in the republic were notably similar to those of the progressive Muslim "Jadidists" in Tatarstan at the same time: both were mildly socialist but basically nationalist, and both desired above all the unity of all Muslim peoples, their liberation from imperialism, and their economic and social development.

But Rasulzade made one great mistake. When, in the early years of the century, a young Joseph Stalin, who was then crossing and recrossing the Caucasus and Transcaucasus as an agitator, incited oil workers to strike in Baku, Rasulzade intervened to save Stalin's life. He would all his life regret that he had done that.

Less than two years after the new Azerbaijani Democratic Republic was formed, at Stalin's orders, the Red Army moved into the Transcaucasus. The budding new nation was brutally destroyed, and its hopes were swept away in the wake of the Soviet terror. Stalin did evince one surprising piece of rare kindliness: he later freed the imprisoned Rasulzade from prison and allowed him to go into exile. The Azeri patriot died in Turkey in 1955.

Even during the darkest days of Soviet rule, the Azeri Communists ran one of the more tolerant and certainly one of the most cosmopolitan republics of the Soviet Union. Baku was the center for Soviet jazz, for instance, which was forbidden elsewhere. Baku's cultured Jewish community felt at home in the worldly air of that city (indeed, 100,000 Jews still live today in Azerbaijan) and liked to tell how, in 1920, two Jewish Bolsheviks, Grigori Zinoviev, head of the Comintern, and the Hungarian Communist leader Béla Kun rallied the Muslim masses of the East to a crusade against the imperialist powers, a week-long rally in Baku with some twenty nationalities from the Middle East and Central Asia. It was typical of the spirit of Azerbaijan that Zinoviev, in what was described as a "spellbinding opening oration," called upon Muslims everywhere to join the jihad or holy war. And the tall, thin, tough mountaineers from Dagestan just to the northwest of Baku made headlines by living to 105 . . . 120 . . . even 140 years old, thus giving the world the idea of a "Fountain of Youth" Azerbaijan that must have some health and longevity secrets to give to the world. (I had gone to Dagestan to meet them in 1971, and they were very tall—and very old!)

Unlike so many of the deadeningly similar, gray, utilitarian cities of the old Soviet Union, Baku had culture and so it had character. Statues of famous Azerbaijani writers—and there are many—still decorate the baroque facades of Baku's Nizami Literary Museum. The rose gardens along the Caspian are enchanting in the summer, and sometimes an avid Azeri sniffer will almost tumble physically right into the flowers . . .

But above all, the sign and symbol of Azerbaijan is fire. Azerbaijan is a land where fire literally bursts out of the land anywhere and everywhere there is the slightest crack in the earth. It is this fire, I became convinced, and not only Azerbaijan's difficult position between Central Asia and the Caucasus, that gives the republic its sinister and angry public face and caused Azerbaijan in earlier centuries to be known as the "Region of Eternal Fire." Twenty miles south of Baku, for instance, there is an astonishing old eighteenth-century building with a tongue-tying name—Atechghiakh—which is a rough stone temple where the Zoroastrians literally worshiped fire. You can still visit the temple, which stands both fearsomely and paganly primitive in its sheer simplicity and power.

Perhaps what is most remarkable, at the turn of the century, Azerbaijan was the world's leading petroleum producer and is actually the birthplace of the oil refining industry. In those years, it

produced more oil than the United States—indeed, it produced
fully 50 percent of the world's oil production!

But the discovery of oil in Azerbaijan was nothing new. As early
as the thirteenth century, Marco Polo, wandering by one day as he
was wont to do, had observed oil seepages in the Caucasus around
Baku. He reported this, too, to a disbelieving Europe and wrote
about it in his *Travels*. As far as we know or can know, he was the
first Westerner to see and report on gas escaping from underground oil deposits and burning spontaneously in what was to
become this entrepôt between Europe and its needs and Central
Asia and its potential untapped wealth.

But behind everything that is happening today with oil and Azerbaijan lies the crucially important story of the 1870s. Early in the
nineteenth century, Baku was home to a tiny government-monop-
oly Russian oil industry in which pits were dug by hand to extricate
the oil. But in the 1870s, Czar Alexander II opened the industry to
foreigners, and the Nobel brothers, Robert and Ludwig, migrated
like eager Midases to unknown Baku. With Azerbaijani oil, they
broke the extraordinary monopoly of John D. Rockefeller's Standard Oil, which was then responsible for fully 90 percent of all the
tins of kerosene in international commerce. (The oil workers called
themselves "Nobelites.")

When the first Russian Revolution exploded in 1905, Baku
erupted in revolutionary and ethnic violence. Author Daniel Yergin tells the story:

> The Tatar workers in the oil fields declared war on the Ar-
> menian managers and entrepreneurs (in an eerie foreshadow-
> ing of today's violence between Azerbaijanis and Armenians).
> The Tatars set fire to the fields—the first but not the last time
> that major oil fields were put to the torch.

Yergin quotes an eyewitness describing the horrors of what happened:

> "The flames from the burning derricks and oil wells leaped up
> into the awful pall of smoke which hung over the inferno. I
> realized for the first time in my life all that can possibly be
> meant by the words 'Hell let loose.' Men crawled or dashed
> out of the flames only to be shot down by the Tatars. . . . It
> was made worse . . . by the ping of rifle and revolver bullets,

the terrific thunder of exploding oil tanks, the fierce yells of the murderers, and the dying screams of their victims."

The Nobel brothers finally had to flee the country disguised as peasants. The Bolsheviks took over their "Russian" oil in 1917, and Azerbaijan's history of outside intervention and investment was over—until now. Azerbaijan, one discovers with a certain intake of breath about her potential, has 700 million tons of reserves under the Caspian Sea, but no technology to extract it.

One day, sitting in the outer office of the Azeri president, one of his young information officers was trying to help me grasp the unusual and often contradictory spirit of Azerbaijan.

On the one hand, the Azeris could be extraordinarily violent; on the other, they were so remarkably tolerant, cosmopolitan, and open to other ideas. On the one hand, observers outside were pointing at Azerbaijan (and at much of Central Asia) and saying, "Watch—watch out . . . Islamic radical fundamentalism will get you!" And then they would say that Azerbaijan would be the likeliest to "go" fundamentalist. Although there were several hundred mullahs from Iran already in Azerbaijan, and although there was considerable Islamic fervor in the slums around the city, I simply did not find this "Islamic bomb."

"Look," the young man was saying, "ninety percent of the people here eat pork, ninety percent drink spirits, and ninety percent do not know Arabic or the prayers. Five percent attend the mosque. We have here a Turkish pattern, where government and religion stay separate from each other. We say that the three religions—Christianity, Islam, and Judaism—are three brothers. Before Islam we had the Christian Albanian church here. Before the Arabs invaded, most were Christians and then came Islam. When the Arabs invaded Azerbaijan at the end of the seventh century and the beginning of the eighth, they were able to invade only the low parts. They couldn't risk going up into the mountains, so Georgia and Armenia remained Christian. In fact, a lot of the people holed up in the mountains and remained Christians because the conquerors could not get to them. We even had a Khazar republic on the northwest coast of the Caspian; the Khazars became Judaized and were for a time a real Jewish state!

"The Azeris were formed as a nation on the basis of different religions—that prevents us from being fanatics. That is why we don't have fundamentalism here, because the psychology of the people is very free. There is an excellent attitude toward Jews; even when they leave, maybe to go to Israel, they don't break their ties with Azerbaijan at all. It's just not inherent in the Azerbaijani to live in animosity."

That this historic tolerance has existed throughout much of Azerbaijan's mosaicked history is true. That is still another reason why the sheer horror of what is happening there now is so staggering.

War—war talk—war fear—war fever—war exhaustion: war was everywhere. In the president's outer office, I sat for hours with his young and exhausted top advisers who talked about little other than "Nagorno-Karabakh." It was "a war that could last a hundred years," one of them declared. It was, the great Azeri writer Chengiz Houseinov told me on another day, this time in Washington, a conflict that was "not win/loss; it's loss/loss/loss. It is not postive/negative; it is negative/negative/negative."

It was there that I finally came up against *the* nightmare of all of Central Asia, the prototype of ethnic holocaust that threatened everybody from the shores of Dalmatia to the mountains of Osh and Fergana to the valleys of Nakichevan, North Ossetia, and Chechen-Ingush. Nagorno-Karabakh: of all of them, that six-syllable chamber of horrors was unquestionably the one that has come to symbolize the realities of Azerbaijan and Armenia today.

What was Nagorno-Karabakh? What had happened that this spot on the globe, which virtually nobody in the West had ever heard of, should now be the symbol of a new "time of troubles," not only in the Transcaucasus but in the many disintegrating parts of the world?

The enclave of Nagorno-Karabakh, a small, largely Armenian area located entirely inside Azerbaijan, is today the major example of Stalin's many poison pills to his people. It was not enough in the Transcaucasus that history had placed all these different peoples, languages, cultures, histories, quarrels, and dreams there; man's hand had shaken them up together until one could hardly sort them out anymore or give them time to learn to live together. Stalin had to do still more diabolical things. In order to ensure that these ethnic groups would never come together and threaten the Communist central power, he deliberately created a patchwork of peoples; he moved one tiny part of a people onto another's historic lands; he exiled millions to the ends of Central Asia on whatever pretext he could think of that day.

The first thing one must understand about Armenia is that it is a country with an extraordinarily rich history. This is one of the most ancient cultures on earth, an Indo-European people who adopted Christianity in 314, and who at one time had a powerful-enough kingdom to challenge the Roman Empire. The Armenian Orthodox Church has held the people together with its great pageantry, its exquisite music, its language that is believed to be the language of heaven, and its profound memory of endless persecutions. Not inconsequentially, the Armenians are the only major grouping of Christians besides the Georgians in the sea of Muslims that constantly rises and ebbs around them.

This unusual people survived conquerors from the Persians to the Byzantines to the Arabs to the Bagratids, but it was the Turks who nearly wiped out the entire Armenian people in what was a systematic plan for their extermination. By the time World War I broke out, the Young Turk government of Kemal Atatürk regarded the many Armenians then living in Turkey as a dangerous foreign element that was conspiring with the pro-Christian czarist enemy to upset the Ottoman campaign in the East. The Turkish government's "final solution" was to sentence 1,750,000 Armenians to exile in empty desert regions and leave them there. Many were killed outright. More than one million Armenians died, and hundreds of thousands emigrated to the United States and to Europe. In 1920 historic Armenia became part of the U.S.S.R.

Perhaps the story told by Hedrick Smith, in which he quotes a young Armenian economist, expresses a people's passion best. "In this country," the economist says, "we have only a single right— the right of territory. This is the sole right of the republic, of our nation. . . . So a fight over territory became a fight for our worth, our dignity as a people, as a nation."

Armenia, with its rich history and culture and its uniquely able people, had all the capacities to have been a rare and relative little "paradise" in the former Soviet Union. With its small population of 3.3 million against Azerbaijan's population of 7 million, and its developed industry (not to speak of its famous cognac, Winston Churchill's favorite), Armenia could have done extremely well. Indeed, after independence, in the early 1990s, big upscale international companies like Benetton immediately established factories in Yerevan, which then supplied Benetton's Moscow (and, amazingly, Dushanbe's) branches.

But Armenia's new independence—and its joy at Armenia's historic resurrection as a coherent state—was to be tragically short-lived. For as soon as Gorbachev came to power in 1985, the Armenians began talking about Nagorno-Karabakh or, in hushed or shouted tones, just "Karabakh!" It brought out all the fervor, all the passion, all the xenophobia of their rich and tormented history. Instead of focusing on Armenia's economic development, after 1985 a "Karabakh Committee" was formed to lobby and organize to bring Karabakh back to Armenia.

The trial of "Nagorno-Karabakh" had begun.

But only a few miles away, you had Azerbaijan. In contrast to Armenia, the Azeris were a young people. Dwelling not on ancient churches and monasteries, and less on myth, the Azeris saw as their primary claim to nationhood the sheer territorial integrity of their country. Its new nationhood began in the fall of 1989, when the Communist party was losing its grip and still another popular front of academics and other intellectuals began to agitate for greater political freedom—and to oppose Armenia in its attempts to annex Nagorno-Karabakh. Then, Armenia voted to include the disputed enclave in its annual budget and to allow Armenians living there to vote in Armenian elections. Baku exploded. Thousands of Azerbaijani peasants who had been forced to flee their homes in Armenia because of the conflict launched the first pogrom against Armenians, killing dozens. Soviet troops rolled in on tanks at midnight on January 19, 1990. Horrifying massacres began; "Nagorno-Karabakh" and not new dreams of independence and equality and prosperity became the arbiter of this new age.

In these old, poor, gray, shabby, brooding Armenian and Azeri villages and towns, snuggled in their sooty poverty and festering rage between the mountains, in place of independence there began a nightmare. Freed finally to think and to talk, the first words both Armenians and Azeris (and Serbs and Croats, and Georgians and Ossetians, and Chechen and Ingush) spoke were not words of love and accommodation but words of hate and absolutism. And so, in this area, the ethnic island of Nagorno-Karabakh took on both the symbolic qualities and the burden of the tragedies that were happening in many places. As the war caught fire, a massacre of Armenians by Azeris took place in the Azeri city of Sumgaït north of

Baku. In other places, Azeri villagers had the backs of their heads chopped off with axes. In the village of Khodjaly, for eleven days and nights, lightly clad Azeri villagers huddled in subzero temperatures, eating nothing but snow: half died and a doctor said all the frostbitten survivors would have to undergo amputations. On the other side, Azeris massacred Armenians in Baku and in other cities.

All of this led directly to symbols of death and martyrdom everywhere. Above Baku, on a high hill with a view of the Caspian shore, a park was declared "Martyr's Lane," where victims of the bloody post–cold war clashes were buried. On any afternoon, haunting music, terrifying speeches, and macabre rituals are carried out. On one grave stands a jar containing the pickled heart of an Armenian. One of the dead was a glamorous and popular newscaster, Chingiz Mustafayev, who had filmed his own death in Nagorno-Karabakh in June 1992. Conspiracy theories overlay all of this: it "must be the Russians" who were helping the Armenians, or the Americans, or the Armenian diaspora.

It was a classic case—it was too classic a case—of the idea of "the other," the personification and bringer of evil who could never be trusted, and who finally must be removed. Again in history, it was that "other" who had done violence to one's forebears and who must die in rivers of blood.

Washington and America little understood, our history was so different. In the years of the Reagan and Bush administrations, Washington was awash in hopeful talk about democracy and free markets. To Americans, with their idealistic but sometimes naive notions of history—our vast continent protected by the huge arms of oceans—there was always plenty of space to exercise our energies and keep us from constantly massacring "the other." Frontiers absorbed our "others," although in recent years the frontiers had been dangerously moving in. Indeed, at least until recently America was the celebration of all "the others" come together into one people, universalist in nature and inclusive in spirit.

Summer 1992: more than 1,500 had been killed in four years of fighting between Armenia and Azerbaijan over Nagorno-Karabakh. In Georgia, South Ossetians sought to unite with other Ossetians across the border, with hundreds dead. In Moldova, east of the Dniestr River, Russian and Ukrainian secessionists in the industrial region of the Trans-Dniestr Republic rebelled, fearing that the ethnic Romanian majority in Moldova would unite with Romania; hundreds were killed. In the southern Gagauz region of Moldova, 150,000 descendants of Christian Turks declared their own republic. And the peoples of Chechen-Ingush, an ancient part of Russia in the North Caucasus, wanted to create a confederation of six mainly Muslim territories that stretched three hundred miles from the Caspian to the Black Sea (these were the territories of Abkhazia, Karachayevo-Cherkess, Kabardin-Balkar, North Ossetia, Chechen-Ingush, and Dagestan, with a total of no fewer than 5.3 million people).

A few understood the underlying reasons why this was happening. "There is a process of collapse going on in the former Soviet Union that is just beginning," Chengiz Husseinov, the great Azeri writer, mused with me one day when he was visiting Washington. "It is just at the beginning of its collapse. I have found sixty types of ethnic conflict going on; three years ago, there were fifteen or twenty. Russia has become a kind of new center, and there is collapse there, too. Indeed, collapse is going on so intensively that no one in the world expected it to happen so rapidly.

"It is not something that people can grasp," he went on, "because empires do not usually disintegrate so fast. There is no single master key to unlock all the conflicts."

By the beginning of 1993, historians were saying at conferences that there were no fewer than six hundred ethnic "danger spots" where conflict could break out across the globe.

But how could things have gone so wrong? For decades, indeed since World War I, the West had enshrined "self-determination" in the cathedrals of the democratic mind and soul. The idea was at the very basis of Woodrow Wilson's thinking in World War I. It underlay all of our ideas about nationhood in solving the aftermath of the Great War—and in all of the thinking about the massive decolonialization that followed.

But now I, like many others who eschewed standardized or ideological thought, began to realize that it was not as simple as so many had thought. Here were countries newly freed—newly "self-determined"—and instead of embracing the tolerant, liberal, Western precepts of independence, they were striding in rage back toward the past. They were embracing their worst ancient traditions. It was a question of "folk rights" versus "human rights," something the West chose out of its own experience to believe was long past in the world (with folk rights, nobody settles for anything less than the maximum).

Who, after all, could quite understand that these were peoples who considered themselves "tragic nations"? They had gone from medieval kingdoms to centralized authoritarian Communism to divided and disintegrating ethnic nations within less than a century. They were peoples whose lives were torn and retorn every generation so that there was no time for middle-class or bourgeois life to be developed, as had happened in Europe, whose very different history could produce room for more independent intellectual and educational institutions to challenge medieval doctrines and ways. No, these people had always huddled on the peripheries and on the far horizons of Europe, gazing from afar at the Renaissance and the Enlightenment.

Several sociological developments had matured—ripened—at this point to create such brutality in these new/old "ethnic wars." During the constant invasions from outside during the Middle Ages and even into modern times, some linguistic and religious groups had been caught in the mountains and were largely left alone by the invaders, who preferred the easy valleys for their rampages. These mountain groups became very ingrown in their ethnicity, to the point where they constituted totally "other" peoples from those in the valleys. So it was in Yugoslavia, where the "mountain Serbs" lived alone, culturally different from the urbane "city Serbs" and Bosnians—and hating them. In the Caucasus, by the time I was there, these historic distinctions had led to the formation of a shadowy and fascinating "Confederation of Caucasian Mountain Peoples," which was a group of Islamic mountaineers from roughly fourteen different areas, all united in warfare against the cities and valleys.

Balkan scholar Robert D. Kaplan carries this analysis still further. He talks of "a place like Baku," with its alienated youth and its miles and miles of cement socialist jungles, and says, "You go into the bar and you find young men with nothing to do. They sit around all day and drink and talk. Communism created this Orwellian underclass of violence-prone, semi-criminal peasant males who, as long as there was order, were kept at bay. Then, suddenly, they all got uniforms and became members of militias. One thing that is not emphasized enough about the fight in Bosnia and Baku is the criminal nature of it. The nature between war and unprovoked crime cannot be made enough. Here you have urbanized peasants who don't know who they are but only know who they are by knowing what they hate."

What actually happened was that Soviet Communism had frozen ancient ethnic disputes in time. "It provided no safety valves for the aggrieved parties to dissipate their anger," Enders Wimbush explained. "The Soviet experiment robbed the many peoples of the U.S.S.R. of the lessons learned elsewhere on the globe for resolving ethnic conflict peacefully. Then, when Communism collapsed with its power to compel compliance, some—but actually not very many—disputes continued with renewed vigor as if the seventy years of Soviet Russian rule had never occurred, for it provided no positive examples for mitigating ethnic conflict. Rather, it made ethnic conflict inevitably worse by sequestering real grievances and feuds under the banners of pseudo-brotherhood. In this sense, Communism ironically created nationalism." And this was, other scholars insisted, the "last stage of Communism."

The former American ambassador to Moscow, Jack Matlock, one of the very best Russian/Soviet specialists, further warned that one could not be too cynical about these conflicts, because the "state-owned property of the Communist state set these people up for these conflicts. These wars are not only over economics but politics—the roots are not so much cultural differences as the fight for power." In short, the real question was property; each group and each leader was looking for reasons to get hold of the suddenly released property in the post-Communist world.

(These conflicts were also, always, about how Stalin, in the twenties and thirties, had divided and mixed up these groups the better to control them. Stalin's attitude in terms of always playing the "ethnic card" to the depths of his brutality was shown in one conversation with the great Yugoslav writer Milovan Djilas, who had broken with Tito over socialism. Stalin told him, when they talked about "friendship" with the Balkans: "I'm not interested in Balkan friendship—I can't do anything with that. I'm interested in Balkan hatreds—I can do something with that.")

Or, as Robert Kaplan says, "What we are seeing is indistinct modern regionalisms. Self-determination is an overarching mantra, but the real problem today is identity. The Balkans and the Caucasus were the original Third World before the term was invented; they were worlds of confusion and of ethnic tribalism." Because of the myriad groups—Pliny related over two thousand years ago the story of a hundred tongues and dialects being spoken in a single port city in the Caucasus—Kaplan says that "self-determination means typically one group over another. Self-determination is only a good deal if your group happens to be in the majority. Nothing is more dangerous than an ethnic tribal majority that sees itself as being oppressed." Meanwhile, the criminalization of societies—and the criminalization of wars, as in Bosnia, as in Nagorno-Karabakh, as in Tajikistan—has become still another poison on this world stage.

By the time I got safely home, Central Asia had achieved a modest fashionableness. And at one Washington conference, American diplomat Max Kampelman warned against a too-devouring embrace of self-determination as an overweening moral concept. After all, he averred, "self-determination" is a limited human right encompassing cultural independence, plus freedom of religion, language, and association. "But it does not include the right to change boundaries at will," he said thoughtfully, "because that is destabilizing. Within every majority seeking secession, there is another minority that may want to secede. Where does it end?" He then argued that minorities that did wish to secede have the right to negotiate it, but not to use violence.

Should they opt for the latter, the implicit dangers that could ensue from confct would be theirs, without protection under international law.

The great Baghdad-born scholar Elie Kedourie was even more critical of the supposedly noble idea of "self-determination," calling it a "pillar of international disorder." He pointed out that under the Ottoman and Austro-Hungarian and Hapsburg empires, the collective right of self-determination was suppressed, and yet individual rights could be enjoyed to a greater degree than thereafter. He asked: "Is it faith to say that since Wilson's Fourteen Points, the modern world has laid too much emphasis on collective rights at the expense of individual rights?"

It was a highly complicated subject and one that would engross the world from Nagorno-Karabakh to Bosnia to Tajikistan. It dealt with the question of the very nature of nation-states in a world of disintegrating multinational states, with the real and revivified power of ethnicity, with the rights of peoples as opposed to the rights of individuals, and with the huge question of the right of national self-determination as opposed to the sanctity of existing international borders.

As Central Asia and the Caucasus opened to the world, that opening was initially to be a peaceful one, but looking at these relatively unknown parts of the globe presented the modern world not with the legendary Oriental luxury of a Samarkand but with questions that it thought it had already answered.

But then, lest we forget, that was what this volatile and explosive part of the world historically had often done.

The outer sanctums of the Azeri president's office were uniformly depressing. As with all of these faraway new republics, the presidency was the one big, handsome, modern building in town. All tended toward the same architecture, which of course was Soviet-modern with usually just a touch of the local culture thrown in. Here, there was not even much of that, yet it was a comfortable building. The young men there who were impressive enough as they worked on an interview for me with the president, a stolid old Communist named Ayaz Mutalibov, were bitterly depressed about the war.

They felt, not incorrectly, that every bit of hope they had had for independence—for the potential prosperity and independence that their oil wealth could give them—was bound to be destroyed by the implacable and in the end even pointless slaughter going on in Nagorno-Karabakh. To sit there with them was like sitting at a wake for someone who had not quite died yet, and someone you were not even sure you liked.

Vaqif Rustamov, one of the president's young advisers, was a dark young man, with curly hair, strong and masculine, with an excellent mind. In those hours that we sat around the presidency (where else was there to go in the cold wind?—and besides, I had to "wait for the president"), it was he who really explained to me what the latest economic theories in Moscow were doing to people and to industry out here.

"They've basically destroyed the economy," he began. "It is now common knowledge that they should have dealt first with economics, because economics is the background of politics. Starting with politics breaks the law of nature. The urgent problem of today, at least in my opinion, is to make another try to reestablish the partner relations that we used to have.

"An example: say we have an industrial plant that used to get raw materials from 85 different regions of the U.S.S.R. and sold its product to 252 other regions. When there is a lack of supplies from the other regions, we cannot produce. As a matter of fact, during the seventy years of Soviet rule, all the republics developed their economies under conditions of high integration—and no republic has the complete technology for the entire product.

"If we take agriculture, Ukraine specialized in corn products and cow breeding. Azerbaijan, in wine and cotton. It was a barter community. We sent wine to Ukraine and they sent meat. We also sent Russia cotton and got silk back in return. Now Ukraine needs wine and we have a shortage of bread—in spite of the fact that they have all these materials and we do too. This is simply a fact of life that came along with the breaking of those ties.

"We're not able to agree with one another, and so we are now looking for partners abroad—and the situation gets further aggravated by the speeches of politicians." He paused, shaking his head in more than mock irritation, as though no one could quite believe what was happening. "You must understand that people here are not accustomed to work. So now everyone is engaged in politics—and that is not good. They have no interest in their jobs. Actors are entering politics, and farmers, too. It is not funny, it is a tragedy.

"Azerbaijan annually exported goods worth eleven to twelve billion rubles, but the low quality of today's product will not permit us to export, and so no countries of the world will sign contracts with us. We also don't have any money to get production going. Then there is the overpricing between the republics on what trade we do have. An example: we now have no coordinating organization to settle all the problems. When new tariffs for plane tickets were established, Baku to Moscow was 393 rubles. But from Moscow to Baku, it was 436 rubles. It is really some kind of a mess.

"For about a hundred years now, we have been extracting oil from the Caspian. During that period, we extracted 1,200 million tons of oil. Our ground reserves are exhausted now, but during those years, we created well-organized and large-scale processing plants. When we had the union, Russia and Grozny, the Chechen capital, would provide some pipes from their cities to ours. Oil was processed and sent back; from here, it would be moved throughout the union. Now Russia, when it wishes, marks up the prices for oil and threatens us . . ."

I thought to myself that what they are having here is not free enterprise, certainly as the West understands it, but rather "free-whim enterprise." I complimented myself on the phrase.

"We can always say, if you don't buy at our prices, we'll send the oil to the Western countries for dollars. But sending oil abroad for dollars will settle only part of the problem . . ."

Then he added, almost as an afterthought, that one Azeri boy had actually been exchanged by the Armenians for sixty tons of petroleum. He added that hundreds had already been exchanged in this manner—for oil, food, cattle . . . Napoleon had done the same with his troops.

I thought at this point that I had probably never seen such a wild and strange place. At all times, at least to me, there was a feeling of everything being out of control, ready to explode, on the edge of some psychological abyss. I wondered for a moment what would happen to these people. Yet while I listened to Rustamov, so serious and so cogent (and so depressed), talk about the essential things that had been done wrong, I felt that I had never heard a better explanation of what had happened to them economically than what I got from this intelligent and troubled young Azeri, whose own future as well seemed so terribly and tragically uncertain.

The second night in Baku, the city bitten by the wind, perhaps not surprisingly I awoke to a howling gale from the steppes hitting not only Baku but me! In my bed!

I thought for a moment that I had never been so cold, for the temperature in the room must have been well below freezing. For quite some time I simply huddled in my bed, keeping warm but wondering why, exactly, it was that the room had grown so cold.

Then, suddenly, my mind began to function again, and I realized that the wind was indeed blowing through the room. Shivering, I got up and discovered that somehow I had left the window open, so I closed the window and returned, more comfortable now, to my little Azeri bed.

In the still cool air of the room, with the blackness outside like hell's midnight, I sat there in bed, the little light on, and picked up my beloved Orthodox philosopher Berdyayev's *The Origin of Russian Communism*. For two sweet hours, I sat there calm and self-possessed in one of those rare moments of total peace of soul and spirit, reading the man whom I had always thought said more about Russia than any other writer I knew.

"The religious energy of the Russian spirit possesses the faculty of switching over and directing itself to purposes which are not merely religious, for example, to social objects. In virtue of their religious-dogmatic quality of spirit, Russians—whether orthodox, heretics or schismatics—are always apocalyptic or nihilist . . .

"The doctrine of Moscow the Third Rome became the basic idea on which the Muscovite state was formed. The kingdom was consolidated and shaped under the symbol of a messianic idea . . .

"Western ideas of property were alien to the Russian people; they were but feebly understood even by the nobility. The soil was god's, and all who toiled and laboured at it might enjoy the use of it. A naive agrarian socialism was always an accepted principle among the Russian peasants . . .

"Generally speaking, Russians but poorly understood the meaning of the relative, the fact that historical progress advances by stages, the differentiation of various spheres of culture. Russian maximalism is due to this. The Russian spirit craves for wholeness . . .

"Some, the Slavophiles, dreamed of an ideal Russia before Peter's time; others, the Westernizers, dreamed of an ideal West . . .

"Russian writers, especially the most notable, did not believe in the stability of civilization, in the stability of those principles upon which the world rests, what was called the bourgeois world of their time; they are full of terrible forebodings of impending disaster . . .

"The influence of the West upon Russia was absolutely paradoxical; it did not graft Western criteria upon the Russian spirit. On the contrary, its influence let loose violent, dionysiac, dynamic and sometimes demoniac forces . . .

"The messianic idea of the Russian people assumed either an apocalyptic form or a revolutionary; and then there occurred an amazing event in the destiny of the Russian people. Instead of the Third Rome in Russia, the Third International was achieved, and many of the features of the Third Rome pass over to the Third International . . . also a consecrated realm, and it also is founded on an orthodox faith . . ."

At about four in the morning I went back to sleep, and I enjoyed a perfect, peaceful rest. There are moments like these in voyaging, moments of transcendance that buoy the soul and invigorate the spirit and calm the nervous wakes of life. They are moments when you finally seem to really finally understand something.

I slept so sweetly and so calmly that when I awoke the next morning, I suddenly realized that not even once during that night had I thought about the Turkish Airliner.

They finally arranged the interview with President Mutalibov at ten o'clock Saturday night. I knew that he was an interesting man: although long a member of the Communist party, he called himself a "new Communist," he had dropped "Soviet Socialist" from the name of his country, and he even flew the flag of the independent Azerbaijan of 1918 to 1920.

I was not to see him alone. Susan Goldberger, a smart, funny, tough young American correspondent who was courageously going across the entire Caucasus and Transcaucasus region writing for London's *Guardian,* and I had waited, and waited, and waited. (However, we had awfully good talks with the young Azeris in the outer office, like Rustamov, while we waited.) Susan had been in Georgia, and she was dauntless about traveling through the area; she took trains, stayed with families, and somehow managed to preserve a nice, humorful mien. I liked her.

I was also filled with admiration for her. Although I had done dangerous-enough things in journalism in my youth, I would not have gone to cover the war in Georgia or Tajikistan or (worst of all) Nagorno-Karabakh. Yet she did—and seemed to revel in it.

Susan kept hounding the men in that outer office to *get the interview,* because she was leaving on the nine P.M. flight for Tbilisi, where she could have still more fun covering the nasty conflict there that pitted Georgians of the Gamaskurdia line against Georgians following Gorbachev's former foreign minister, Eduard Shevardnadze. It was Georgians against Ossetians (North and South), and now, Chechens against Ingush, and God knows who against whom next . . .

"I *must* get that plane at nine," Susan kept saying, leaning against Rustamov's desk and trying to look viciously determined (she didn't quite, thank God). Poor guy, he would then look appropriately pained, stare at the paint on his desk for several minutes, and finally look up at her with a cocker spaniel's helpless and dependent look.

"What can I do?" he would ask (this had been going on for several hours). "It is the president who must decide." Then he would send his assistant somewhere to check, only to return to face Susan's wrath yet again.

When it came close to 7:30—the time when Susan had to leave for the airport, if indeed she were actually to travel to an even more misery-ridden part of these worlds than this—she got up and announced she was leaving. Enough was enough! At this point, one of the outer-office corps (why had nobody thought of it before?) suddenly had a bright idea. "I ought to try to call the airport," he said.

We all looked at him. Actually, we stared at him—then we laughed uproariously.

The very idea that an "airport" in wherever we were—and whatever wherever we were now was (for the moment) called—would actually *answer* the phone (if there was a phone) was so stunningly original that we giggled. We laughed. We guffawed. We behaved like idiots. But—surprise!—the joke turned out to be more on us than on them.

Because, yes, they *did* answer the phone. At least, someone did. It was the answer that was so infinitely amusing: there was no plane to Tbilisi—none at all. At this point, Susan showed her ticket, and it was then that we truly laughed till we cried, cackling wildly at this ridiculous situation, in this end-of-the-world new republic, where we all so amazingly found ourselves.

At this point, Susan drew herself up and proudly insisted that she would leave by train.

They tried to call the train station for Susan, to find out when a train for Tbilisi was leaving. The phone rang, and rang, and rang . . .

So there we were, doomed to sit and wait in the outer offices of an Azeri president who would be peacefully replaced in three weeks, to wait, and wait, and wait for words that would therefore mean nothing in the world.

At 10:00 P.M. precisely, we were ushered into the beautiful, wood-trimmed office of President Ayaz Mutalibov, pouter pigeon in physique, former Communist in résumé, free-thinking jazz connoisseur in his imagination. It was a pleasant-enough room, with bannered flags and blond wood furniture (yes, it was blond, just like the furniture of our Chicago childhoods). Mutalibov himself was very, very formal. In his good gray suit and with a very stiff demeanor, he at first stood up like some old cardboard Communist figure from another era, ready to greet us in the old style as "fraternal brothers and sisters from around the socialist world."

But in this new day and age, instead, he got Susan and me!

And so, after all that waiting or because of it, we sat there stiffly, seated around a blond table, with Mutalibov sitting ramrod-straight behind his blond desk. He went on and on about Armenia—in truth, it obsessed everyone there—about how Azerbaijan had "made many initiatives . . . all were rejected . . . certain people were interested in only escalating the conflict . . . with the aim of creating a second Armenia, right on the territory of Azerbaijan . . . and the worst thing was that it was the international media which was trumpeting the idea that it was the Azeris, and not the Armenians, who were violating human rights in this area . . ."

Despite the advertisements of "new," Mutalibov was the very soul of Old Red: stiff of body, unsmiling of expression, deadly bureaucratic, and unimaginative of spirit and soul. To tell the truth, I was already sick and tired of this new war; for twenty-eight years, I had covered every war, revolution, civil disturbance, riot, militant-expression-of-inferiority-acted-out, cry of pain, shriek of bloodlust, and simply uncontrollable rapacious desire of someone to kill anyone who got in his way. I was sick of fanatics; I was out of patience with wimpy, complaining, histrionic professional historic "victims"; and, in my peaceable spirit of the moment, for my part I had become personally ready to wipe out people who were unendingly determined to wipe out others.

It quickly became clear that he intended to speak only and forever about Nagorno-Karabakh, until suddenly he would say, "Time is up," and we'd be out on our little rear ends, Susan hitchhiking to Georgia or hunting for a midnight plane and me lurking around the hotel dining room looking for errant steaks and loose caviar.

At moments like this in an interview, I just *do* something—and I did.

When our gray man of rivers of words finally took a breath and I had a second's entry point, I jumped right in with the most important question of the night. But first, I fixed him with a kind of terrifying unflinching gaze that scared him into silence; then I struck.

In assessing the room at the beginning of the interview, I had noticed that he had an entire array of phones behind the desk. Indeed, there were eight of them, mostly in pinks and blues but one in white.

So I asked him: What were the "new Reds" doing with all these phones?

His dour face brightened at once (perhaps he, too, was glad to have an excuse to get off the subject of Nagorno-Karabakh, I thought, ungenerously to be sure; or perhaps in this "new Azerbaijan" one recognized, by his phones, a man of the world). Indeed, he grew downright pleasant as he contemplated his myriad, brightly colored, cheerful phones, and probably he was also moved by the pride and pleasure of showing a foreign visitor how "civilized" he and his new country were.

"These three are internal systems," he said, pointing to three and revealing his enthusiasm with smiles and general good cheer. "This one goes to the former Soviet Union, this one is a space communications satellite for overseas—and this one goes directly to Ankara."

Directly to Ankara! How interesting! Here, again, I had found the precious—the treasured—the sought-after Turkish connection. I had to bite my tongue not to ask him whether he would call Ankara to see if the Turkish Airliner would come on Monday; but somehow, through a herculean act of will, I restrained myself.

It was not easy.

I then attempted—successfully, I might add—to move him away from Nagorno-Karabakh and onto the new "Great Game" in Central Asia and the Caucasus, which of course was supposed to be Iran versus Turkey. And he bit. "Our relations are good with Iran and Turkey and with all our neighboring countries," he said, "but Turkey is the country that speaks the same language we do. Of course, in Iran, there are a lot of Azeris, we have common borders, so we have to maintain relations. But the political situation of Iran and Turkey is different; Turkey is a civilized country, and we follow the Turkish model. The problem with Iran is that when a people feels itself isolated in solitude and it feels it has been badly treated, then there is only one way out—to worship. But ours is a country of full literacy, and we have everything possible to help us create a civilized country.

"There are certain circles today that declare that, before 1985, we lived much better under Communism. But we are a civilized nation, with our own language, history, and culture, although we are as well very respectful to world culture." Suddenly his voice began to soar in enthusiasm. "Did you know that in the late fifties, when our Iron Curtain began to fall, the biggest jazz musicians were in Baku? It was the center of jazz of the former Soviet Union—and I was one of the best musicians." Now the cardboard man was smiling broadly; he was excited, almost happy. "I was a playboy—I danced to jazz—I played the piano, guitar, classical, jazz, spirituals . . ."

For just a moment, Mutalibov seemed a truly happy man.

For my part, I was happy to see him so happy. "Mstislav Rostropovich is from Azerbaijan, you know," he went on. I did know; the great maestro lives in my building in Washington, and is the most charmingly classic "Russian," always hugging us beautiful women in the building and giving us sweet busses on both cheeks. A small world?

Before we left, Mutalibov, a man transformed, now the soul of joviality, told us that he had just come from the World Economic Forum in Switzerland. Henry Kissinger was there, and U.S. Senator Bill Bradley. "Kissinger asked me who was my suitmaker," Mutalibov said proudly. "He said, 'We know a little about you.' " He was obviously thrilled.

Mutalibov also revealed to us that he had that very day signed an agreement—a historic one—with Amoco, the powerful Western oil company, for extracting the oil under the Caspian Sea. It was the biggest Amoco deal in its existence, he said, a long-term agreement for thirty years, with $10 billion to be invested in what is effectively a joint venture. The terms were 70 percent of the profits to go to Azerbaijan and 30 percent to be reinvested.

It had obviously been a good day for Ayaz Mutalibov. It had not been a bad day for us. At 10:15, we said good-bye to the Top Ex-Red and headed for the hotel for a good dinner with Rustamov. At eleven o'clock, Susan bustled off to the train station; she still persisted in thinking there were trains. I don't know what happened to her; I didn't see her again, but I did wish her all the best in her odyssey through the legendary Caucasus, with its eternal beauty and its diabolical destructiveness.

It came to be Monday, it actually did. And that was the day I was to leave, after all those long, difficult, and unforgettable weeks. Monday morning I awoke with one thought in my mind: would the

Turkish Airliner really come, land, go, keep going, and take me to Istanbul?

I tried to be calm. But I suspected that, at breakfast, everyone was looking at me, saying, "Look at her! Look at how foolish she is! Pitiful girl, she actually thinks that a Turkish airliner is going to sweep in here, like some Haji Baba, and carry her to legendary Istanbul! Imagine, she thinks that tonight she will actually be at the Hilton Hotel in Istanbul, sipping a Manhattan and looking over the Bosporus and forgetting all of us—all our miseries and our hopes! Poor child, poor poor child! We'll never let her go."

I, of course, ignored them and tried to pretend that all was normal, and that, of course, everyone knew that the Turkish Airliner would come at 5:00, when it was supposed to come, and leave at 7:30, when it was supposed to leave. But in my heart, I wondered.

It was only normal—it was only cautionary—it was merely the behavior of a meticulous and precise person—to leave breakfast and to once again hightail it over to the Azeri travel office.

The same pleasant and efficient young lady served me. "Yes, Miss Geyer, the Turkish airliner is expected on time today at five P.M. at the Baku airport," she repeated, with a perfectly hateful and patronizing patience.

She smiled, waited a moment, then added, "As always!"

True, she was nice enough, but again I wondered, What did she *really* know?

But before Monday came, I had a wonderful Sunday—perhaps the very nicest day of my entire trip—seeing old Baku with a charming English professor I had met at the Azeri news agency.

Molla Haji Mollayev was a tall, gray-haired, handsome man, probably in his early sixties, an Avar from the Dagestan region northwest of Baku, and his English was that careful, precise, deliberate English that was taught as a foreign language earlier in this century. A cultured man, he was also tremendously gentle and kind. At the news agency, the young blood called him "the old man," but in truth he was not old, only distinguished, which of course made him seem strange in this tortured land.

In short, I liked and appreciated him tremendously, and when he asked to take me on a tour of old Baku on Sunday, I was more than pleased to agree.

On my entire trip, in those rare minutes when I could or would pause to think, I had the gnawing realization that I was not meeting people who had ever been happy or led satisfied lives in these faraway, unknown (to us, of course) parts of the world. It was not at all unusual that we journalists tended to meet men and women of politics, of economics, of social and/or military importance. In general, these were at heart malcontents. And in fact, it was not at all difficult to understand that we weary travelers should meet the misery-ridden, the unassimilated, the discontented, the haunted, the unquenchably ambitious, and the warriors-against-time.

But with Molla Haji Mollayev, at last out in this other world, I finally met a happy man—a man of inner balance—a man of considerable spiritual depth. And, for a few hours, I even had fun!

You see, I had not expected picturesqueness, much less fun, in Baku with its wars-upon-wars threatening always just over the horizon. I had settled for the nice, Oriental section of downtown right around the hotel, and I was satisfied. But Molla Haji Mollayev introduced me to the "old town" of Baku that Sunday morning. We strolled like tourists around the small medieval part of town, first stopping at the round, heavy, gray Bastion of the Maiden tower of the eleventh century, the Palace of the Shirvan Shahs of the fifteenth century, and numerous mosques. We strolled in the sunlight, we laughed, we explored caverns underneath the Muslim ruins, we visited the Museum of Azerbaijani Carpets and Applied Folk Art, and I wanted to buy every single carpet. I wanted—my God, how I wanted!—to visit the Fire Worshippers' Temple Museum, which was a Zoroastrian temple with oil-fed fires, but it was twenty miles outside the city and nobody had enough gasoline to go that far. No matter; I would not have wanted to drive that far with any of the Azeri drivers I had met—no, I correct that—with *any* Azeri driver!

And after we had walked slowly through the old streets, stopping to sit quietly in the sun and even pretend that we were normal people in normal times, we went to the Caravanserai restaurant, a charming place in a restored caravanserai in the old city. It was a lovely scene. We had a small, private, cavelike room, one of the rooms that travelers in those ancient times would have taken for the night.

A small fire gleamed in the fireplace, and we drank red wine and consumed a lunch of many plates of typical meat, chicken, and vegetable combinations that cost me as much as the average Azeri earns in a month (roughly five hundred rubles or five dollars). And it was then, in that evocative setting, only tens of miles away from the terror of Nagorno-Karabakh, that Molla Haji began his story.

In truth, I had the distinct sense that he was relating his life to me in the same narrative, emotional style of the storytellers who had for so many centuries passed down truths from person to person in this part of the world.

Strangely enough, our conversation began as we talked about agricultural reform.

"I will tell you a story about land," he said, as I sipped some cognac. "I came from a village in the north, from Dagestan," he began. "After World War Two, my brother had a small plot of land. Stalin had said, 'Grow food!' So we grew enough for chickens all year. But now, no one is plowing the land. I asked my brother recently why people don't do that anymore. And he said, 'Well, we don't know if someone will come and take the land. They've lost interest and initiative. Today the peasants still have the collective farms. That means that the government takes their wheat and says it will give them bread; but in truth, everything rots in storage.' Do the peasants even have the mentality to change anymore?" He shook his head sadly. "I doubt it . . ."

Why had he turned out so different from the men, also from this world, who were only dozens of miles away slaughtering and scalping one another in Nagorno-Karabakh? How had he come to master and to so love the English language, which came to him from worlds so far distant?

"I was born in Dagestan . . ." And so first he told me about Dagestan, which means "mountain country," and which is to be found at the eastern end of the great Caucasus range, beside the Caspian Sea and the Kuma River. It is a land of crests of the Caucasus mountains, a dry climate, and of course is home to those Dagestani tribesmen who often live to 120, 135, 145 years of age. Russians had penetrated the area as early as the fifteenth century, but they did not annex it until 1813. Now Dagestan was again in the news—even in the great papers of London, New York, and Tokyo—and this was because of the persecuted Chechen-Ingush people. Busy Stalin had deported them, too, in 1944, when he accused them of collaborating with the Germans.

But in 1957, the Chechen-Ingush Autonomous Soviet Socialist Republic was once again formed here, and some of their lands were returned.

Ah, but that was not the end of it. First, Chechen-Ingush declared its own independence from Russia, the first group inside the Russian federation to do so. But by the time we were talking, the two persecuted peoples were now fighting each other.

"There are more than one hundred thousand Avars in Dagestan, all Muslims," Molla Haji went on, "and they speak a different language than Azerbaijani, but we have the same religion and names. It is the same way of life. They say it is a Caucasian-Iberian language, but who knows? No great linguist has ever studied these languages, not that of the Lezghians, nor the Ossetians . . ."

But let us get back to his English, let us please get back. "Well," he began, "when I was a child, I had a teacher who taught me to read. I read everything, I studied exams. Then I was taken into the Russian army—and in six months, I learned Russian. My love for reading continued in my free time and I read a lot of Russian books. I read Victor Hugo, and when there were some phrases in English, I would copy them. I saw that it was a little difficult to study in this way . . .

"Then I tried to learn English with a dictionary. That was a vain matter. Finally I began working in an industrial plant, and by chance I happened to be in a bookshop and I saw some books in English. One was named *Coral Sea,* I remember. With the help of a dictionary, I began translating it into Azerbaijani.

"The shop manager saw this, and he naturally reproached me, saying, 'Why don't you enter the Foreign Language Institute?' I did and I got satisfactory marks. My parents did not expect this at all. They had never been in English-speaking countries; they had never been out of the Soviet Union. When foreign students would ask me why we never went out, I would answer appropriately, saying, 'Well, our country is so beautiful . . .'

"Later on, I saw that French was very beautiful and I wanted to learn it. Two years ago, I got a textbook on Arabic and began studying. I listened to the singer Ferouz—I'm mad about her singing and language . . ."

Then, as the little fire danced and we sipped cognac in our dark cave, with the sun shining in through the door that often brought in the resourceful waiter with more engrossing little dishes, handsome, dignified Molla Haji reminisced about his childhood—about his happy childhood. "We had a simple life in those days," he began. "There were not even any trains. We remembered by ourselves what was remembered to us. The fruits, the hazelnuts! In the evening, people would come to our house from other houses, and Father would send us up to the attic, because that was where we stored things. I would bring down a bucket of apples and we would all eat. We had jars of mulberries, of grapes, of pears. Mother would make concentrated juice by boiling the fruit until it was thick. It was very good to feed babies with . . ."

He smiled a perfectly beatific smile, a gesture of memory and (or so it seemed to me) of thanks to his loving parents. "It was a wonderful time," he said softly. "It was not a bad time. Then, after the war, we had shortages, but we didn't feel that too much either. Life was very natural in those days."

At this point—I suddenly realized that we had been there for three hours—we reluctantly got up from the table and wandered slowly out into the sunshine. It blinded me for a moment, coming out of the comforting darkness and memory. Then we strolled about in the old city for another hour, and Molla Haji, who had embraced "the other" throughout his life while so many around him were destroying it, suddenly stopped in his tracks. Seeming rather modestly pleased with himself, he then duly offered his answer to the economic problems of Azerbaijan.

"Look at what we have," he said—announced, really. I tried to look around the old streets and parks but, frankly, I saw only garbage.

"Yes, garbage!" he virtually shouted. "That is what we have. We can get a grant or a loan from the West and pay people to pick up the garbage. Most of it can be used to feed cattle . . ." He then spun an absolutely astonishing yarn about the many uses to which the garbage that filled the streets could be put!

Once again on this unique trip, I stood there, dumbfounded, struck with wonderment at the audacity of it all.

"If we really had a free economy," he finally pronounced, "people would have to think about ideas like this!"

Monday morning, I packed up, just in case the Turkish Airliner really did come. It was with an unexpected sadness that I put the Hearty Okura Slippers into my suitcase; after all of this, they were just as neat and good as they were the day I got them nine years ago in Tokyo (which should tell you something about who is going to rule the world and why). I felt very grateful to those noble scuffs!

I packed the picture of George Bush that had served me so well and which had given these myriad peoples such an unexpected sense of respect. I left my dark green and black flannel nightgown and one dress; I was surely tired of them.

I packed away my odd books on Tatarstan, on Jadidism, and on all the things that I had had no idea about until I took this trip, and I carefully wrapped the little Kyrgyz figure that the People's General had given me. I was ready, and I was even surprised to find myself sad to be ready.

At eleven o'clock, they began to come. My translator came to say good-bye; and he sat there very sadly, wondering aloud whether *he* would ever be able to get out and have a future. Molla Haji came, carrying a wonderful bouquet of red carnations, which I carried all the way to Istanbul and put into a vase in my room, where they lived two full days before they wilted. Then the others from Radio Liberty came and took me in a taxi to the airport.

To my amazement, I was checked through in only five minutes, and all they asked was did I have any gold or rugs; but then, Turkish Airlines had its own small terminal and its own priorities. I couldn't believe how immaculate it was; there were comfortable chairs, truly clean windows, tables with flowers, and lovely pictures of Turkey. And when I went to the ladies' room, it was clean too! The room even had pleated curtains.

I realized at that moment that it was now this world that was strange to me and to which I was unaccustomed.

As people poured into the Turkish Airlines lounge from five o'clock on (the plane was due to "come and leave by 7:30 P.M."—I kept repeating that little litany to myself), one felt suddenly an air of excitement about the room. Soon the windows began to steam because of the cold outside and the breaths of many travelers inside. Amoco men and women were all over the place, as our warm breaths turned the room into a tight little steam bath. Some had (wisely) brought Georgian wine and were drinking it while I died of thirst, staring pitifully at them for mercy. They only exchanged stories.

"We just came back from Georgia," one trim, good-looking young woman geologist from Houston told me at one point. "You could not believe it. We went with some of their men who work on oil. It snowed like perfect hell and we were in this cabin up in these wild mountains overnight. It was . . ." Her voice trailed off. "Well, they insisted upon killing a steer right there before us. They stabbed it in the neck and the blood was all over. Then we had to eat it . . ." Her voice dropped off again, she blinked her eyes, then slowly shook her head.

Why was I not surprised?

The plane did not come.

But more travelers came, and all seemed extraordinarily gay and mirthful—and, of course, why not, for they were leaving!

Still the plane did not come.

I was beginning to get over that strange initial sadness that overtook me earlier and to sink back into the reason for my ostensible terror: *it would not come.* Meanwhile, as the sun went down in winter's early February days, the outside grew totally black, for there were no other planes. And all the while, we sat in this cozy, well-lit, hopeful little lounge, which, as I truly knew, was an only barely welcome interloper and tease from another world.

Finally, after I had been there for more than three hours, I could just begin to see a small light in the sky. The light was slowly but steadily approaching us.

Yes, it was the Turkish Airliner, and Marco Polo could surely not have been more thrilled had he seen the Great Khan walking out to meet him, even when he discovered the khans' great capital of Karakorum in Mongolia, or when he finally returned to his beloved Venice, to die having told "only half of what I saw." At precisely 8:25, the giant plane ground to a halt in front of the terminal, and a belch of oil people, Turkish businessmen, and missionaries came spluttering out.

But before we could actually get into the plane, Azeri police kept pushing our group of travelers back, with that same violence that I had felt across the entire society, and I was reminded again what a gratuitously violent part of the world this is.

The plane took off at nine o'clock—from Baku to Istanbul and points west. Your friendly Turkish pilot was smiling. Your pretty Turkish Airlines hostess was brisk and efficient, there to serve you, thank you! Your passenger from the East was mistrusting. Long after we took off, and after I finally felt some assurance that we really were not going to circle and go back to Baku, I still kept myself safely swathed in my World-Famous Lodencloth Cape-Coat, for most of me was still "out there," somewhere in Central Asia, wondering why this miserable part of the world fascinated and consumed one so.

I was leaving behind human beings I had never dreamed existed: sensitive, generous Molla Haji; searching philosopher Tynchtik-bek; smart, decent Western/Oriental Askar Akaev; sweet, savvy, and sad Rimzil of Kazan; Dr. Bang, who somehow wound up in Alma-Ata on his way from North Korea to San Francisco; sacrificial Marilyn Beaney, who was destined to teach all of Kazakhstan business ethics; pretty little Dania, who despaired of ever finding a husband; Tahir of the funny hat; that proud but nameless scrub-woman of Tashkent who so courageously pioneered a new method of "cleaning" the floors of the world; gorgeous Mohammed Salikh in his white Hemingway-Havana suit; cameo-faced Nurilla, who will surely end up the Ivana Trump of Central Asia; valiant Feliks Kulov saying that courage wasn't really very difficult, presenting me with an archeological figure to remember little Kyrgyzstan; wily "Mayor Daley" Nazarbayev in his sleek offices in Alma-Ata; Dr. Tcho, he of the "ideas" and the dirty Krambds offices, who will design new economies for all of Asia; President Mutalibov of Azerbaijan with his white phone to Ankara and his yen for jazz; Kenny-the-Kyrgyz, who will someday operate a fleet of taxis in Bishkek; the great "Stock Market Turkestan" in legendary Samarkand; the Crimean Tatars who were going home—not to forget the engrossing Old Russia of Kazan, the mellow parks of Alma-Ata, the unlikely decency of gray Bishkek, the new sophistication of Tashkent, the throbbing sensuality of Baku, the baths of the Tatars. . . .

And, of course, winter.

"What would you like to drink?" the hostess asked. In fact, she said it three times—I was not quite yet "out" and so did not know exactly how to respond to such a curious offer.

I looked at her suspiciously. No one in Russia or most of its environs ever asked you what you *liked,* ever! Then I realized for the first time where I really was and I decided to test her, demanding, "Two scotch and sodas, please, and a glass of red wine."

"Fine," she said, and off she went to actually get the drinks.

And so, slowly, I took off my World-Famous Lodencloth Cape-Coat, with some of the clean syringes still in the pockets, and I finally folded it up on the empty seat next to me. As I did that, I noticed, strangely enough, that my rings were loose. It seemed that during these weeks my fingers had somehow grown thinner.

Then I remembered something that my mother had told me once when she realized that her youth was behind her and that life would now be very different. She told me that, when you get old, your fingers grow thin.

Epilogue
"Others Will Come"

I am back in my comfortable, cozy, warm condominium in downtown Washington, with my sweet little Japanese Bobtail cat,
Nikko, curled up at my feet. (Occasionally I discuss with him Kazakhstan's or Kyrgyzstan's facing toward Asia instead of Russia;
naturally, he applauds the idea.) I have plenty of hot water to bathe
with now, and in my gray marble bathroom I treasure a chest of
gorgeous soaps, oils, and perfumes. (In short, I could not be further
removed from the great Hotel Ala-Too in Bishkek, whose reputation I sullied with the treacherous "affair of the stolen glasses.")

But I am still wearing my Hearty Okura Slippers, which would
surely deserve a "Hero of Socialism" medal were there still Soviet
socialists and were they still awarding them. Oh, I did have a bout
with giardiasis, an intestinal disorder caused by a nasty micro-
scopic parasite, endemic now from St. Petersburg to Tashkent, and
which makes your insides feel very endlessly sickish indeed; but it
was treated by my doctor and now even my stomach seems normal
enough again.

And so we have moved on to very different worlds—winters.

Now, when I think back on that other—that unforgettable—
winter of 1992, Central Asia sometimes seems so long ago and so
impossibly far away as to have been almost some dream that I have

now awakened from, like those empires that gleam most brilliantly just at the moment that they are no more.

I have received letters only from "the old man," handsome Molla Haji, from Baku. He wrote a long and angry letter, in perfectly scripted English, about what dogs, savages, barbarians, thugs, murderers, rapists, and liars the Armenians were! (Frankly, I wished he would have instead told me more about how his garbage-recycling scheme was going.) No matter, I did not really expect to hear from any of them: we had briefly and wondrously met, but now they were in their world, I was back in mine. (Besides, the mails are terrible!)

But in the spring of 1993, there was a break in the silence— another symbolic breakout from Central Asia—when President Akaev of Kyrgyzstan made an official visit to the United States. He was the same all-smiles but tough, charming, and determined leader whom I had spent so many interesting hours with in Bishkek. I was delighted to sit next to Akaev at a dinner for him and for Kyrgyzstan at the Freedom Forum in Arlington, Virginia, and I was especially tickled and honored when I heard he was telling people that I was his "best friend in America" (at least since "Great Roosevelt" is dead).

But even as I quickly resettled into my life here, in the very bosom of "the most powerful nation in the world," one question kept echoing in the recesses of my mind: why does Central Asia so beguile so many of us?

Much of Central Asia is, in fact, ugly. Its poverty is of such magnitude that the misery sometimes makes one gasp with the hopelessness of it all. There are relatively few strikingly beautiful Nurillas or really strikingly handsome Molla Hajis. Most of the "Kyrgyz eyes" would not in truth have excited the discriminating Thomas Mann, and, as they all said, so many of their best people had been killed. Remember too, when I was out there, it was cold, freezing, ambiguous winter.

And yet, Central Asia remains—to journalistic gourmands like me and to adventure-gourmets alike—a Lorelei singing a distant and an unlikely siren's song.

When the Turkish Airliner landed in Istanbul that night, I found it hard to believe that I was "out," that I was "free" and back in the "Western world."

I have always loved Istanbul. Indeed, it has always been my favorite city. I love the haunting foghorns on the Bosporus that call to you through the mists that protectively embrace the ancient city; the historic horizons where the caliphs built their graceful minarets; the dignity of the tough and upright Turks . . .

I had expected to walk off the Turkish Airliner in my World-Famous Lodencloth Cape-Coat, show my passport with the single visa that took me through five countries that did not really exist, and take off for the Istanbul Hilton (where I would soon be spotted sipping a chilled Manhattan on the rocks while staring out over the Bosporus and vaguely remembering that somewhere out there there was a place on the map called "Bishkek").

"Why, hello, Miss Geyer."

That would be the barman, whom I knew from the many times I had stayed there.

"And where did you come from this time?" he would ask brightly.

How astonished he would be when I told him! How impressed he would be with my exploits and adventures! (He might even remember or remind me that there were 50 to 55 million Turkic-speaking folk out there, now constituting one fifth of the world and in contact with Turkey for the first time since the ninth century!) He would tell me proudly, "It was all ours once, you know!" and I would nod, with an appropriately wistful little smile.

I would fax my office in Kansas City. I might even phone my editor, Elizabeth, and how happy and relieved this fine young woman would be to know that I was safe and drinking Manhattans by the Bosporus.

In short, I would immediately fall back into my old life with all the ease and alacrity of someone who had not really ever been gone.

Only that did not happen.

That first night, even the Istanbul airport jarred me. Why was it so neat, so orderly, so clean? (Was there perhaps something *wrong* with the Turks?) When I got to my room at the Hilton, I busied myself with my old habit of "making a nest" and settling in, but it did not work. In the first good, clean bed I had had in six weeks, I could not sleep—why was it so comfortable, so civilized?

The first morning, out of odd feelings of needing to be reattached to the "heartland of empires," I phoned Ilter Turan, a prominent and prestigious professor of international relations at

Istanbul University whom I had known from earlier visits. He immediately dropped by the hotel to chat. Ilter had always had about him a distinguished handsomeness, and it had not abandoned him, although he was grayer than when I had seen him eight years before. To my delight, he was quite "up" on Turkey and her new relations with her Turkic children "out there"—and his words and company helped immensely in bridging the many little chasms I was feeling inside me.

"Turkey is everywhere," Ilter told me, as we sat by one of the Hilton's huge windows overlooking the Bosporus. "We are restoring an old building in Baku for our embassy. The Turkish PTT, our telecom monopoly, has set up a direct phone exchange with special Ankara numbers for Central Asia; they have a 2,500-line capacity for each of the five republics. Turkish firms are bringing their own workmen into their industries, because there is no floating labor force out there . . .

"You probably don't realize it, but even before the Soviet collapse, Turkey had already oriented itself toward the Eastern and Soviet blocs," Ilter went on, pausing occasionally to glance out at the darkness gathering over the romantic waterway. "They had decided to link up Turkey with the Soviet gas system. Turkish construction companies had already gone into the Soviet Union. They have established a good reputation in Europe, next to Germany . . ."

Then Ilter ticked off a fascinating list of contacts, ties, and projects that Turkey now had or would soon have with Central Asia. "A Congress of Turkology meets now in Turkey very year. But everything has changed. Before, the Turkish Communists were interested in the Soviet government, while the religious Turks were interested in Central Asia. Then, in the eighties, there was a drive in Turkey to increase exports—and the Turkish commercial people began looking 'out there.' In Ukraine, a steel mill produced rails, and the Turks struck a deal for rails in exchange for other products . . ."

Ilter did not mention it, but I soon found out for myself that every Sunday, at the crenellated old wharves along the Bosporus and the Golden Horn, where the Turkish fishermen fried their fish aboard their boats to sell to buyers on shore, there was now a bustling "Eastern people's bazaar"—Romanians, Crimeans, people from as far away as Odessa on the Black Sea and Baku on the Caspian. All now came, opened their rickety suitcases, and sold everything from soccer balls to extension cords.

And, enterprisingly, the "Natashas" (as the Russians called them) came. These were generally Romanian and Russian prostitutes, and they were all over Istanbul in still another example of Western free-marketeering.

Indeed, even during the two days that I was in Istanbul, the announcements of deals being made between Turkey and her "children" were little less than extraordinary. More than one hundred members of a delegation of Turkish and American businessmen, bankers, and diplomats had just been in Baku. Turkish banks like Vakifbank, Halkbank, and Ziraatbank announced that they would soon open branches there.

As the wise and far-seeing late Turkish president, Turgut Ozal, told me later in Washington, "The key to the Central Asian countries is communications and transportation. They should go to India, to China, through Turkey to Europe, and through Iran to the Persian Gulf. If that is provided and their oil is able to move, they have the possibility of being really independent."

That was the rational and hopeful summing-up of Turkish thought about their "Turkic brothers," sadly lost to them for so many long centuries in that vast wilderness where the Turkic peoples roved.

Perhaps most amazing of all, while I was in Istanbul, it was duly announced that branches of the posh Italian fashionwear chain Benetton were going to open in Ashkabad, the capital of Turkmenistan. If that could happen at the end of the world, anything could!

The second afternoon in Istanbul, as I was really preparing to go "cold turkey" on my heartland of empires addiction before I left for the States the next day, Nadir Devlet, professor at the Turkic Studies Institute at Marmara University, dropped by. Here was not only another charming man, but a Turk who had actually out–Marco Poloed all of us modern wanderers! To my delight, Devlet told me how, in the spring of 1991, he and other academics from across the world had taken a 12,000-mile UNESCO bus trip across all of Central Asia—from Ashkabad to Bukhara and Samarkand, through Dushanbe and up to Osh, Bishkek, Alma-Ata, and the Chinese border.

"I have been working for twenty years on this topic of Central Asia," he recalled dreamily, as again we sat at a window of the

Hilton overlooking the magic waterway that linked the Mediterranean and its progressive Westernism to the Black Sea and its endless sagas of elusive Golden Fleeces. "I had a lot of information, but this was the first time I could check whether I was right.

"At that time, the central powers were still strong, the KGB was still there; people were beginning to be open, but not too open . . ."

I had thought that my trip was hard. But those two hundred professors not only traveled by bus, they were in places that were so poor and so ecologically poisoned that in many towns they could not even safely wash their faces with the water. Nevertheless, he had remarkably reasonable expectations. "They have a very young generation," he said at one point, "and if they educate their young people correctly, there is hope. But they need a lot of help."

His own institute had already organized a conference on contemporary Arabic alphabets. It had brought twenty-eight scholars from the former Soviet Union—Tatar, Bashkir, Chuvash, Kurguz, Turkmen—and they discussed a common alphabet. "Especially," he went on, "the Tatars and Azeris were willing to accept the Roman alphabet. So now we are trying to send them books and typewriters. They are all searching for something. They are building huge mosques and the people are paying for them. This is largely a reaction to the past, although there is always the danger that some scholastic-minded religious man could create some problems . . ."

And everywhere he had gone, because of the same linguistic roots of the varied Turkic languages, despite Stalin's insufferable meddling into people's psyches (and alphabets), after all these centuries he and the many peoples of Central Asia could understand one another.

Marco Polo dead? Not at all. The great Venetian was clearly being replaced by a new generation of searchers and seekers, with new ideas of adventure, who could move proudly in his footsteps (so long, of course, as they did not have to go Aeroflot).

But as I settled into my life in Washington, it soon became clear that much of the promise that I had seen that winter—the excitement that I found everywhere, the breathtaking feeling that the Central Asians were finally really opening to the world and were prepared to take their place in the larger world—was also being overtaken by dire and clouded events.

In Mother Russia herself, the situation seemed to grow only darker and darker, even under reform-minded President Boris Yeltsin. (And Russia, of course, was still, despite everything, "the center," whose every move and twitch influenced all of the other republics.)

By the winter of 1993, the economy had grown so bad that Sovietologist Peter Reddaway was able to say that, in Russia, "democracy has become a swearword." With their lack of any historical tradition or philosophy to make capitalism or democracy workable systems, the Russians had managed to pass no fewer than sixteen thousand laws—and observed none of them.

The problem was simple in statement, but difficult in application: neither democracy nor free enterprise was in any way natural to the Russians. They had not gone through the Reformation, the Renaissance, or the Enlightenment; they had no organic development of the advanced social theories behind these historic high points. Decades before, Berdyayev had said it all.

To me, the problem seemed to be primarily one of values, with the jury still out on the terrible question of whether societies in the process of transformation from totalitarianism to freedom must have the internalized value systems and civil moral principles necessary for the difficult shift to free enterprise and free politics. If they did not, I was convinced, we were standing squarely on the dangerous edge of a new age that most had not counted on. This could then become not an age of liberty and economic growth but an age of the return to still more virulent types of chauvinistic dictatorship. That, in turn, would mean the discrediting of the capitalist system and of democracy itself in these fragile and vulnerable parts of the world.

Perhaps worst of all, in Russia but also in the new republics, was the horrific situation of the environment, of the destruction of the very physical earth-plant upon which anything they now built had to be constructed.

In October 1992, Vladimir Pokrovsky, head of the Russian Academy of Medical Sciences, walked out into a press conference in Moscow and shocked the world with his frankness. Of the old Soviet Communist regime, with its "brotherhood" of man, he said, "We have already doomed ourselves for the next twenty-five years. The new generation is entering adult life unhealthy. The Soviet economy was developed at the expense of the population's health."

Pokrovsky then ran down the list of staggering data: 11 percent of infants with birth defects; half the drinking water and a tenth of the food supply contaminated; 55 percent of school-aged children suffering health problems; Russian life expectancy falling . . .

The ecological disaster was turning out to be much worse than anyone had previously believed. Basically, the very life-giving water system of Central Asia was drying up. (The destruction of the Aral Sea, as serious as that was, was turning out to be just a warning of what lay beyond.) The area's two great rivers—the Amu-Darya and the Syr-Darya—could give no more. The area's water supply could not be increased further, because the only solution would be to divert water from the Siberian rivers—and those were now inside Russia.

The recent independence of the Central Asian republics had made even such diversion impossible because of new sovereignties and borders. *The Economist* of London, in a special report, editorialized gloomily:

> In short, Central Asia is a rare case of a region facing Malthusian disaster. Its population is rising. Its capacity to grow food is determined by the availability of water. And water supplies are fixed or falling. . . . The next round of the Great Game . . . will be a quagmire of Central Asian squabbles, deepened by rifts between styles of Islam, into which the old local empires will be sucked . . .

On top of this was the new and often overwhelming persistence of unchecked crime, of criminal activities so flagrant that by 1994 the racketeers (the so-called Russian mafia) had virtually taken over the economic life of many cities in the former Soviet Union. Meanwhile, analysts were describing Central Asia as "one vast gray area." By that, they meant that the law was neither black nor white, but gray. Central Asia was by then the most important base for raw materials for the former Soviet Union's illegal drug market, most importantly a major supplier of Indian hemp, whose buds are used to prepare hashish. Afghanistan, with great influence on Central Asia's southern borders, had itself become one uncontrolled "free zone," where drugs and training in any kind of weaponry now ruled that all but destroyed country.

"Criminal gangs have no religion, no ideas," was the way Colonel Jurabek Aminov, deputy chief of Tajikistan's security police, characterized the situation. "They remain with those who pay them well and with those whom they feel influential." Indeed, his words could have been a metaphor for all of the sinking into criminality that worried me—and that was occurring from Moscow to Kazan, from Baku to Yerevan, from Bishkek to Kiev. These peoples and cultures simply had few historical principles and virtually no internalized ethic to face an age without the iron hand of autocracy, much less to move them forward into the immensely more complicated, nuanced, and internally disciplined cultures of democracy and free enterprise. Once that autocracy began to crumble . . .

And stunning too, on the negative side, were the changes coming in Russia itself. The amazing electoral showing of nationalist xenophobe Vladimir Zhirinovsky in elections in the fall of 1993 not only showed the extent to which the Russians were direly humiliated by the West's intrusions and were sinking into their own purgatory, it also showed the attempts by certain groups within the Russian military and the Russian political spectrum to rethink and remake the Russian Empire.

Moscow, never historically satisfied to be only a city or only a country but needing always to be the "Third Rome" again and again, was reclaiming its "near abroad," which is to say the newly independent republics that were formerly within the Soviet Union. By the spring of 1993, Russian military units were active in Georgia, finally forcing Eduard Shevardnadze's regime to accept their suzerainty; Russians were decisive in Azerbaijan in replacing the elected Azeri president, Abulfez Elchibey (who quickly succeeded my presidential interviewee, Mutalibov), with an old-line Communist they could control; and Moscow had openly intervened in Tajikistan to defeat the democratic and Islamic forces and install another Communist. Meanwhile, the Russian military had carved out the strategic slip of land called the "Trans-Dniestr Republic" between Moldova and Ukraine, where all the old Communists and KGB operatives were gathering to plot their return to power.

Some said that a "new Russian Empire is in the making." Others saw Moscow engaged in the "third round of its Caucasus wars in the last three centuries, by proxies, with the aim not so much of reestablishing imperial borders but of turning the Caucasus into an indirectly controlled protectorate." What was certain was that the Russians were not simply going to give up and allow these bustling new republics to go their own way; and that threw a very different light over them than was the case when I was there.

The two Central Asian republics that I had not visited showed most clearly what the new Russian policies could engender.

Interestingly enough, I had come upon Tajikistan once from the other side—from Peshawar in Pakistan during the Afghan war. That war also involved Central Asia because tribes like the Tajiks had members both in the Soviet Union and in Afghanistan.

One day, talking to the mujahideen leaders in Peshawar, an astonishingly strange and wild city where all the tribes of Central Asia come together and from where the mujahideen attacked into Soviet-held Afghanistan, they mentioned to me that they had "membership cards" among their Tajik brothers and cousins inside the Soviet Union. I was astonished, because those Communist borders were supposed to be impregnable, but I became convinced that it was true, and I wrote it in a column.

The next week, in Washington, within the space of an hour, I received not one but two calls from the Soviet embassy, which in those years never called *anybody*. They were terrified of the idea of the unifying of these tribes across borders (many of the Tajiks in Afghanistan had fought with the anti-Soviet Basmachi guerrillas in the 1920s). As it turned out, my story was correct and presaged many of these later developments.

That was my only contact with Tajikistan, a little country of 76,641 square miles of desert that stretched along the borders of Afghanistan, China, Kyrgyzstan, and Uzbekistan, and produced cattle, sheep, fruit, and hydroelectric power. Unlike all the other Central Asian republics, its language was not Turkic but Persian, although the Tajiks were Sunni Muslims. The situation in Tajikistan was bad, even worse than that of Nagorno-Karabakh.

Basically, what had happened there was *the* final nightmare for the whole area. In September 1992, the old Communists, with forces loyal to President Rakhmon Nabiev, began fighting an odd constellation of forces of Tajik intellectuals, Islamicists, and tribesmen. By winter, eighty thousand refugees were encamped, freezing and starving to death, on the Tajik-Afghan border, tens of thousands had died, and many parts of the capital of Dushanbe were sadly in ruins.

Tajikistan, while barely missing a historic breath, had gone from

Moscow-controlled buffer zone to Moscow-controlled buffer zone; from total Communist control to total Communist control. Sometimes, in some geographically unlucky places on earth, the more things change, the less they change.

Then there was Turkmenistan. There, surely, you also had a strange-enough place, a land of barely seven inhabitants per square mile, with fully 90 percent of its landmass made up of the great Kara-Kum desert, a country so remote and singularly uninviting that it lured a mere 302 émigrés in 1990, at the very height of its hopefulness!

And yet that dry and faraway place—the real heartland of that ancient dream of Turkestan that still found some resonance in the hearts of men—was faring surprisingly well. With only 2.5 million Turkmen nomads still wandering about, herding their sheep and raising their famous, sturdy, square little horses, their culture boasted beautiful art objects for warring—swords, saddles, and fine weavings.

But one found in Turkmenistan something else besides interest in the past. From being one of the most backward of the Soviet republics, it had moved under independence to become one of the most promising. The reason was simple: the discovery of readily exploitable gas and oil deposits so rich that President Saparmurad Niyazov declared his country, perhaps a bit prematurely, a "second Kuwait."

In the spring of 1992, when the nasty war in Tajikistan was beginning, I happened across a segment on television on our "new American embassy staff in Dushanbe, Tajikistan." And there was Ed McWilliams, who had opened that first American embassy in Central Asia in Kyrgyzstan that February, my friend from Bishkek—looking as happy as little Nurilla had she just married Michael Jackson—obviously cooking over an open fire in his hotel room in Dushanbe with other obviously equally crazy American diplomats.

When the war got too bad, I heard that they had all been evacuated—and I could imagine how disappointed that made Ed! However, he went back to Dushanbe again—it was surely the kind of place he wanted to be. And I hoped to meet him again, too.

Something else important happened in Turkmenistan that would serve as a kind of example of what was pending elsewhere: two weeks after the Russian elections in the fall of 1993, President Niyazov agreed to permit the country's 400,000 Russians to have dual citizenship, a step he had long opposed. The Russians in Turkmenistan formed no less than 10 percent of the population and included a large military community. This step marked another measure of the renewed and renascent force of Moscow on her borders and of the militarization of foreign policy toward the former republics. Not unimportantly, both Tajikistan and Kyrgyzstan followed course; now, they could do little less than respond to Moscow's worries about its Russian minorities in the "independent" republics.

This new remilitarization on the southern borders affected the big republics like Uzbekistan as well. Uzbekistan had been doing relatively well when I was in Tashkent and Samarkand, but soon it, too, was suffering from the Tajik war and from the threat of its spreading elsewhere. Fearful that the Tajik conflict would overflow into Uzbekistan, the Uzbek president actually sent troops to the border to seal it off from refugees. Amazingly, President Akaev of Kyrgyzstan joined him in sending troops, showing how serious the entire thing really was. These developments, not unexpectedly, did overflow into Uzbekistan, and the government soon outlawed Birlik, the independent movement.

But it was too easy—and too cheap—to focus only on the negative developments, for in truth serious problems were always inevitable. Central Asia was coming out of a long and bitter trance that had eaten away her historic energies; it had to have problems—and dire ones. Central Asia's new fight was a fight against all the odds—and a struggle for centralness and for centeredness again as well. And, in truth, there was still much to be happy and optimistic about in Inner Asia, the heartland of empires, the "capital of the world," Tamerlane, the Mongol khans, the Tungans, Khazars, and Avars and all their brothers and sisters.

For the undeniable fact was that between 1985 and 1989, when glasnost and perestroika began there, and since the elections that occurred across Central Asia between 1989 and 1991, that world had changed beyond recognition.

Even in the year since my visit, untold dreams had suddenly been realized. Major airlines from the "outside world" now flew directly into Central Asian and Eastern Siberian cities: Lufthansa from Europe to Alma-Ata; Alaskan Airlines from Alaska to Khabarovsk; Turkish Airlines now flew regularly into most Central Asian cities. (Pakistan International Airlines was going into Tashkent once a week, and "the story" was that its flights mainly ferried Islamabad's jet-setters to the fleshpots of Tashkent—i.e., Tashkent's cheap wine and available men and women. I, of course, had seen and tasted only the cheap wine!)

As to Tatarstan—and all of its hopes of independence from the Russian federation—those hopes were still frozen in time, stymied by the Russian "near-abroad" hopes not only to keep maverick areas like Tatarstan and Eastern Siberia *in* the federation but to actually bring back nominally independent states like Ukraine, Kazakhstan, and Uzbekistan. Still, Tatarstan was moving slowly and inexorably forward.

The hoped-for Tatarstan Community College—the one that the former minister of education had so enthusiastically outlined to me—was indeed coming into existence. By 1994, it had a board of directors, an administration, and even a faculty; it had taken over a vacated public building and had all of 250 students. It was proudly named the "American-Kazan Community College," and was being aided in America by the Community Colleges for International Development, an organization of sixty-five community colleges across the country. Indeed, the Tatar emanation was progressing so hopefully that its founders were thinking seriously of extending the idea to various communities in Siberia.

The community college idea was being taken particularly seriously in the former Soviet Union because one of their most dire necessities—the upgrading of an adult workforce that was now basically nonfunctional in a global economy—could be met by just the community college philosophy that peculiarly addressed that problem.

Tatarstan was also about to *actually get a phone system that would be operational and that would open the area to the world!* Hughes Networks Systems, Inc., a subsidiary of Hughes Aircraft Company, was finishing up its cellular network and fixed wireless telephone system in Tatarstan—they expected it to be operational by 1995.

Tatarstan—and, indeed, all of the new republics—had also found a spirited and intelligence benefactress in America in the person of Susan Eisenhower, Ike's beautiful granddaughter who had married the Soviet space genius Roald Sagdeev. Susan, through her Center for Post-Soviet Studies, was enthusiastically and intelligently working with the former republics, with her talented husband. (And they seemed to have no intention, despite the corny jokes of my Kazan colleagues, of creating any copresidency of Tatarstan, like some steppe Clintons.)

In Kazakhstan, meanwhile, the Kazakh government changed the name of Alma-Ata to Almaty, for reasons that never seemed very clear. But President Nazarbayev was very clear indeed; he came to the United States in the winter of 1994 and gave press conferences, surrounded by American industrialists and oilmen who were obviously most interested in his big and potentially rich country. Still, he had not yet clarified the rights the oil companies would have in Kazakhstan, and so, although the Chevron deal over the Tenghiz oilfields had once again been signed, oilmen and women said openly that it could again be rescinded and that, if that happened, all the oil companies would pull out.

There was another reason now, however, for such foolish hesitation: The Russians were putting pressure on Kazakhstan, as with the other "independent" republics, by refusing to allow its oil to flow through Russian pipelines. That could stop the entire progress of the republic. After all, "White Nights," which had been so hopefully pumping oil in eastern Siberia when I was there, had folded under the constant demands for more money and the lack of legal statutes assuring land or mineral rights ownership.

But if the oil companies still found it hard to make a (realistic) deal with the Kazakhs or the Uzbeks, a classic risk-taking man like the big investor Shoul Eisenberg of Tel Aviv was able to make deals on a big scale. One was a $160 million agreement to make and install advanced irrigation equipment in the south of Kazakhstan.

Devout, dedicated Marilyn Beaney had weathered her first year and was actually sent out—expenses paid by the Kazakhs—to get others to come.

Things had begun to change in Alma-Ata in the spring after I was there. Marilyn wrote in her pep-talk "newsletter" to her friends back home:

"As the sun warmed the air and people began to emerge from their residences, little commercial enterprises began to appear on the streets. More and more consumer goods were making their way into Alma-Ata, and new stores with attractive window displays and a variety of items appealingly presented were 'discovered' and 'welcomed' with enthusiasm . . .

"The World Bank and International Monetary Fund were sending delegations; discussions were being held and plans made to develop the international airport and to perhaps build a second facility just outside of Alma-Ata; embassies from countries around the world were opening, not only physical sites but also windows to the outside world . . ."

Most amazing of all, Marilyn went into the central department store, Tzoom, and *"polite clerks offered to assist me in my selections!"* (Her emphasis.)

Young Tatars were now seeing Arnold Schwarzenegger's *Terminator 2* before it was even out on video in the States (a questionable surge forward in culture, to be sure). And Maxim's had opened a restaurant in Alma-Ata.

Ten thousand young Central Asians from all the new states were studying in Turkey alone, and some analysts still persisted in believing that Tenghiz and the Tarim Basin could transform the region into another Saudi Arabia by the mid-1990s.

Indeed, by 1994, the two early contesters for the modern will of Central Asia, Turkey and Iran, had both slipped in importance next to China and the rest of the "authoritarian democracies" of Southeast Asia, where Nazarbayev and most of the leaders from the very beginning were looking for models and for help. By the end of 1992, China ranked as Uzbekistan's leading trade partner outside of the Russian-dominated Commonwealth of Independent States, which seemed like more and more of a euphemistic name. China had even signed ten economic agreements with strife-torn Tajikistan.

On the structural and metaphysical level, it had become utterly clear that China, Singapore, and South Korea, with a central autocratic economic and political control having been maintained until the economy was transformed into versions of free market (when supposedly the political system could change), had won out as the model of preference in Central Asia and, indeed, most of the world.

Jeffrey Sachs, the personable young Harvard economist whom I had interviewed that snowy morning in Moscow while the harpist played in the Metropole dining room and the Russians stood in breadlines out on the streets, had simply been proven wrong. It was much too much to "shock" the economy with draconian free-market shock therapies. Far better would it have been to gradually transform the creaking enterprises, little by little, instead of bankrupting and destroying the economy and the people's sustenance—and, by the way, bringing out all the lurking chauvinistic and hatred-filled Russian fear of the outside world, which had been my greatest fear when I saw all those Novotel, American Express, and Christian Dior signs there in 1992!

The ones who had been right were men like Professor Boris Mihailov at the Institute of the U.S.A. and Canada in Moscow, when he told me that "it was more important to privatize first, to establish readjustment training, and to use state procurements to fill the market in the first phase. . . . What happened was the prices are free, but the shops are still empty. . . ." The ones who were right were men like my friend Vaqif Rustamov, one of the Azeri president's young advisers, when he told me that "now they've basically destroyed the economy. It is now common knowledge that they should have dealt first with economics, because economics is the background of politics. Starting with politics breaks the law of nature."

But the one bad thing that had not happened was that extremist and radical Islamic fundamentalism, which was threatening countries like Algeria and Egypt, had never really become a real threat in Central Asia at all—the threats from the economy and from the ecology were the great, gnawing threats.

Would the Far East of Russia come to a point where it would break off from historic Russia and form some sort of new regional nexus? It already had.

It was the larger psychological and spiritual questions that were so much harder to answer than the sheer economic ones: How do you find moral and ethical renewal after such years of plague? What do peoples do with such a burden of history and of oppression? How does one address the burdens of guilt and forgiveness? Is justice possible after such depradations? Where does one even go for renewal, much less resurrection?

In all my wanderings, I found only equivocal answers to those questions. But at least now there were people free to think, to speak, to write, and to address them—and thus, for the first time in half a millennium, there existed the *possibility* of answers.

Oh, I almost forgot one major step forward in Central Asia from the time when I crossed it. The new Chinese-built hotel had actually opened in Bishkek, and the next time I visited my friend "Great Akaev," I would not have to stay at the Ala-Too. (I simply assumed that "Kulov's men" would be securely protecting it, and how happy I would be to see those, my good big friends, again!)

American economist Carl Bucher once said, "Every advance of culture commences with a new period of wandering." That was what had suddenly happened in Central Asia, as it opened to the world that winter, and that new period of wandering also brought with it—amazingly, wondrously, miraculously—a modern-day revival of the once romantic Silk Road.

What we were seeing was the opening of palpable, productive new Silk Roads all around us: the foreign airlines, the oilmen, the Israeli industrialist, the journalists, the missionaries, the new explorers and adventurers . . .

My friend Edwin Bernbaum, always seeking out his beloved "Sacred Mountains" from China to Central Asia, went to the mountains of Hunza, the epicenter of the "Great Game," and played cards on the very border where the Great Gamesmen had set out. "I was leading trips on the Silk Road," this attractive young scholar told me one day when we exchanged stories and feelings on the "whys" of having to explore "out there" where others had not yet gone, "and I spent a week on the Tai Shan, the holy mountain of China. It was the main sacred mountain that the emperors would climb—and Confucius as well. . . . A lot of the problem we have in the world is that people feel trapped—they need that openness. Going into the mountains is like going back into memory. I feel I'm in touch with my inner self . . ."

Another dear friend, *Wall Street Journal* correspondent Frederick Kempe, in the summer of 1991 took a trip down the remote Siberian Ob River, where the ice floes in the spring poured like watery avalanches into the Arctic Sea. His group sailed on a specially rigged riverboat for five weeks, met Khantys, Mansis, Komis, and Nenets (Siberia's native peoples), found "Big Bill" Haywood's town of Kemerovo (where the famous Chicago labor organizer went in the 1920s to found a utopian workers' colony), and saw suspicious KGB men and pious Lutheran ministers, and the diaphonous bodies of people massacred by Stalin, which after all these years were suddenly being spewed up by the river. (Kempe still had that special manic spirit of the great foreign correspondent—part champagne and part Friedrich Nietzsche.)

In September 1992 there was even an auto rally from Paris to Moscow to Beijing, all across vast Central Asia. The rally took European auto enthusiasts from Paris to Warsaw to Bukhara to Bishkek to Aksu to Beijing. People along the way, the auto enthusiasts said, had never seen anything like it, and one can pretty well rest assured that that was true.

("Others will come," the inscription on the fortress in Kazan had read.)

But above all, we could now see real and intensive efforts to actually reconstruct the fabled Silk Road itself.

New-style hawkers on one new Silk Road were suddenly being seen on the streets of New Delhi in India, as white-skinned, blond-haired, and blue-eyed Russians and Ukrainians suddenly came overland selling watches, cameras, vodka, and dolls; the ruble was so low that the Russians and Ukrainians could undercut the heavily taxed Indian goods and still show a profit.

"In centuries past," *The Economist* of London opined, "one of the silk routes ran through Alma-Ata and Tashkent to Delhi. The silk has now been replaced by consumer goods, and the camels by specially chartered flights. But thanks to India's economic policies, the route is profitable again. Guesses put the value of this burgeoning trade at maybe $150 million a year."

But what really illustrated the renewed fascination in the Silk Road was the resurgence of archeological and historical interest in "the road."

New discoveries in 1993 revealed that Chinese silk was apparently present in the West long before the Han emperor started organizing trade on the road. New archaeological findings suggested that trade across Eurasia may have begun some centuries earlier than previously thought.

But perhaps the most exciting development of all lay in the fact that plans were afoot for satellite surveys of the entire vast Taklamakan desert region for lost cities on the route. For the first time, spaceborne radar systems with remote sensors would apply the latest technology to identifying buried settlements along the entire Silk Road. This imaging radar system, long tested on space shuttle flights, is capable of penetrating the desert to reveal everything from ancient riverbeds to the actual ruins of cities and towns. Scientists talked excitedly about "doing a radar job on the entire Silk Road" almost with the same air of expectation with which the early travelers had talked of "doing the road."

So that winter of 1992—and my funny little trip—and all the strange, and wondrous, and utterly banal people that I had met—were in truth just the beginning. My special winter seemed in some measure long past; and yet I had been there at that special moment of purity, at the instant when the tightly closed bud began to open, at that turn in history when change seemed so impossibly daring that all one could do was draw in one's breath at the very "unthinkable" thought of it!

And adventure, too, had changed. Most early books of exploration were written to uncover the verities of the past, to find treasure or power. Today's adventure was to understand the new, to preserve what was left, to help people advance, and to rummage around in the memories of minds long closed in order both to link us to realities long forgotten and to discover ways to forget and overcome the times of trouble.

The old Silk Road, after all, was a world of caravans that exchanged silk for glass for gems, a canvas where Buddhists and Zoroastrians buffeted each other, a world that beckoned to the West with the promise of the luxurious Oriental gardens of Paradise. But it was also a road of conquest, of violence, and of mass destruction.

Today's new Silk Roads instead are voyages in the air, voices on the radio waves, new Turkish telephones hooked up to Ankara, foreign images on television and CNN that carry man's most advanced technology and exchanges of culture (and the "advanced" world's most appalling cultural depths as well), and finally even radar that will uncover the past more swiftly than any poor patient archeologist's shovel. Yes, that "new period of wandering" had surely begun, surely opening a new and pregnant period in man's history.

And I only told half of what I saw.

Selected Reading

Bacon, Elizabeth. *Central Asia Under Russian Rule.* Ithaca, New York: Cornell University Press, 1966.

Bennigsen, Alexandre A., and Chantal Lemercier-Quelquejay. *Islam in the Soviet Union.* London: Pall Mall Press, 1967.

Bennigsen, Alexandre A., and S. Enders Wimbush. *Muslim National Communism in the Soviet Union: A Revolutionary Strategy for the Colonial World.* Chicago and London: The University of Chicago Press, 1979.

———. *Muslims of the Soviet Empire.* Bloomington, Indiana: University of Indiana Press, 1985.

Berdyayev, Nicholas. *The Origin of Russian Communism.* Ann Arbor, Michigan: The University of Michigan Press, 1969.

Bernbaum, Edwin. *Sacred Mountains of the World.* San Francisco: Sierra Club Books, 1990.

Bobrick, Benson. *East of the Sun: The Epic Conquest and Tragic History of Siberia.* New York: Poseidon Press, 1992.

Brzezinski, Zbigniew. *The Grand Failure: The Birth and Death of Communism in the Twentieth Century.* New York: Charles Scribner's Sons, 1989.

Diuk, Nadia, and Adrian Karatnycky. *The Hidden Nations: The People Challenge the Soviet Union.* New York: William Morrow and Company, 1990.

Doder, Dusko, and Louise Branson. *Gorbachev: Heretic in the Kremlin.* New York: Viking Penguin, 1990.

d'Encausse, Hélène Carrère. *Decline of an Empire: The Soviet Socialist Republics in Revolution.* New York: Newsweek Books, 1979.

Feshbach, Murray, and Alfred Friendly, Jr. *Ecocide in the USSR*. New York: Basic Books, 1992.

Geyer, Georgie Anne. *The Young Russians*. Homewood, Illinois: An ETC Publication, 1975.

Heller, Mikhail, and Aleksandr M. Nekrich. *Utopia in Power: The History of the Soviet Union from 1917 to the Present*. New York: Summit Books, 1985.

Hopkirk, Peter. *Foreign Devils on the Silk Road*. Amherst, Massachusetts: The University of Massachusetts Press, 1980.

————. *The Great Game: The Struggle for Empire in Central Asia*. New York, Tokyo, London: Kodansha International, 1992.

————. *Setting the East Ablaze: On Secret Service in Bolshevik Asia*. Oxford: Oxford University Press, 1984.

Kempe, Frederick. *Siberian Odyssey: A Voyage into the Russian Soul*. New York: G. P. Putnam's Sons, 1992.

Kennan, George F. *The Marquis de Custine and His Russia in 1839*. Princeton, New Jersey: Princeton University Press, 1971.

Lamb, Harold. *Genghis Khan: The Emperor of All Men*. Garden City, New York: International Collectors Library, 1927.

————. *Tamerlane*. New York: Bantam Books, 1944.

Li Man Kin and Editors of Kingsway. *Marco Polo in China*. Hong Kong: Kingsway International Publications, 1981.

Longworth, Philip. *The Cossacks: Five Centuries of Turbulent Life on the Russian Steppes*. New York: Holt, Rinehart and Winston, 1969.

Maclean, Fitzroy. *Back to Bokhara*. New York: Harper & Brothers, Publishers, 1959.

Olcott, Martha Brill. *The Kazakhs*. Stanford, California: Hoover Institution Press, 1987.

Pipes, Richard. *The Formation of the Soviet Union*. Massachusetts: Harvard University Press, Cambridge, 1957.

————. *The Russian Revolution*. New York: Alfred A. Knopf, 1990.

Polo, Marco. *Travels of Marco Polo*. London: Penguin, 1958.

Remick, David. *Lenin's Tomb*. New York: Random House, 1993.

Rorlich, Azade-Ayşe. *The Volga Tatars: A Profile in National Resilience*. Stanford, California: Hoover Institution Press, 1986.

Schuyler, Eugene. *Turkistan: Notes of a Journey in Russian Turkistan, Khokand, Bokhara and Kuldja* (2 vols.), 1876.

Smith, Hedrick. *The New Russians*. New York: Avon Books, 1990.

Stark, Freya. *The Valleys of the Assassins and Other Persian Travels*. Los Angeles: J. P. Tarcher, 1936.

Vambery, Arminius. *Travels in Central Asia* (2 vols.), 1864.

Wimbush, S. Enders. *Soviet Nationalities in Strategic Perspective*. London and Sydney: Croom Helm, 1985.

Wolfe, Bertram D. *Three Who Made a Revolution*. New York: The Dial Press, 1964.

Yergin, Daniel. *The Prize: The Quest for Oil, Money and Power*. New York: Touchstone Books, Simon and Schuster, 1992.

Index

GEORGIE ANNE GEYER likes best to be described as an "adventurous wanderer" or as a "courier between cultures." For eleven years, she roved the world for the legendary writers' paper, the *Chicago Daily News,* as the first woman foreign correspondent of our era. In 1975, she became a syndicated columnist; her thrice-weekly column on foreign affairs now appears in more than 125 major newspapers in the United States and Latin America. She speaks five languages and has written six books on various parts of the world, her most recent being the acclaimed *Guerrilla Prince,* a biography of Fidel Castro. Ms. Geyer is in great demand as a speaker and was featured at the Smithsonian Institution's winter 1993 series of lectures on the Silk Road.